Influence
without
Authority

Influence
without
Authority

SECOND EDITION

ALLAN R. COHEN

AND

DAVID L. BRADFORD

WILEY

John Wiley & Sons, Inc.

Published by John Wiley & Sons, Inc., Hoboken, New Jersey.
Published simultaneously in Canada.

For general information on our other products and services please contact our Customer Care Department within the United States at (800) 762-2974, outside the United States at (317) 572-3993 or fax (317) 572-4002.

Wiley also publishes its books in a variety of electronic formats. Some content that appears in print may not be available in electronic books. For more information about Wiley products, visit our web site at www.wiley.com.

Library of Congress Cataloging-in-Publication Data:

Cohen, Allan R.
  Influence without authority / Allan R. Cohen and David L. Bradford.—2nd ed.
      p.   cm.
  ISBN 0-471-46330-2 (cloth)
  1. Organizational effectiveness.   2. Executive ability.   3. Interpersonal relations.   I. Bradford, David L.   II. Title.

HD58.9.C64 2005
658.4'09—dc22

                                                              2004027078

Printed in the United States of America.
20 19

To our wives, Joyce and Eva,
who, as our toughest and most supportive colleagues,
have taught us the essence of mutual influence
in strategic alliances.

Acknowledgments

From the First Edition

Many people have influenced us in positive ways, and we are deeply indebted to them. A number of colleagues read portions of the manuscript in draft form and made helpful suggestions, including J.B. Kassarjian, Lynne Rosansky, Les Livingstone, Jan Jaferian, Farshad Rafii, and Roy Lewicki. Rosabeth Moss Kanter, Barry Stein, Richard Pascale, Jerry Porras, and Jean Kirsch provided useful stimulation over many years. National Training Laboratories gave us the opportunity to develop and test our ideas in a series of workshops for managers. Many wonderful friends and clients provided the rich examples we have used, but regrettably, most must remain anonymous to preserve confidentiality. We thank former students Tom Greenfield, Marianne McLaughlin, Spencer Lovette, and James Wiegel, and good friend Leslie Charm, for their contributions. In addition, our students and clients have been a continuous source of learning. Our editor, John Mahaney, went far beyond the call of duty in helping to shape this book, and we're almost sorry for all the grief we give him. We very much appreciate the perspective he brought. Sydney Craft Rozen and Louann Werksma buffed our prose, and Nancy Marcus Land's cheerful wisdom made the production process more than bearable. Tom Hart gave us valuable advice on contract issues. We want to thank Sydney Cohen for preparing the index.

We are very grateful to Babson's Vice-President for Academic Affairs, Gordon Prichett, the faculty nominating committee, and Ex-President Bill Dill, for choosing Allan to be the first occupant of the Walter H. Carpenter Chair. The selection was perfectly timed to permit concentrated writing effort just when the book needed it, and we literally couldn't have finished without this opportunity. Although the miracles of word processors let us do most of the typing ourselves, several people at Babson were incredibly helpful in producing draft after draft of the manuscript; for their support we thank Margie Kurtzman, Jim Murphy, Sheila Faherty, as well as George Recck and his angels of computer mercy, Ara Heghinian, Scott Andersen, and especially John Walker, who promptly and patiently rescued lost files and answered countless questions. The Graduate School of Business at Stanford also provided valuable support.

Our extended families have also played an important part in helping us, not only by their encouragement but also by the lessons on influence they teach as we interact with them. For their contributions to our ongoing education, we are forever grateful to our wives, children, parents, brothers, in-laws, aunts, uncles, and cousins—a veritable army of informal instructors.

ADDITIONAL ACKNOWLEDGMENTS
TO THE SECOND EDITION

We are grateful to an additional group of colleagues and managers who have provided us with feedback and examples. Andrea Corney, Anne Donnellon, PJ Guinan, David Hennessey, James Hunt, Martha Lanning, Carole Robin, Phyllis Schlesinger, Mike Smith, Neal Thornberry, and Yelena Shayenzon have built our ideas and helped with the manuscript. Eric Arcese, Timlynn Babitsky, Suzanne Currey, Brian Duerk, David Garabedian, Mary Garrett, Doug Giuliana, Mike Glass, Tony Greco, Fran Grigsby, Jan Jefarian, Sandi Medeiros, Akihiro Nakamura, Efren Olivares, Dan Perlman, Ethan Platt, Carole Robin, Nettie Seabrooks, Scott Timmins, Jim Salmons, Paul Westbrook, all contributed examples in one form or another. We are also deeply appreciative to the hundreds of managers with whom we have worked, who provide criticism, hard-nosed assessment of the utility of our ideas, and wonderful examples of how they struggle with or use influence at work.

The vagaries of publishing have brought us several Wiley editors since the first edition, all of whom we enjoyed, but we worked most closely with Paula Sinnott, Richard Narramore, and Emily Conway. We thank them for forcing us to make the manuscript ever more accessible and useful.

Alas, despite our profound gratitude to a lengthy list of helpful influencers, we can not escape final accountability for the results of their splendid efforts. Only we had the authority to complete this book, and we are responsible for its contents.

A. R. C.

D. L. B.

CONTENTS

PART I

INTRODUCTION

CHAPTER 1

WHY INFLUENCE: WHAT YOU WILL GET FROM THIS BOOK

One of the biggest challenges facing us in UBS-IB (UBS Investment Bank) is the ability to influence others over whom we have no direct authority. Flatter structures, globalization, and cross-functional teams have brought fresh challenges and having to influence people who have different styles or views makes the task even harder.

Being able to influence one's boss, peers, or top management is often quoted as a key reason for the success or failure of individuals. We all know what we want to achieve, yet are often unsure how to go about it or even who are the key people needing to be influenced.

—Rationale for Course on Strategies for Influencing and Persuasion, MAST, UBS-IB

This is a book about influence—the power to get your work done. You need to influence those in other departments and divisions, that is, people you can't order and control. You need to influence your manager and others above you, and you certainly can't order and control them!

But you are not alone: Nobody has the formal authority to achieve what is necessary, not even with those who report to them. It is an illusion that once upon a time managers could make their direct reports do whatever was needed. Nobody has ever had enough authority—they never have and never will. Organizational life is too complicated for that.

Yet, it is possible to have enough influence to make things happen—and this book will tell you how.

3

You will learn how to move others in order to accomplish important objectives, in a way that benefits them as well as you and the organization. We build on a way of working that you already know, though it is easy to lose sight of how to create win-win trades when you are in difficult situations, or have to deal with difficult individuals, groups, or organizations in order to be effective. The book teaches you how to stop doing the things that get in the way of influence, and how to do what's required in these tough situations. It can dramatically increase your ability to get things done.

When we first started writing about influence in the 1980s, we had to justify why we thought this was important to people at all levels of organizations. The leadership and managerial focus was on how to command better, how to give clear directions and ensure compliance. But the world was changing, and there was greater need for managing laterally and upward—along with less ability to just give orders downward. Today, we meet no one who works in an organization larger than 10 people who does not understand that gaining cooperation through influence is the lifeblood of contemporary work life. Anyone who has ever been charged with coordinating the efforts of many others knows the importance of influence and just how maddening it can be to need others to get work done, but not be able to move them. We have lost count of the people who hear the title of this book, *Influence without Authority,* and instantly say, "That's my life."

Do you recognize your organizational life in any of these challenges?

- You have been asked to head a cross-functional task force and have to get people outside your area committed to the project, but they are not cooperating.
- You are on a cross-functional task force and are caught between loyalty to your department and the emerging recommendations of the task force.
- You are on a task force or workgroup assignment, and other members are leaving all the work to you, despite your pleas to pick up some of the slack.
- You are in product development and need the cooperation of a key person or department in marketing to test out a new product you are developing.
- You are in marketing, but can't get the regional managers or salesforce to think about the brand in any coherent way.
- You are in human resources, and have all kinds of ideas about how managers could be better at developing their employees, but they claim they are too busy to attend your programs.

- You have a great idea, but are in a lower organizational position and need approval from management to pursue it. Even if you could figure out who to talk to, they don't understand the problem and probably won't listen to you.
- You see how the company could be much more efficient in dealing with customers or suppliers, but other departments would have to do things differently—and they like things the way they are.
- You often have to ask colleagues to shift their priorities, to pay attention to your requests—giving you some of their precious "mindshare"—even to sacrifice a portion of their resources or to take a risk and use up some of their credits with others in the organization.
- You could be far more effective if you could figure out how to get your controlling boss off your back.
- You can't get the attention of your boss for anything; she is far too busy at endless meetings and dealing with "crises."
- You need your boss to support you and be willing to provide "flight cover" on the approach you want to use to handle a difficult customer.
- You have a talented person reporting to you who won't listen to your advice about how to handle difficult colleagues; as a result, he is far less effective than he could be.

As these examples (and the endless number of others like them) illustrate, the organizational world is getting increasingly complex. (See Table 1.1 for the forces causing the greater need for influence.) Few people can get anything of significance done alone; as in the Tennessee Williams play, we are all "dependent on the kindness of strangers" [and colleagues]. This

Table 1.1 Forces Increasing the Need for Influence Skills

The increasing rapidity of technological change and shortening of product cycles.
More competition (including internationally).
Complex problems require smarter employees, more input from specialists and more need for integration. This makes it difficult to command excellence.
More information is needed, and more is accessible via information technology.
Lower organizational slack due to downsizing and cost-cutting, so more use of all employees needed.
Greater emphasis on quality and service, so "getting by" doesn't get by.
Fewer middle managers as a result of technology and downsizing.
Fewer traditional hierarchies, more lateral organizational forms, including product-based, geographical, customer-focused, matrix, virtual, and networked organizations.

requires influence in three directions. Along with death and taxes, an inevitable certainty of organizational life is that everyone has a boss. In a flat organization, the boss may be a distant and benevolent resource and, in a more hierarchical one, the boss may be breathing down your neck: but no one escapes having a person officially responsible for him or her. Even CEOs have a Board and one or more sources of financing they must influence, not to mention the financial markets, the press, and other organizations needed to create or sell company products.

Similarly, virtually everyone in organizations has peers to deal with. There are very few jobs where a person works completely solo. Most are dependent upon, and important to, a variety of colleagues.

Finally, some people also have responsibility as supervisors of others—the bosses to all those subordinates just mentioned. These managers are expected to utilize the talents of their subordinates to see that the work their area is assigned gets done.

Therefore, those who keep their heads down and only work within their immediate areas will slowly become extinct. Whatever your job, you are expected to join your colleagues in doing important work, which will lead you to influence and be influenced. You will need to know how to sell important projects, persuade colleagues to provide needed resources, create satisfactory working relationships with them and their managers, insist that your boss respond to issues that may not appear important to him or her, and, in turn, give thoughtful responses to requests associates make of *you*. The person asking something of you today may be the very one you'll need next week.

With so much interdependence required, wielding influence becomes a test of skill (Table 1.1). Going hat in hand to throw yourself at a colleague's mercy with a request is seldom a powerful or very effective option. Of course, trying to bull your way through by sheer nerve and aggressiveness can be costly as well. Antagonizing crucial peers or superiors is a dangerous strategy, since they can so easily come back to haunt you.

When you already know how to get needed cooperation, just do it. But if you are stuck, or frustrated, or want to be sure how best to approach someone, then this book has a universal model that can be applied in any organization, to any person or group, in any direction, to get results.

What we have to teach you is based on a few core premises. These are not exotic or unfamiliar, though we have seen hundreds of people abandon what they know when they get stuck, or turned down too often:

- Influence is about trades, exchanging something the other values in return for what you want.

- Relationships matter; the more good ones you have, the greater the odds of being able to find the right people to trade with, the odds of having some goodwill to help the trades along.
- Influence at work requires that you know what you are doing, have reasonable plans, are competent at the task at hand—but that often isn't enough. It is just the price of admission.
- You have to want influence for the ultimate good of the organization. In the short term, that may not be necessary, but genuine care for the organization's goals makes you more credible, more trustworthy, keeps you from being seen as only in it for yourself, and prevents those whom you have influenced from ruining your reputation or seeking retaliation.
- Your difficulty with influence often rests, unfortunately, with you. Sometimes it is just a matter of not knowing what to do, and that is relatively easy to fix. But at certain critical moments, all of us do things that keep us from being as effective as we could be. While occasionally the other party is truly impossible, far more often, the source of the influence deficit is something that you are doing—or failing to do.
- Just about everyone is potentially much more influential than they think they are.

WHY AN INFLUENCE MODEL?

You already know a lot more about influence than you realize. Some of the time, you can just ask for what you need, and if the other person or group can respond, they will. Sometimes you have to work a little harder to figure out how to get what you want. You may not think about it, but you instinctively understand that when someone helps you, you are expected sooner or later to somehow pay them back, in some reasonable way. This kind of give and take—formally called exchange—is a core part of all human interaction, and the lubricant that makes organizations able to function at all.

Although the concept of give and take is in many ways simple and straightforward, the *process* of exchange is more complicated. When you already have a good relationship, you don't need conscious diagnosis, careful planning of your approach, or subtlety of implementation. Like the person who discovered that after all these years he was unknowingly speaking "prose," you probably already are instinctively doing much of what we describe here, especially when things are going well.

Table 1.2   Barriers to Influence

External	Internal
Power differential too big	Lack of knowledge about how to influence
Different goals and objectives, priorities	Blinding attitudes
Incompatible measures and rewards	Fear of reactions
Rivalry, competitiveness, jealousy	Inability to focus on own needs and benefits to others

Remember, an influence model—including careful diagnosis of the other's interests, assessment of what currencies you command, attention to the relationship—is only necessary when:

- The other person or group is known to be resistant.
- You don't know the other people and are asking something that might be costly to them.
- You have a poor relationship (or are part of a group that has a poor relationship with the group the other person belongs to).
- You are asking for something that could be a big burden to give.
- You might not get another chance.

But look at all the times when these are the conditions you are facing, so that your natural understanding of give and take leaves you stuck. Despite your enthusiasm for what you are trying to accomplish, the harder you push the more you are met with resistance.

We're going to show you how to get out of this kind of maddening bind, how to step back and figure out a way that will work.

BARRIERS TO INFLUENCE

So why is it so hard to get influence at those times when your natural instincts and knowledge of how things work leave you stuck? (See Table 1.2 for a summary.)

Some of what blocks influence is external to you, for example:

- *Too great a power differential between you and the person or group you want to influence.* All of the focus on influence assumes that you have no better than equal formal power (a position that gives you the right to give orders) in relation to those you want to influence. The book teaches you to find ways to increase your resources. But sometimes the difference is so great that you have little to offer.

- *The people you want to influence have different goals and objectives from yours, leading to different priorities, and you can't find common ground.* By their organizational roles, some people will not care about what you are trying to accomplish, because they have such different expectations. Sometimes they just have completely incompatible personal goals.
- *The people you want to influence have incompatible performance measures and rewards.* Similarly, by organizational role, they may be held accountable for and rewarded for things that won't let them respond to what you want. The measurement system may leave them with little latitude.
- *The people you want to influence are rivals, or feel competitive and don't want you to succeed.* If your success will be seen as somehow interfering with their success, you may not be able to get help even when they know it would be good for the company. Also, they might have such strong personal animosity toward you or your area that it clouds their judgment.

These are objective reasons why it can be hard to get what you need for doing the good work you want to do. Occasionally, you can't overcome these barriers, no matter how skilled an influencer you are. However, we have discovered that far more often, the barriers are *inside* the influencer. You may not have the needed knowledge of the situation and skills to move the resistant person, or may not have the required attitudes and courage.

These internal barriers include:

- *Lack of knowledge of how to go about influencing when there are objective difficulties.* As instinctive as some kinds of influence are, many people do not have a very conscious idea of how to go about it when the other person or group is not responsive. They don't think of influence as a kind of exchange, and don't understand how important it is to deliver something of value to the *other* person, rather than what they themselves value. They revert to emphasizing how wonderful what they want is, and forget that it has to appeal to something the other person or group cares about.
- *Attitudes that blind you to important objective information that would help you.* Do you think that you shouldn't have to try to influence

others; they should just recognize truth (or a better mousetrap) and give in? Another attitude that gets in the way is the rapid writing off of anyone who doesn't quickly go along with a request, assuming that they are deficient in some important way. We will have a lot to say about this all-too-common barrier and how to overcome it. And another handicap is knowing what would move the other person but you can't stand people who want that, so you back off or become hostile.

- *Fear of the other person or group and how they might react.* Frequently, people recognize that to have influence they would have to say something that might get the other person or group angry, or wanting to retaliate. Out of fear, usually untested (and often unfounded), they decide they can't go ahead. Even the idea that pushing might make the other person not like you can paralyze some people.
- *Inability to focus on what you need and how the other person could benefit from that.* Sometimes people who want influence aren't very clear about exactly what their goals are, who they have to influence to accomplish their goals. This leads to stressing the wrong things and getting hung up on secondary, often symbolic, issues.

OVERCOME THE BARRIERS: USE AN INFLUENCE MODEL TO GUIDE YOU

Can you get past these kinds of barriers? We are going to help you step back and use some new guidelines. The challenge will be to overcome your own feelings and reactions, so that you do a better diagnosis of just what is called for, and learn to get past the fears and misconceptions that block you. In the next chapter we introduce the Cohen-Bradford Influence without Authority model, and build your learning from there.

The model starts from the observation that all influence is about the person being influenced getting something valued in return (or avoiding something disliked) for willingness to give what is requested. This kind of trading—formal or informal—can be examined systematically, so that you can better figure out what others want, clarify exactly what you want, identify what you have to offer, and build a mutually influential relationship to produce win–win trades. The price of admissions is doing good work. That is basic because it creates trust that you are a dependable performer. But that is seldom enough; you also need to have a wide set of good relationships, often way before you draw on them, and enough self-awareness to avoid the many self-traps that can keep you from effective influence.

This may sound calculating—and it is. But it is deliberate planning about how to get work done; not calculation for your own personal benefit. If people perceive you as interested only in your own advancement or success, they will be wary, resistant, or go underground to retaliate later. In this way, influence in organizations over time goes to the sincere, those genuinely interested in the welfare of others, those who make lots of connections and often engage in mutually profitable exchanges. Machiavellian, calculating, self-seeking behavior may work for a short time, but eventually, it creates enemies, or lack of interest in being helpful, and renders you ineffective. When someone wants to get you, they can trade negative actions for your behavior, and this kind of payback can be unpleasant. If you are in an organization that has developed a negative culture where only self-seeking gets rewarded, it eventually suffers and declines. People who care about the organization's objectives get disenchanted and leave as soon as they can, and those who stay spread bitterness.

THE BOOK'S ORGANIZATION

Here's how we do it. This chapter has introduced the need for influence, and the benefits of learning a more systematic way of thinking about how to get it. Chapter 2 spells out the core influence model, and Chapters 3 through 7 go into more detail about each stage of the model. Then in a series of Practical Application chapters, we use the influence model in familiar situations to demonstrate how to get what you need to do good work. You may want to read selectively among these chapters to fit your current situation, and then return later as you move into other, more complex settings.

In addition, we offer on our web site seven extended examples of people who had to go through many obstacles to acquire influence (http://www .influencewithoutauthority.com). (For more detail about these examples and the lessons we draw from them, see Appendix A on pages 291–295.)

We show how Nettie Seabrooks, an African American who started as a librarian in the 1960s, slowly gained influence during her long career at General Motors.

You can read about Warren Peters, a manager who thought he was following procedures, yet gets into and out of a tangle with a more senior manager who gives him a hard time about a person Warren wants as an employee.

Or look closely at how Anne Austin, a low level sales forecaster at a Fortune 100 consumer goods company, figured out how to get her product idea accepted, and as a result, managed to cross the usually impenetrable marketing department barrier into a product manager's job.

You can hear from Monica Ashley how she tackled a complex matrix organization and a powerful but negative senior researcher to introduce a revolutionary new product—and ended up being removed from her product management role even though she was eventually proven right.

If you want to see how a lone person managed to work in a new community to build interest in and support for a radical idea like wind power, we have included the saga of a minor miracle in Montana.

For a good example of using influence to make change, we include the story of Will Wood, a training and development person who learned to speak the language of finance in order to gain support for expensive software needed for innovative online training.

And Fran Grigsby tells how she managed to navigate the political waters at Commuco to end a pet project of an important manager without ruffling too many feathers.

These extended examples allow for a more complete telling and situational analysis if you like to learn from that kind of comprehensive opportunity. Again, you can find all of them at http://www.influencewithoutauthority.com.

This is a book that can help you get ahead, by showing you how to make good things happen for the organization and for those you will be dealing with. More power to you.

PART II

THE INFLUENCE MODEL

CHAPTER 2

THE INFLUENCE MODEL: TRADING WHAT THEY WANT FOR WHAT YOU'VE GOT (USING RECIPROCITY AND EXCHANGE)

I have done enough for you, Apollo; now it's your turn to do something for me.
—Rough translation of inscription on a Greek statue of the
God Apollo, 700–675 B.C., demonstrating ancient
understanding of the concept of reciprocity.[1]

*It is not always evident when you are going to make a withdrawal from the
favor bank of politics, . . . but it is always obvious you are making a deposit.*
—From "Giuliani Plays Major Role on Bush Campaign Trail,"
Jennifer Steinhauer, New York Times *(August 12, 2004), p. A1,*
demonstrating contemporary understanding of reciprocity.

To address the kinds of challenges we have described in Chapter 1, how can you influence those over whom you have no authority? The short answer is that to have influence, you need resources that other people want, so that you can trade for what you want. This key to influence is based on a principle that underlies all human interaction, the Law of Reciprocity.

IGNORE THE LAW OF RECIPROCITY AT YOUR PERIL

Reciprocity is the almost universal belief that people should be paid back for what they do—that one good (or bad) turn deserves another.[2] This belief about behavior, evident in primitive and not-so-primitive societies all around the world, carries over into organizational life. One form it takes in work settings is, "an honest day's work for an honest day's pay."

People generally expect that, over time, those people they have done things for "owe them," and will roughly balance the ledger and repay costly acts with equally valuable ones. This underlying belief in how things are supposed to work allows people in difficult organizational situations to gain cooperation. A classic study of prison guards found that the guards could not control prisoners, who greatly outnumbered them, by threats and punishments alone.[3] The guards did many favors for the prisoners, such as overlooking small rule infractions, providing cigarettes, and the like, in return for cooperation from prisoners in keeping order. All the formal authority in the world can't keep rebellious prisoners in line; they exchange their cooperation for favors that make their confinement more tolerable, not out of respect for "the rules."

Even at much higher levels of organizations, little gets done without similar give and take. One manager alerts her colleague that their CEO is on a rampage and should be avoided today. Eventually, the grateful colleague repays the favor by telling the manager what he learned at a conference about a competitor's IT strategy. Soon after, the manager hears about a potential new customer who she refers to the colleague; when the colleague has the chance, he initiates a joint project that can cut several steps out of the billing process and save the manager considerable money. The give and take of their relationship makes organizational life better for both.

Give and take can also be negative. The trade can be a loss of a benefit for lack of cooperation, or a cost that results from an undesirable response. Negative trades can be expressed as threats about what will happen in the future, or can result in both parties losing.

EXCHANGE: THE ART OF GIVE AND TAKE THAT PERMEATES ALL INFLUENCE TACTICS

There are numerous ways of categorizing influence behavior. You can influence people by methods such as rational persuasion, inspirational appeal, consultation, ingratiation, personal appeal, forming a coalition, or relentless pressure.[4]

Although it is tempting to think of each of these methods as a separate tactic, we believe that exchange—trading something valued for what you want—is actually the basis for all of them. In *every* form of influence,

Table 2.1 Examples of Reciprocity at Work

You Give	*You Get*
Work that job description calls for	Standard pay and benefits
Willingness to work on weekend to complete project	Boss praises you, mentions extra effort to higher-ups, suggests you extend vacation
Support for a colleague's project at a key meeting	Colleague gives you first shot at project results
A difficult analysis requested by colleague not in your area	Colleague tells your boss how terrific you are

reciprocity is at work and something is being exchanged.[5] For example, rational persuasion works because the person persuaded sees benefits from going along with the argument; inspirational appeal works because the person gets to feel part of a cause, or that something good will result; ingratiation works because the person receives liking and closeness for willingness to be influenced, and so on. None of these tactics succeed, however, if the receiver does not perceive benefit of some kind, a payment in a valued "currency." It is valuable to have a wide repertoire of ways of trying to influence others. You should use those tactics that will work in a given situation; *the underlying principle is giving something valued by the other(s) in return for what you want or need (or withholding something the other values—or giving them something they don't want—if you don't get what you need).*

This kind of reciprocity is constantly taking place in organizational life. People do things and get something in return (Table 2.1).

Why an Influence Model?

Although the *concept* of exchange in many ways is simple and straightforward, the *process* of exchange is more complicated. When you already have a good relationship with another person, there is no need for such conscious diagnosis of the situation and thinking through the appropriate approach. You just ask, and if the colleague can respond, he or she will. This doesn't mean that our model doesn't apply. It does; it just means you are instinctively using it.

But there are other times when it is not so easy to influence the other person, and a more deliberate and conscious approach is needed. That is why this influence model—a careful diagnosis of the other's interests, assessment of what resources you possess, and attention to the relationship—can be so valuable. Table 2.2 on page 19 lists the conditions that require a more systematic way of diagnosing your influence approach.

Reciprocity Naturally Takes Place
in Organizational Life

Dr. Stanley Snyder, scientist, inventor, and entrepreneur, is an untenured senior scientist at a leading Midwestern university. As a maverick and self-described organizational outsider, Dr. Snyder learned to gain necessary influence through difficult experience. Dr. Snyder had been for a long time an adjunct member of the biology department, a natural home because he had his PhD in molecular biology. In that department, he had developed several patented technologies for the university and paid his own way through royalties and grants. However, he had been a thorn in the side of the Assistant Provost for Research, who Dr. Snyder believed had been looking for an excuse to get rid of him for some time.

The anthrax scare immediately following 9/11/01 provided the precipitating excuse for a confrontation. Dr. Snyder's work had principally involved biology, but when the U.S. government had started the search for a quick test to determine the presence of anthrax, and a company approached Dr. Snyder for assistance in developing such a test, Dr. Snyder "came to the rescue." He worked with a colleague who had an anthrax strain in her research collection and had previous experience culturing these bacteria. They rather quickly came up with an inexpensive and practical detection method for anthrax. Dr. Snyder then went to the University Provost to announce the good news and to help arrange a corporate license agreement, with royalties to go to the University. Instead of welcoming the news, the university administration, according to Dr. Snyder, "went ballistic," prompted by the high anxiety over anthrax. He and his colleague were subjected to a university investigation, and then were investigated by the local police and the FBI as if they were reckless scientists and criminals. They were placed on administrative leave (a very negative exchange!).

Dr. Snyder had liked working at the university where he had colleagues and research collaborators. He did not wish to leave, and at first could only think of fighting the university. During this stressful period, a leading member of the physics department, Dr. Zelikoff, whom Dr. Snyder had previously helped in writing a patent application, met with him. As they were discussing Snyder's employment problem, Dr. Zelikoff offered to explore the possibility of having him join the physics department. A bit of an individualist himself, but skilled at working within the university organization, Dr. Zelikoff wanted to help both Dr. Snyder and the university resolve a difficult situation. He studied the policies and procedures and realized that he could invite Dr. Snyder (who would be self-funding anyway), to the department. Dr. Zelikoff would get a useful colleague and the department would receive a share of Dr. Snyder's royalties. Dr. Snyder would gain a degree of protection and oversight as well as laboratory and office space. Resisting the efforts of the Assistant Provost for Research to terminate Dr. Snyder, they worked out a deal with the Provost (manager of the Assistant Provost) that was beneficial to Dr. Snyder, the department, and the university. Dr. Snyder is currently hard at work on applied research and new inventions.

Table 2.2   Conditions Requiring Conscious Use of an Influence Model

Use an influence model when faced with one or more of the following conditions:

- The other person is known to be resistant.
- You don't know the other person or group and are asking for something that might be costly to them.
- You have a poor relationship (or are part of a group that has a poor relationship with the group the other person belongs to).
- You might not get another chance.
- You have tried everything you can think of but the other person still refuses what you want.

Conscious attention to this model isn't necessary at all times, but when useful, think of the model as analogous to a pilot's checklist, which is followed routinely when undertaking a flight. Pilots know what to do, but going through the checklist makes sure they cover all the bases. Such an influence checklist is especially helpful when faced with an anxiety-provoking situation that tends to narrow your focus and constrain the alternatives considered. We have built a model of influence (Figure 2.1) to guide you when you are in difficult circumstances.[6] Let's look at the parts of the model.

Assume All—the Other Person or Group—Are Potential Allies

One of the greatest challenges to influence is trying to influence someone who isn't cooperating. Rather than writing that person off prematurely assume that everyone you want to influence *could be a potential ally* if you work at it. When you need something from someone who has no formal obligation to cooperate, begin by assessing whether you could form an alliance by discovering where there might be overlapping interests. Failure to do that by assuming the other person will be an adversary rather than an ally prevents accurate understanding, leading to misperceptions, stereotypes, and miscommunication, and can create a self-fulfilling prophecy. Treating the other person as an enemy produces adversarial responses. This same mind-set of assuming the other person is a potential ally also applies to your manager; if you assume that managers are partners in the organization with subordinates, then it is also part of your responsibility, along with the manager, to figure out how to make the relationship mutually beneficial. (In Chapter 12, we explore in detail how to do that.)

Figure 2.1
Summary of the Cohen-Bradford Model of Influence without Authority

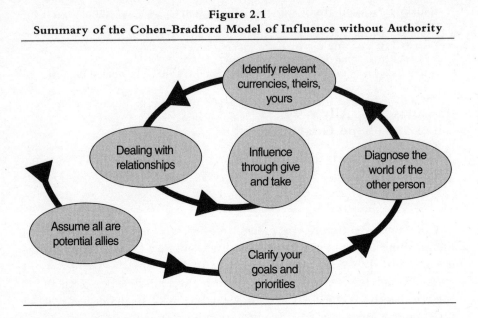

Clarify Your Goals and Priorities

Knowing what you want from the potential ally isn't always easy. The dimensions that affect the choice of how you should proceed are:

- What are your primary versus your secondary goals?
- Are they short-term or long-term objectives?
- Are they "must-have" needs or "nice-to-haves" that can be negotiated away?
- Is your priority task accomplishment or preserving/improving the relationship?

You need to think hard about your core objectives, so you won't get side tracked into pursuing secondary goals. Just what do you require, what are your priorities among several possibilities, what you are willing to trade off to get the minimum you need? Do you want a particular form of cooperation on a specific item or would you settle for a better relationship in the future? Would a short-term victory be worth the creation of hard feelings, or is the ability to come back to the person in the future more important?

Too often, the person desiring influence does not sort personal desires from what is truly necessary on the job, and creates confusion or resistance.

For example, if you are overly concerned about being right at all costs, humiliating the other person, or always having the last word, your personal concerns can become central and interfere with other more important organizational goals. Would you rather be right or effective?

Diagnose the Ally's World: Organizational Forces Likely to Shape Goals, Concerns, and Needs

The challenge here is to determine the organizational situation of the potential ally that drives much of what he or she cares about. These forces usually play an even greater role in shaping what is important to them than their personality. If for any reason you can't ask that person directly, examine the organizational forces that might shape goals, concerns, or needs. For example, how a person is measured and rewarded, the manager's and peer's expectations, where the person is in his or her career, and so on, have a powerful effect on what the person might want in exchange for cooperation, and what the costs would be for giving what you want.

This diagnostic activity helps overcome the tendency to blame bad personality, character, or motives for behavior that you do not like or understand, and can help to see the person behind the role. Understanding the pressures that person is under can help you avoid "demonizing," and start seeing a potential ally.

Identify Relevant Currencies (What Is Valued): The Ally's and Yours

We have named the things that people care about "currencies," because that equates something of value you have that you can trade for something valuable they have. Most people care about more than one thing (e.g., prestige, money, being liked). If you can identify several applicable currencies, you will have a wider range of possibilities to offer in exchange (Table 2.3).

Table 2.3   Sources of Currencies

Sources	Examples
Organizationally determined	Performance, how to behave, reward system
Job determined	Meeting measures, doing required work well
Personally determined	Preferred style, reputation

Assess Your Resources Relative to the Ally's Wants.   It is not unlikely that your ally wants some things that you can't offer. Therefore, it is important to know what resources you command or have access to, so that you can use a currency that fits. Because many people underestimate the resources they can muster, they jump to the conclusion that they are powerless. But a careful look at the many things you can do without a budget or formal permission—the alternative currencies you command—can reveal potential bargaining chips. Employees lose influence, for example, by failing to see the wide range of currencies they can offer their manager, such as getting work done on time, passing on important information from other areas, defending their manager to others, alerting the manager to potential disasters, and so on.

Dealing with Relationships

This has two aspects: (1) What is the nature of your relationship with that person—positive, neutral, or negative? (2) How does that person want to be related to?

You might have a prior relationship, and if it is a good one, then it will be easier to ask for what you want without having to prove your good intentions. If, however, the relationship has a history of mistrust—whether for personal reasons or because you represent departments in conflict—or there has been no prior contact, proceed with caution. You will need to pay attention to building the requisite trust and credibility.

Each person has preferred ways of being related to. Some like you to bring a thorough analysis before you launch into discussion with them, while others would rather hear preliminary ideas with a chance to brainstorm. Some want to see alternative solutions, whereas others want only your final conclusion. Be careful not to relate in the style you most prefer without taking into account the other person's preferences. You will have more influence if you use an approach the other person is comfortable with.

Determine Your Trading Approach: Make Exchanges

Once you have determined what goods or services can be exchanged, then you are ready to offer what you *have* in return for what you *want*. Your approach will be shaped by:

- The attractiveness of your resources
- The ally's needs for what you have

- Your desire for what the ally has
- Your organization's unwritten rules about how explicitly people can express what they want and need
- Your prior relationship with the potential ally, as well as the preferred style of interaction
- Your willingness to take chances to pursue what you want

This helps you plan an approach that has the best chance of being judged on its merits. We will discuss all of these issues in more detail later in this book, but for now it is important to understand that expectations of reciprocity are vital in gaining influence.

Outcomes of Exchange: Task and Relationship Are Both Important

In organizations, all influence attempts simultaneously contain both a task and a relationship component. There is the work at hand and the nature of the relationship: In addition, people seldom interact without past experience or knowledge of each other somehow shaping the discussion. (In fact, it isn't even necessary for you to have actually interacted with someone to have your reputation from other interactions a factor in how the person will deal with you.) Furthermore, ideas about the results for the relationship in the future are likely also to affect the discussion. Ignoring the future, risks winning the battle, but losing the war. You can choose to ignore the history, or the consequences of your exchange attempts on the relationship, but that could be a problem if you have to deal with the same party again, as usually is the case in organizations.

Trust plays an important part in achieving influence. If other people perceive you are too calculating or interested in influence for your personal benefit rather than for organizational work, they will be wary, resistant, or go underground to retaliate later. In this way, influence in organizations over time goes to those genuinely interested in the welfare of others, those who make connections and often engage in mutually profitable exchanges. Machiavellian, calculating, self-seeking behavior may work for a short time, but eventually it creates enemies, or lack of interest in being helpful, making the person who will do anything to win ineffective.

Because good relationships make it easier to gain cooperation, it pays to be generous and engage in win–win exchanges. Doing good work together, living up to what you say you will do, or just providing what is valued by the other party, improves relationships. Making successful trades tends to make people feel better about one another.

Make Connections Early and Often.   There are times when a poor relationship makes it almost impossible to get others to make task exchanges, even when it might be in their best interest. Then time has to be spent rebuilding the relationship before any task work can be done. To prevent this, find a way to make relationships before they are needed. Suppose you want a special analysis from a colleague in order to proceed with your new product planning. If the relationship has been strained, you may first need to relieve the strain and reestablish the relationship. This will ease the conversation about the information you need and aid in finding a basis for getting the help you want.

Finally, a discussion of what you want and the quality of the relationship are always concurrent. Pay attention to the *process* of discussion about exchange. If you focus only on the task outcome—getting your way—you may not only harm future dealings, but you may lose the deal.

Making many relationships and creating a positive reputation means that your credit will be good, and you will have longer to pay back the help received. Having a good reputation is a form of saving for a rainy day, like making a goodwill deposit in a bank, so that you have the capacity for drawing on it later. Try not to mortgage the future; you never know when you will need to call in your chips.

Exchanges Can Be Positive or Negative

As mentioned earlier, exchanges can be positive or negative. If positive they take the form, "I do something beneficial for you and in turn you do something that is of value for me." But you can also exchange negatives for negatives, as in, "I have little inclination to go out of my way for your requests since you won't do that for mine."

Note two forms of negative exchange: (1) implicit or explicit threat of what you might do, or what might happen as a consequence of the other person's responses; and (2) negative retaliation, in which both sides end up losing. Negative payback can feel unpleasant for both the sender and the receiver, but it can be necessary if positive exchanges are eventually to occur. Lose-lose retaliatory exchanges are the least desirable, to be used only as a last resort. If the organization has developed the kind of negative culture where only self-striving gets rewarded, it suffers and declines. People who care about the organization's objectives get disgusted and leave as soon as they can.

You May Occasionally Need to Use Negative Exchanges. Even offers of positive exchange, however, implicitly contain a message about the negative consequences that will result from not accepting it. If compliance will result in mutual benefit, there is always the underlying possibility that *not* complying will lead to negative results for both parties. You can make clear or leave unsaid how you will repay refusal with a comparable future refusal to cooperate, or a willingness to inflict something negative. "If you help me I will give you my undying gratitude," can also mean, "if you do not help me I will not give you any gratitude (and may even be upset)." Similarly, "If you can loan me that chemical engineer, I can complete this essential project," implies that failure to comply will stop the project and something valuable will be lost. Finally, you can use negative exchanges to gradually up the ante, making it increasingly undesirable not to cooperate.

Being overt about the possibility of a negative exchange can be useful in moving things along, putting teeth into the request. It shows seriousness and can be a powerful way to move others—if the threat is real and the other person cares about it.

While the threat of negative consequences is a less friendly way to make exchanges, it may be necessary in difficult situations. The mule may need a whack with a two-by-four to get its attention when no amount of coaxing will move it. When mentioning negative consequences, it is usually helpful to also hold out a carrot: "I don't want to have to resort to this, I would much prefer X, but if that can't occur, I will be forced to . . ." We have more to say about this in Chapter 7 on making exchanges.

A problem arises, however, when frustration with lack of cooperation—now or in the past—causes you to *open* with threats of negative exchanges, not out of careful diagnosis but out of aggravation. Feeling stymied can force people to move rapidly to negative ways of operating, relying on threats as a first resort rather than a distant last one. That may cause a negative reaction in itself, getting in the way of the possibility of making a deal.

Have a Bias Toward Positive Exchanges. Although negative exchanges can be powerful influencers, we encourage beginning with the positive side of exchange. There are some people who find it more difficult to get tough when necessary, but we believe that a positive emphasis will expand the influence repertoires of most people.

Taking a negative approach may create its own form of reciprocity, one in which the other person feels compelled to oppose you. You create a self-fulfilling prophecy. Threatened people often automatically start to fight fire with fire, increasing their resistance. The person becomes more difficult, reinforcing your negative opinion, which induces you to be tougher. The negativism escalates until each of you is irritated and unlikely to bend. Even worse, if you gain a reputation for the negative, some potential allies will take a negative posture toward you *before* you do anything to them. The potential threat of your setting fires causes them to burn you first.

Another reason for accentuating the positive is that peers and superiors may be stronger; they may have at least as many resources available to retaliate as you do, which heightens the potential dangers from getting into a spitting contest. They may salivate at the chance to show who is tougher. Positive expectations, on the other hand, create an atmosphere that makes win-win outcomes more likely. Much of what transpires after you make a request depends not only on the extent to which you speak to the person's needs, but also on how much the person trusts you—a product of your past actions and the extent to which the person views you as a good corporate citizen.

Furthermore, you need to think beyond the present. The pace of change in modern organizations makes it hard to know what your future relationship will be. You may one day find yourself in the position of the other person's subordinate, manager, or dependent peer. If it is at all likely that you will have to deal with anyone again, act as if you probably can find mutual objectives and outcomes. By doing that, you give them credit for being as interested in good results as you are. Should the assumption later prove to be untrue, you can fall back on other strategies and assumptions.

SELF-CREATED BARRIERS TO INFLUENCING

We have described a straightforward model for diagnosing what to do and executing it to achieve desired influence. Over the years, we have taught many people to use this model successfully. But we have also observed many failed efforts at each stage of the model, whether or not the person was aware or conscious of using it. Either the person desiring influence manages to make things worse, gives up prematurely, or doesn't even try in

Table 2.4   Common Self-Created Barriers to Influencing

Not assuming other person is at least a potential ally.
Not carifying your goals and priorities.
Not diagnosing ally's world: organizational forces likely to shape goals, concerns, needs.
Not determining the ally's currencies.
Knowing but not accepting the ally's currencies.
Not assessing your resources relative to the ally's wants.
Not diagnosing your relationship with the potential ally (and fixing it if necessary).
Not figuring out how you want to make trades—and making them.

frustration from anticipated failure. Before we expand in subsequent chapters on how to use each of the important parts of the model, here are the most common ways that people block their own effectiveness at each stage. Table 2.4 can serve as warning alerts to monitor yourself as you try to make things happen at work.

***Barrier: Not Assuming the Other Person Is at Least a* Potential Ally.** Failure to think in a positive way about people who are difficult to influence is perhaps the deadliest of self-created traps. It usually starts with a request that is turned down. You want something that to you is clearly important, and well within the capacity of the other person to deliver. Sometimes this is followed by a second request and, if you are really determined, a third. Few people can be turned down two to three times without walking away from the interaction convinced that there is something fundamentally wrong with the other person. (Psychologists call this *attribution*.)[7] There is a defect of character, motives, or intelligence, or the person is a "perfect representative of that miserable group of incompetents from . . . (the offending group)." The negative attribution doesn't have to be spoken out loud ("Just another empty suit from marketing." "Another engineering nerd." "A numbers-obsessed shark from finance." "A soft-headed bleeding heart from HR." "A green eyeshade accountant who doesn't have the personality to be an actuary."), but it gets communicated anyway.

The problem is that once you even think such a thing, whether or not you verbalize it, the targets sense that you believe they are defective, and close off. Who wants to be influenced by someone with the equivalent of a red neon sign on the forehead that says, *"I think you are a jerk!"* The difficulty is that once you think the person is a jerk (or worse), it is hard to find a big enough cover for the neon sign.

Classic Joke on the Hazards of Assuming the Worst of Someone You Want to Influence: The Story of the Jack

A man was driving an unfamiliar country road late at night, when his tire blew. He intended to change the tire, but discovered that he had no jack in the trunk. After fuming a while, he decided that his only choice was to walk until he found a farmhouse and borrow a jack. As he walked, he began to worry that it was late, dark, and he would be a stranger waking up the occupant in the middle of the night. But lacking any alternative and feeling cold, he kept walking. Finally, he saw a farmhouse, but as he got closer, he grew more and more concerned about the likely reaction from the person he would be waking. "He's going to be really upset, he'll be angry, and might have a gun," and so on. Finally he got there, knocked, and yet again imagined how upset the farmer was going to be. After a lot of knocking and a long wait, the light went on and door opened. The traveler punched the farmer, shouted, "You can keep your damn jack!" and stomped off.

Separate your frustration at the moment (which is real) from the conclusion that this person could never be an ally. Even though he or she may think there is a rational reason for opposition, search for some common ground. Try not to write off anyone, no matter how difficult they appear. If after all efforts you fail, there is plenty of time to be dismissive.

Barrier: Not Clarifying Your Goals and Priorities. You may be tempted to build up a long list of what you desire, especially from someone you haven't had success with or anticipate resistance from, but that only causes overload and makes people back away. Another mistake we see often is the mixing together of personal and organizational objectives. Not only is some resource or support requested, but also personal recognition, or extra attention, or in the case of someone who is in an organizational minority, admission that the minority person (such as a marketing expert in a technical organization, a woman in a male-dominated organization, an African American in a White-dominated organization), is truly a worthy equal. Getting good work done, over time, usually eventually brings you the personal acclaim desired; mixing it into the work-related request can cause a reaction to the mixed messages and reduce the chances of getting what you most need.

Another important barrier arises when your intense *personal* needs—to win, not to lose face, to do the other in, to show how smart you are, to get ahead, and so on—get in the way of the other person being sure that you

---

**Example of Failing to Take into Account
Organizational Forces Driving Resistant
Behavior at an International Software Company**

A product manager is frustrated because the Country Manager in France won't push his salesforce to try an important new product. But it turns out that the Country Manager is measured by total country sales and it is much more work for his salesforce to explain and sell a new, low list-price product than to make a few big sales of existing ones. The new-product manager pushes, but gives up in frustration. Lack of cooperation isn't the inevitable result. One mistake is failing to diagnose this difference in objectives in advance and blindly bumping up against it, and the second is even when it is understood, ignoring the other things that might be attractive to the recipient. Perhaps the country manager cares about the prestige of being the first to develop a good market for the new product, or wants to be involved at an earlier stage of market planning, which the product manager could offer.

---

really want the cooperation to get the work done more than a victory. Is personal triumph so important that you are willing to jeopardize the task or relationship? If the answer is "yes," that's your right, but you should be making a conscious choice, not just acting reflexively.

Barrier: Not Diagnosing Ally's World—Organizational Forces Likely to Shape Goals, Concerns, and Needs.   Everyone responds to the situation they are in, especially within organizations. A major source of failed influence is that people in another department are measured for different accomplishments than you are, and they are therefore unwilling to do what is requested. Instead of trying to accommodate to what they inevitably see as very important, you just push them harder to do what you know is important to the organization, and to you.

Barrier: Not Determining the Ally's Currencies.   Even more fundamental is the common failure to pay attention at all to what the person or group to be influenced cares about. Those desiring influence are often so excited about what they are trying to accomplish, so in love with the accomplishment they wish to bring to life, so sure that the value is self-evident, that they ignore what the other person values. We call this "missing by a mile," and every reader has seen, if not personally committed, this self-inflicted limit. Think of the soccer enthusiast trying to sell the game to a basketball or American football fan by raving, "It's such a subtle game of skill and tactics that there is very little scoring, and if you watch long enough, you will see how beautiful it is!" That argument hasn't worked yet, though some keep using it.

Another common major barrier is failing to recognize the possible range of currencies that people can value, assuming that everyone likes only what you like. It isn't only Henry Higgins of *My Fair Lady* fame who can't understand why a woman he wants to influence can't be more like a man, that is, more like him.

A variation of this problem is assuming that the other person only likes one thing, one important currency, and when you don't have any of that, you are stuck, as with the boxed example of the product manager and the French Country Manager. Almost everyone has a valued portfolio of currencies, and even though some are more valued than others, trade-offs are often possible.

Barrier: Not Accepting the Ally's Currencies. Sometimes the influencer does understand what the other person cares about, but doesn't accept those as desirable currencies. It is one thing if what the other person wants violates deeply held values or ethical principles, but often it is just differences. A go-getter with entrepreneurial skills can have difficulty accepting the colleague who focuses on structure and procedures, leading him to want to change the colleague instead of accommodating to what is important to him. Influence by exchange is about giving what the other person wants in return for what you need, *not* about changing what the person wants.

Barrier: Not Assessing Your Resources Relative to the Ally's Wants. The biggest barrier here is failing to recognize that many of the desired currencies held by others are ones that you have in abundance. You don't need anyone's permission to give recognition, show appreciation, confer status, give respect, be understanding, help the other person, and so on. If the only currency the other party will accept is a transfer of budget dollars and you do not yet have a budget for your project, you might be at a dead end, though sometimes creative horse-trading can overcome even that limitation. But most people have more at their disposal than they recognize.

Barrier: Not Diagnosing Your Relationship with the Potential Ally (and Fixing It If Necessary). We have already mentioned that ignoring the benefits of positive relationships can block making exchanges. If you are not trusted, it can be very difficult to get a potential partner to take any risks in working together. Those desiring influence make the mistake of focusing only on the task benefits of transactions, or suddenly trying to be nice at the last minute, which comes across as phony.

Alternatively, some people desiring influence fake interest in the other person, go through the motions of making relationships, or are so instrumental in their approaches to others at every stage of attempting influence, that they are seen as manipulative, creating distrust in the process. No technique works well when the person using it is perceived as *only* self-interested. Our influence model doesn't work when it is used in a way that appears to be only about the influencer's benefit, and not at all about the organization's true needs. This problem is compounded by Machiavellian game players who cloak all requests in the "it's-good-for-the-organization" mantle, as if no one notices their self-orientation.

Barrier: Not Figuring Out How You Want to Make Trades—And Making Them.
Again, failure to create trust is a major barrier to influence. Coming across as a person who makes everything into a tit-for-tat exchange—a wheeler-dealer or a compulsive exchanger who can never rely on mutual goodwill and liking—can cause even attractive deals to get turned down. Occasionally, an influencer goes too far in the other direction, presuming that past positive exchanges and a decent relationship should cause the person being asked for cooperation to completely go against self-interest, and then gets angry at the ally who says that the request is too much. The anger then interferes with the relationship, and future as well as present influence is lost.

Another common barrier is failing to adapt your style of interacting to one preferred by the potential ally. This can be caused by interpersonal blindness, in which, for example, you don't notice that the other person likes concise solutions so you blather on about the complexities of the problem. Sometimes you might recognize the other person's preferred way of being interacted with, but stubbornly stick to your own preferences as a misguided way of "being true to yourself." By defining interaction style as a matter of personal integrity, people wipe out the rights of others to have their own preferences, and cause annoyance, if not worse.

See the boxed example for lessons from an otherwise competent manager failing to get what he wanted because he lacked an appropriate guiding model to help him determine action. Then we begin a series of five chapters that help flesh out the Influence without Authority model. We start with a deeper discussion of currencies and their meanings.

Why Won't He Listen? An All-Too-Common Example of Failed Influence—And How Using the Influence Model Could Have Helped

Bill Heatton* is the director of research at a $250-million division of a large West Coast company. The division, which makes exotic telecommunications components, has many technical advancements to its credit. In the past several years, however, the division's performance has been spotty at best. Despite many efforts to become more profitable, it has racked up multi-million-dollar losses in some years. Several large contracts have been big money losers, causing each part of the division to blame the others for the problems. A major cause of the problem, Bill feels, is Roland, a program manager in Marketing.

Note Bill's frustrations as he talks about his efforts to influence Ted Lowry, his peer and the division's director of marketing. Ted is the direct supervisor of Roland, who has been given the responsibility for an important new contract that marketing and research (along with production) will work on together:

> Another program's about to come through. Roland, the program manager, is a nice guy, but he doesn't know squat and never will. He was responsible for our last big loss, and now he's going to be in charge again. I keep fighting with his manager, Ted Lowry, to move Roland off the program, but I'm getting nowhere. Ted doesn't argue that Roland is capable, but he sure as hell isn't trying to find someone else. Instead, he comes to me with worries about my area.
>
> I'm being a team player here. I responded to their requests by changing my staffing plan, assigning the people they wanted to do the research on Roland's program. I even overruled my own staff's best judgment about who we should assign to the program. But I'm still not getting the progress reports I need from Roland, and he's never "available" for planning. I'm not hearing a lot of argument, but there's not action to correct the problems, either. That's bad, because I'm responding but not getting any response from them. There is no way to resolve this. If they disagree, that's it. I could go for a tit-for-tat strategy. I could tell them that if they don't do what I want, we'll screw them next time. But I don't know how to do that without hurting the organization. That would feel worse than the satisfaction I'd get from sticking it to Roland!
>
> Ted, Roland's manager, is so much better than the guy he replaced that I hate to ask that he be removed as director of marketing. We could go together to our mutual manager, the general manager, but I'd really hate to do that. You've failed in a matrix organization if you have to go to your manager. I have to try hard before I throw it in his lap.
>
> Meanwhile, I'm being forced into insisting that Ted get rid of Roland, but I'm afraid it's in a destructive way. All I want to do is yell. I don't want to wait until the program has failed to be told I've blown it!

---

* All names in this example are disguised, but all else is real.

Bill is clearly angry about the situation and frustrated about his inability to influence Ted Lowry. He finds himself behaving in ways he doesn't feel good about. Bill's failure to use the law of reciprocity lies at the heart of his inability to influence Ted. Because Bill believes he has gone out of his way to help Ted, he expects Ted to reciprocate automatically and remove Roland from the project. When Ted does not act, Bill's anger reflects his belief that, by changing his own staffing patterns, he has created an obligation in Ted. He has established a "credit" with Ted, and Ted should honor that credit and agree to replace Roland.

Bill is also worried about a negative exchange—being blamed unfairly for project failures when he has done his part. He has strong feelings about what credit he should deserve for his efforts; to be judged harshly after extra effort would violate his sense of justice.

Failure to See Others as Potential Allies

Like other managers who very much want to influence someone who is not cooperating, Bill narrows his sense of possibilities by seeing Ted, his potential ally, as an intractable enemy, attributing negative motives to Ted. Because he doesn't know how to get what he needs from Ted, Bill is beginning to leap to dangerous conclusions about why Ted is ignoring his efforts.

Also, he had already written off Roland as a worthwhile ally; and he saw his manager, the general manager, only as a court of last resort rather than as a possible resource for problem solving. Thus, Bill isolated himself from potential allies and felt incapable of affecting any mutually satisfying solution.

Failure to Clarify His Own Goals and Priorities

Bill had a lot of trouble sorting out his goals and priorities. He wanted to get rid of Roland, but that was actually a means to a more important end: improving the project management process and reversing the division's current slump. Bill wanted Ted to acknowledge his needs; but he focused on one particular response, not joint problem solving. He wanted revenge, but he didn't want to harm the organization. He wanted the problem resolved, but he didn't want to involve the general manager because that would look weak. No wonder Bill was unable to muster influence; he had not figured out exactly what mattered most to him. As a result, he was unable to develop a plan of action.

Failure to Diagnose Ally's World and Resulting Currencies

As a result of the very human tendency to focus on self-interests, Bill missed seeing the issue from his potential ally's world and point of view. For example, Bill did not think about what costs Ted would incur if he were to remove Roland from the project.

(Continued)

Bill could easily have determined these interests of Ted:

- Minimize project management costs.
- Utilize existing talent.
- Keep his department from feeling that he doesn't protect them from outside attacks.

Had he been thinking about diagnosis, Bill could have first asked himself the following questions about the situation:

- Does Ted have anyone better?
- Does Ted believe that he can coach Roland into a better performance on this project?
- Does Ted even agree that Roland did a poor job on the last project, or does he blame the project's failure on other departments' shortcomings?
- Is Ted trying to save face with his other subordinates?
- Does Ted fear he will set a precedent by allowing R&D to determine his staffing?

Bill was so intent on telling Ted that he should get rid of Roland that he never bothered to assess what Ted's perceptions might be or to consider how it would affect Ted to go along.

Finally, Bill never even asked Ted why he had not responded. Perhaps Ted was being measured by different criteria or pressured by the general manager in some way that made it impossible to respond to Bill's request. Instead of fuming and dreaming of revenge, Bill might have set out on a fact-finding mission to learn what he could do to fashion an exchange worthwhile from Ted's point of view as well as from his own.

Bill might have approached Ted in a friendly, nonthreatening manner and said, "Ted, I'm really baffled. It seems to me that you are reluctant to address my concerns about Roland. Obviously, my view of him is different from yours, so help me understand where you are on this." Such a first move might have at least broken the ice. Without knowledge of the potential ally's world, it is difficult to pinpoint what would produce the desired response.

Failure to Determine Exchange Strategy

Bill is so frustrated that he misses many possibilities for exchange. Although he believed that he acted in good faith by juggling assignments in his own area, thereby creating an obligation in Ted, it isn't clear that Ted realized that Bill was reacting to his requests, or that Ted got something he wanted. It isn't even clear that Ted knew that Bill expected anything in return. Although Bill altered his own organization in anticipation of a comparable response from Ted, he did not make it clear to Ted how inconvenienced he was by this accommodation. As a result, Bill gave but he didn't get. What is the sound of one side exchanging? Resentment.

While Bill's values prevented him from striking out in a way that would hurt the organization, he seemed completely unaware of the resources he could muster for a positive exchange. His relationship to the general manager was a card he hated to play, but there might have been ways to do it without appearing weak and un-managerial. Could he have used the general manager as a sounding board on how to approach Ted? Could he have suggested that the general manager meet with him and Ted, not as the final arbiter but as a problem-solving consultant?

Furthermore, Bill appeared to have only two styles of interaction: nice or nasty. When nice did not work, he thought only of turning to nasty. More moderate styles—inquisitive, calmly insistent, or speculative—did not seem to occur to him. With a scientific background, Bill probably was capable of calling on such alternative styles, but he did not look carefully enough at his behavioral options to get any use from them. Thus, he had far less impact than he could have had.

Because he had no model of how to influence, and therefore no useful way to organize a diagnosis, he could only stew in his own frustration. He didn't know what to ask Ted or how to initiate a dialogue about Roland that could guide him to a workable strategy. This is an apt illustration of social psychologist Kurt Lewin's maxim, "There is nothing so practical as a good theory"—or, we might add, so impractical as the lack of a good one.

CHAPTER 3

GOODS AND SERVICES: THE CURRENCIES OF EXCHANGE

Mugger: Your money or your life.
 —*Notorious cheapskate comedian, Jack Benny: (Silence)*

Mugger: Well?
 —*Jack Benny: I'm thinking!*

COIN OF THE REALM: THE CONCEPT OF CURRENCIES

The Cohen-Bradford Influence model is based on exchange and reciprocity—making trades for what you desire in return for what the other person desires. Influence is possible when you have what others want. The metaphor of currencies—which stands for something that is valued—can help you determine what you might offer a potential ally in exchange for cooperation. Because currencies represent resources that can be exchanged, they are the basis for acquiring influence. If you have no currencies in your treasury that the other person values, you have nothing to exchange. In this chapter, we look more closely at how currencies work, which ones are common to organizational life, and how to understand their use.

FREQUENTLY VALUED CURRENCIES

To make trades, you need to be aware of many things people care about and all the valuables you have to offer. At least five types of currencies are at work in a variety of settings:

1. Inspiration-related
2. Task-related
3. Position-related
4. Relationship-related
5. Personal

Although the list is by no means comprehensive and is somewhat arbitrarily grouped for convenience, it does provide a broader view of possible currencies than many organizational members conventionally think about. Having this framework can alert you to possible currencies valued by others or available to you to offer. Table 3.1 on page 38 summarizes our starter list of currencies.

Inspiration-Related Currencies

Inspiration-related currencies reflect inspirational goals that provide meaning to the work a person does. They are increasingly valued by people at all levels of organizational life.

Vision.   Vision is perhaps the grandest of currencies. Portraying an exciting vision of the company's or department's future and imparting a sense of how the ally's cooperation will help reach it can be highly motivating. You can help overcome personal objections and inconvenience if you can inspire the potential ally to see the larger significance of your request.

Excellence.   The opportunity to do something really well and pride in having the chance to accomplish important work with genuine excellence can be highly motivating. In this sense, craftsmanship is not dead; it is only in hiding, waiting to be tapped. There are many people who want to do high-quality, polished work, and knowing how to offer a chance to do that can be a valuable currency.

Moral/Ethical Correctness.   Probably most members of organizations would like to act according to what they perceive to be the ethical, moral, altruistic, or correct thing to do. But they often feel that isn't possible in their job. Because they value a higher standard than efficiency or personal convenience, these people respond to requests that let them feel they are doing what is "right." Their self-image is such that they would rather be personally inconvenienced than do anything they think inappropriate. This lets them feel good about themselves, so virtue becomes its own reward.

Table 3.1   Currencies Frequently Valued in Organizations

Inspiration-Related Currencies

Vision	Being involved in a task that has larger significance for unit, organization, customers, or society
Excellence	Having a chance to do important things really well
Moral/ethical correctness	Doing what is "right" by a higher standard than efficiency

Task-Related Currencies

New resources	Obtaining money, budget increases, personnel, space, and so forth
Challenge/learning	Getting to do tasks that increase skills and abilities
Assistance	Receiving help with existing projects or unwanted tasks
Organizational support	Receiving overt or subtle backing or direct assistance with implementation
Rapid response	Getting something more quickly
Information	Obtaining access to organizational or technical knowledge

Position-Related Currencies

Recognition	Acknowledgment of effort, accomplishment, or abilities
Visibility	The chance to be known by higher-ups or significant others in the organization
Reputation	Being seen as competent, committed
Insiderness/importance	A sense of centrality, of belonging
Contacts	Opportunities for linking with others

Relationship-Related Currencies

Understanding	Having concerns and issues listened to
Acceptance/inclusion	Feeling closeness and friendship
Personal support	Receiving personal and emotional backing

Personal-Related Currencies

Gratitude	Appreciation or expression of indebtedness
Ownership/involvement	Ownership of and influence over important tasks
Self-concept	Affirmation of values, self-esteem, and identity
Comfort	Avoidance of hassles

Task-Related Currencies

Task-related currencies are directly connected to getting the job done. They relate to a person's ability to perform his or her assigned tasks or to the satisfactions that arise from accomplishment.

New Resources.   For some managers, especially in organizations where resources are scarce or difficult to obtain, one of the most important currencies is the chance to obtain new resources to help them accomplish their goals. These resources may or may not be directly budgetary; they could include the loan of people, space, or equipment.

Challenge.   The chance to work at tasks that provide a challenge or stretch is one of the most widely valued currencies in modern organizational life. Challenge is consistently among the top items in surveys of what is most important to employees about their jobs. At the extreme, some people in professional roles will do almost anything to have a chance to work on tough tasks. In many technical organizations, it is a running joke that the reward for killing yourself 80 hours a week on a tough project is that, if it is successful, you get the chance to do it again on a tougher, more important project. For those people, the challenge itself is its own reward.

It is usually not difficult to figure out ways of offering challenge. Asking your potential ally to join in the problem-solving group or passing along a tough piece of your project for him or her to work on are ways you can pay in the currency of challenge (and, if the person is at all competent, probably get back more than you expected).

If your boss values challenge, it would be sensible to share information about tough issues you are facing, go to him or her with tough decisions to talk over, or suggest major issues that he or she could tackle with colleagues or higher-ups. (The boss who hates challenge, however, will value being protected from dealing with complex issues.)

Assistance.   Although large numbers of people desire increased responsibilities and challenge, most have tasks they need help on or would be glad to shed. Perhaps they personally dislike those tasks, are swamped by the current difficulties they face, are in unreasonably demanding jobs, or for some reason have decided to disinvest in the organization. Whatever the reason, they will respond particularly favorably to anyone who can provide relief.

Another important type of assistance involves products or services provided by one department to another. These products or services can be customized to fit the needs of the recipients rather than designed for the convenience of the provider. Staff groups can create the currency of assistance by first making a sincere attempt to learn about and adjust to departmental needs before demanding compliance with a new program.

Organizational Support.   This currency is most valued by someone who is working on a project and needs public backing or behind-the-scenes help in selling the project to others. It can also be valuable to someone who is struggling with an ongoing set of activities and who will benefit from a good word with higher-ups or other colleagues. Since most work of any significance is likely to generate some kind of opposition, the person who is trying to gain approval for a project or plan can be greatly aided by having a "friend in court." A positive word dropped at the right time to the right person can be very helpful in furthering someone's career or objectives. This kind of support is most valuable when the person receiving it is under fire and a colleague takes a public stand in support of the person or the project.

Rapid Response.   It can be worth a great deal for a colleague or boss to know that you will respond quickly to urgent requests. Managers in charge of resources that are always needed "yesterday" soon discover that helping someone avoid the waiting line builds valuable credit that can be drawn on later. Sometimes, people in this position get carried away and try to make it seem that they're always doing the other person a big favor, even when they have spare capacity. This tactic works only as long as those with urgent requests don't know the true backlog; a secret that is likely not to be secret for long. Be careful; overdoing your burdens not only depreciates a valuable currency, but builds mistrust.

Information.   Recognizing that knowledge is power, some people value any information that may help them shape the performance of their unit. Answers to specific questions can be valuable currency, but broader information can be equally rewarding. Knowledge of industry trends, customer concerns, top management's strategic views, or other departments' agendas is valued for its contribution to planning and managing key tasks. And insider information may be even more valued. Who is getting ahead and who is in trouble? What are top management's latest concerns? What are the hottest industry trends or the newest customer developments? Information junkies will go out of their way to help anyone who can give them a fix of insider information, even if it does not help them with immediate tasks.

This hunger for information can create opportunities for anyone who has access to valuable knowledge and is willing to share it. If your boss values this kind of information, you have an extra incentive to develop wide-ranging relationships throughout the organization. In addition, keeping your ear to the ground will provide a wealth of extra-valuable currency to offer to the information-hungry boss. Paradoxically, the higher a person's position, the less likely he or she is to be aware of what is really going on in the organization and the greater the gratitude for being kept informed.

Position-Related Currencies

These currencies enhance a person's position in the organization and, thereby, *indirectly* aid the person's ability to accomplish tasks or advance a career.

Recognition. Many people gladly will extend themselves for a project when they believe their contributions will be recognized. Yet, it is remarkable how many fail to spread recognition around or withhold it for only very special occasions. It is probably not a coincidence that virtually all the managers identified in a major research study as having successfully accomplished innovation from the middle of their organizations were very careful to share the credit and spread the glory once the innovation was in place.[1] They all recognized the importance of paying people off in this valuable currency.

Visibility to Higher-Ups. Ambitious employees realize that, in a large organization, opportunities to perform for or to be recognized by powerful people can be a deciding factor in achieving future opportunities, information, or promotions. That is why, for example, task force members may fight over who will be allowed to present the group's recommendations to top decision makers.

Reputation. Yet another variation on recognition is the more generalized currency of reputation. A good reputation can pave the way for lots of opportunities while a bad one can quickly shut the person out and make it difficult to perform.

A person who has good press gets invited to important meetings, is consulted about new projects, and is considered to be important to have on your side when trying to sell ideas. A talented person with bad press, even one in a nominally important position, may be ignored or not asked for opinions until it is too late to make a real difference. Note that actual ability is only partially related to reputation, at least in larger organizations, because few have direct knowledge of anyone's actual capacities. Accurate or not, however, reputation carries potent consequences. And, having no reputation—being essentially invisible—means not being asked to participate even when you could be very helpful.

Often, people at lower levels, who think they have very little clout, don't realize how much they can do to influence the reputation of a manager who has more formal power. Speaking well or ill of the manager can make an enormous difference in reputation and, therefore, effectiveness. Aware sales personnel go out of their way to be nice to secretaries or other support staff members. They realize that a nasty comment about them from a secretary to the boss can create a bad impression that is difficult to overcome.

Insiderness.   For some members, being in the inner circle can be a most valued currency. One sign of this currency is having inside information, and another is being connected to important people. The chance to be included in important events, tasks, or plans can be valuable in itself. Some people gain their own sense of significance from being close to the action and extend themselves to obtain that kind of access.

Importance.   A variation on the currency of inside knowledge and contacts is the chance to feel important. Inclusion and information are symbols of that, but just being acknowledged as an important player counts a lot for the large number of people who feel their value is under-recognized.

Contacts.   Related to many of the previous currencies is the opportunity for making contacts, which creates a network of people who can be approached when needed for mutually helpful transactions. Some people have confidence in their capacities to build satisfactory relationships once they have access. The organization member skilled at bringing people together benefits from facilitating introductions.

A Contact-Creation Master

Our friend, Alice Sargent, an organizational consultant, was the world's greatest contact facilitator. Alice's address book—built through expertise; a friendly, open style; willingness to extend herself; and a profession that put her in the position of meeting many new people—was at the service of hundreds of people, including us, and she always knew someone we "should talk to" no matter what we were working on. She was selfless in her desire to be helpful; and we were always grateful for her knowledge of who was doing what, her energy in increasing her range of acquaintances, and her willingness to share them. Even on her unfairly premature deathbed, she was still searching for just the right contact to help a friend's daughter decide whether to go to Pomona or Bryn Mawr, an author find an audience for his message, and a company to help package the author's training program. Many consultants and organizational members benefited from her generosity and still miss her. Among the many things we learned from her is the potency inherent in helping people connect to one another.

Relationship-Related Currencies

Relationship-related currencies are more connected to strengthening the relationship with someone than directly accomplishing the organization's tasks. That in no way diminishes the importance of the tasks.

Acceptance/Inclusion. Some people most value the feeling that they are close to others whether an individual or a group/department. They are receptive to those who offer warmth and liking as currencies. While they may or may not place closeness over other, more task-related currencies, at the very least they won't be able to sustain satisfactory transactions with anyone who does not preface serious task discussions with warmth and acceptance.

Understanding/Listening/Sympathy. Colleagues who feel beleaguered by the demands of the organization, isolated, or unsupported by the boss, place an especially high value on a sympathetic ear. Almost everyone is glad at times for a chance to talk about what bugs him or her, especially when the listeners seem to have no axe to grind or are not too caught up in their own problems to pay attention. Indeed, sympathetic listening without advice is a form of action that many managers do not recognize because, by the nature of their jobs and personalities, they are oriented to "doing something." They don't recognize that being listened to, in and of itself, can be a valuable currency.

Personal Support.   For some people, at particular times, having the support of others is the currency they value most. When a colleague is feeling stressed, upset, vulnerable, or needy, he will doubly appreciate—and remember—a thoughtful gesture such as dropping by his desk to inquire how he is doing, a kind word, or a hand on the shoulder. Some people are intuitively brilliant at figuring out just the right touch with a colleague in personal stress, sensing who would appreciate flowers, who would like to be asked home to dinner, and who would respond best to a copy of a meaningful article or book. The item itself is far less important than the gesture, no matter how awkwardly it might be expressed.

Unfortunately, such personal gestures could miss the mark or be misconstrued as signs of more intimate interest or personal friendship than might have been intended. An invitation to dinner at your home, for example, could come across as an intrusion to a very private person. Although caution is in order, genuinely kind gestures usually transcend misinterpretation.

Personal Currencies

These currencies could form an infinite list of idiosyncratic needs. They are valued because they enhance the individual's sense of self. They may be derived from task or interpersonal activity. We mention only a few that are common to many individuals.

Gratitude.   While gratitude may be another form of recognition or support, it is a not necessarily job-related one that can be valued highly by some people who make a point of being helpful to others. For their efforts, some people want appreciation from the receiver, expressed in terms of thanks or deference. This is a tricky currency because, even to those who desire it, it is easily devalued when overused. That is, expression of gratitude for the first favor may be more valued than a similar expression of gratitude for the tenth.

Ownership/Involvement.   Another currency often valued by organizational members is the chance to feel that they are partly in control of something important or have a chance to make a major contribution. While this is akin to other currencies, for some people the chance to get their hands into something interesting is its own reward. They do not need other forms of payment.

Self-Concept.   We referred earlier to moral and ethical correctness as a currency. Another way of thinking about currencies that are self-referencing is to include those that are consistent with a person's image of himself or herself. "Payments" do not always have to be made by someone else. They can be self-generated through action consistent with your idea of who you are and awarded to yourself to fit personal beliefs about being virtuous, benevolent, or committed to the organization's welfare. You might respond to another's request because it reinforces your cherished values, sense of identity, or feelings of self-worth. Payment is still interpersonally stimulated, generating this kind of self-payment by asking for cooperation to accomplish organizational goals. But the person who responds because "it is the right thing to do" and feels good about being the "kind of person who does not act out of narrow self-interest" is printing currency (virtue) that is self-satisfying.

Rosabeth Kanter, a leading researcher on change, discovered a number of innovative middle managers who had worked long and hard to make significant changes that they knew would not be rewarded.[2] Several had been punished by the organization for fighting through valuable changes that upset cherished beliefs or key executives. Furthermore, they had been aware that their efforts would get them in trouble, but they proceeded anyway because they saw themselves as the kind of person who would do what (they think) is needed whether or not anyone else agreed.

Comfort.   Finally, some individuals place high value on personal comfort. Lovers of routine and haters of risk, they will do almost anything to avoid being hassled or embarrassed. The thought of having to make a public fuss, be the target of notoriety, or the recipient of anger and confrontation is enough to drive them to the ends of the earth. They are far less interested in advancement than in being allowed to do their job with a minimum of disturbance; you do them a valuable favor by protecting them from being bothered or by restricting outsiders' access to them.

Negative Currencies

Currencies are what people value. But it is also possible to think of negative currencies, things that people do not value and wish to avoid

Table 3.2 Common Negative Currencies

Withholding Payments
Not giving recognition
Not offering support
Not providing challenge
Threatening to quit the situation
Directly Undesirable
Raising voice, yelling
Refusing to cooperate when asked
Escalating issue upwards to common boss
Going public with issue, making lack of cooperation visible
Attacking person's reputation, integrity

(Table 3.2). These are less desirable to use because they can set off repercussions you don't want, but they are sometimes potent or necessary. Negative currencies come in two forms:

1. Withholding payment of a known valuable currency
2. Using directly undesirable currencies

Insofar as a currency is valuable to an ally, its absence or threatened removal can also be motivating. Because too many people think only of the possible negative effects when seeking influence, we have stressed the positive side of currency use; but it would be needlessly self-limiting to overlook the power of withholding a valuable currency you control. Refusal to give resources, recognition, challenge, or support can move an ally to cooperate. Used in the right situation, the threat of quitting—removing the benefits of your staying in the situation—can be potent.

The directly undesirable currencies are fraught with danger because they can be quite unpleasant forms of payment to the recipient. Although different people value different currencies, few like to be yelled at, have their behavior on display to the boss or others, want to be exposed for their behavior and attitudes, or want to have a colleague attacking their reputation. These negative currencies, or the threat of using one or more of them, can be exactly what is necessary for you to move the other person into action.

The danger is that the action will be retaliated—at once or in the future. You don't want to enrage a person who has more ammunition than you do or who is willing to go down in flames while dragging you along. Using negative currencies risks setting off a war or winning influence in the short term but creating an enemy who looks for chances to retaliate when you least expect it.

Therefore, it is the better part of valor, even when employing the negative variation of currency exchange, to look for a positive way to frame the currency. "I know you wouldn't want to be left out" probably will get a more positive response than "If you don't cooperate, I'll see that you're left out." In both cases, however, it is the absence or withholding of the currency that is being used as exchangeable merchandise. If you have to directly use a negative currency, try to tie it to a future, more desirable state in which the negatives won't be necessary.

USING CURRENCIES: COMPLEXITIES AND RESTRICTIONS

Even if you do not underestimate the number of currencies you have available, there are still complex issues around implementation.

Establishing Currency Exchange Rates: How to Equate Apples and Oranges

If it is true that everyone expects to be paid back in one form or another, then it is important to address the question of "one form or another." What will it require to make an offer in a currency that the other person considers equivalent?

In the economic marketplace, everything is translated into monetary equivalents, which makes it easier to say what a fair payment is. Does a ton of steel equal a set of golf clubs? By translating both commodities into dollars (or their equivalent in euros, yen, or rubles), strangers can arrive at a fair deal. In the organizational marketplace, however, calculating the payback is more complicated. How do I repay your willingness to help me finish my report? Is a simple "thank you" enough? Will it be sufficient for me to say something nice about you to your boss? And what if your idea of fair repayment is very different from mine? We may place very different values on the same thing. Absent an established standard value, exchanging for influence is a complicated process.

A useful way of conceptualizing what is important to potential allies is to examine the goods and services they trade in. What do they seem to care about? What do they signal by their language? What do they talk about first when explaining why they do not want to cooperate? Does your analysis of their world and how they are measured and rewarded help? Can you ask directly—in a collaborative way, aimed at finding ways to help them so they can help you? Be careful not to load your own weights for their currencies. It isn't how you value the goods and services, it is how they do.

Occasionally, members of organizations know exactly what they want in return for favors or help at work, but more often they will settle for very rough equivalents—provided there is reasonable goodwill. It may, therefore, be more important to identify the currency the potential ally likes to trade in and offer to pay with goods that you have translated into that currency than it is to determine the exact right amount. In other words, think about the nature (quality) of the currency in each transaction before you worry about the quantity.

Different Strokes: Few Universal Currencies

Because interests vary from person to person, currencies are valued differently. *The value of a currency is solely in the eye of the beholder.* While one manager might consider a thank-you note a sign of appreciation, another might see it as an attempt to flatter, and a third might dismiss it as a cheap way to try to repay extensive favors and service. (And we can say from experience, don't try even friendly East Coast irony with the straightforward, nice folks from Minnesota!)

Furthermore, the same currency that is successful several times with the same person or group can eventually become devalued by them, so that it no longer works. After a while, for example, praise can sound hollow if you are giving it for constant favors that take a lot of time.[3]

One Act: Multiple Currencies, Multiple Forms of Payment

Currencies of the kind discussed here are not exact and fixed; they are also a function of perception and language:

- *A particular "good," for example, an offer to create a special analytical report, may be translatable into several different currencies.* To the receiver, it may be a performance currency ("When I have the report, I'll be able to determine which products to push."); a political currency ("Getting the report will help me look good to my division president."); or a personal currency ("Although getting the report certainly won't hurt my decision making, more significant is the fact that it really shows you recognize my importance."). The same good may be valued for different reasons by different people—or by the same person.

- *One currency can be paid in many different forms.* For example, you can pay in appreciation by verbal thanks, praise, a public statement of support at a meeting, informal comments to peers, or a note to the person's boss.

- *The changeable nature of the value of currency makes it even more necessary to understand as much as you can about what is important to each potential ally—not only what he or she values but also the language that reflects that valued currency.* Sometimes a different way of talking about your offer—based on what you know about the ally's style and priorities—will make it more attractive. Don't needlessly exaggerate; if you don't have the right goods, hype will only offend. Nevertheless, it is worth careful thought about how to talk about goods that are available.

Currencies Can Be Organizational, Not Just Personal

For convenience, we have discussed currencies completely in terms of what is important to the individual you want to influence. But another, less direct, kind of currency is departmental or organizational benefit. When an employee identifies strongly with the welfare of his or her group, department, or organization, exchanges that provide a benefit to the unit rather than to the individual can be very important.

At the same time, the person gets the psychological satisfaction of "being good," or of "doing what is right," which are by no means trivial currencies. The sense of self as a good citizen and benevolent, loyal person is indeed a powerful currency for many. This is a potent payoff to them, even when at first glance what they must give does not appear to be in their self-interest.

In fact, in some organizations, the acquisition of a reputation for being willing to do things that are not of immediate personal benefit is precisely what develops an influential, positive reputation. These are the kinds of organizations in which altruism reigns supreme. We have watched a large number of upper middle managers at Blue Cross Blue Shield of Massachusetts, for example, focus on what the organization can do for members and the uninsured and resist talk of narrowly construed self- or departmental interests. Managers who can think creatively about helping customers are listened to and valued.

In such situations, a strategy of encouraging the potential ally to cooperate for personal gain is a serious breach of etiquette. That the person's reputation will be enhanced is considered a by-product, one not to be overtly touted.

Although there may be a few situations where blunt, "I'll do this if you will do that," trades are expected, as in a tough New Jersey construction firm we know, in most organizations it is more about *how* what you want is described in a way that appeals to your audience. Paying attention to the culture's ways is important in addition to looking at the individual. If, however, you are dealing with a maverick, a countercultural approach may be just the thing.

Reframing: Fit the Language to the Culture

How explicitly you position self-interest is different from organization to organization. For example, in numerous high-tech companies, members are expected to be direct about what they want from others. Employees talk freely about wheeling and dealing for resources. But at IBM, the language is expected to be far less direct, with requests couched in terms of organizational benefits, not personal gains. No one at IBM is likely to say, "If you help me on this project, your career will be advanced." Instead, they will say something like, "Your area's help will increase the value of the product, and that will aid your group's getting the recognition it deserves for its outstanding efforts." The result might be the same, but the language used to get results is different.

Sometimes a good idea can be stymied because it has been described with loaded language—words whose connotations turn off the people whose support is most needed. Inappropriate language can convert what might have been valuable to a potential ally into undesirable currency. One of the authors remembers vividly getting completely tuned out at the old, polite Hewlett-Packard for talking to human resources people about "ways to get clout." They wanted to shape managerial practice, but clout sounded far too crude. (And they were too nice to tell him until after easing him out of the program.)

Make Long-Term Investments

It is all too easy to forget about the future when you are focusing on your current job and all the ways you need more influence. But try to think longer term, anticipating future currencies of relevant colleagues (or possible future colleagues). If your job, for example, interfaces with operations and you are aware that your organization is facing cost pressures and will need to consider outsourcing some activities to India or China, you might want to learn something about the difficulties of outsourcing even though no one has asked you to. If you build knowledge in advance, you might have something valuable to the operations person who suddenly gets dumped with the problem, and you can create credit that will serve you later.

SELF-TRAPS IN USING CURRENCIES

While the notion of exchange seems simple, there are many ways in which people go wrong and miss by a mile (see the Checklist for Avoiding Currency Traps).

Checklist for Avoiding Currency Traps

Don't underestimate what you have to offer. What do your training and experience give you?

Your Resources	Who Would Value the Resource?
☐ Technical	_____
☐ Organization information	_____
☐ Customer knowledge	_____
☐ Political information	_____

What do you control that requires no permission to spend?

☐ Reputation	_____
☐ Appreciation	_____
☐ Visibility	_____
☐ Gratitude	_____
☐ Recognition	_____
☐ Respect	_____
☐ Your personal help on tasks	_____

Pay in what the other person values, not what you value.

☐ Fit with what you know about the person.
☐ Fit with the way the person likes to be approached.
☐ Give what the other person wants, even if you don't like it.

Are you willing to do more than is required?

☐ Go beyond job description.

Don't exaggerate or lie.

☐ Can you deliver what you promise?

Underestimating What You Have to Offer

Start with what you know. What has your training and experience given you access to that could be valuable to others?

- Rare technical knowledge?
- Organizational information such as where expertise resides, what departments are interested in your department's activities, or who holds resources that aren't being used?
- Customer knowledge such as who a key customer is playing golf with, what problems they are having using your company's products, how they have improvised new uses for your products that might be of interest to other customers. Potential clients who are not being attended to now.
- Political information such as who is unhappy, planning to leave, on the rise, or close to key higher-ups.

What do you control that requires no permission from anyone to "spend"? As suggested earlier, sometimes people who feel impotent have been thinking too narrowly about what resources they command. They think only of budget dollars or promotions as relevant resources and, lacking these, assume they have nothing of value to trade. You can give gratitude, recognition, appreciation, respect, and help—many things that are valuable to others. No supervisor or higher-up has to empower anyone to write a thank-you note, publicly praise another, or rush responses to a request. Often, valuable goods or services are at your disposal if you cast your net wide enough.

Pay in the Currency of Other Values, Not Just What You Would Value

This is a completely understandable trap because it is both easier to know what you like and to assume that because it is so valuable to you, everyone else must want the same. Sure, there are some universals that almost everyone wants—self-worth, recognition for good work, connection—but even for those, it is tricky. Many people like positive attention and gratitude, but some do not like the spotlight or being thanked for favors that they consider a routine part of their job. Others just want to be left alone. But even worse, people often are so preoccupied with what they want that they don't pay close attention to or totally ignore the signals the other is sending about what matters to him or her. These signals are heard as excuses or barriers or are just plain tuned out.

We have seen many people, even at high levels, who are so certain that it would be impossible to influence their manager that they completely miss something as obvious as the manager's desire for proposals to be made in writing. For example, the subordinate wants early feedback, but she is so sure that the boss won't like her idea that she doesn't bother to put it into a concise memo and send it ahead before the meeting. Creating a memo is within the subordinate's control, but she never sees how crucial that is to her reflective and busy boss, so she fails to take a simple but effective step to gain influence. (For more on how to tune in to signals sent, see Chapter 4.)

Worst of all, when frustrated influencers hear what the other wants but don't like it themselves, they don't want to give any of it to the other. The colleague who craves status, for example, can set their teeth on edge, and they do everything possible to make that person be seen as small. Or, they resent ambition so they try to thwart it rather than work with it and help the ambitious colleague get ahead. Remember, reciprocity is about paying with something the other person values.

Resenting Having to Go Out of the Way

Some people limit their influence by refusing to do what might be needed to move others in desirable ways because it isn't their job. They stand on principle: "That shouldn't have to be my job, and my colleagues should just be persuaded by the power of my arguments and what (I see) is right!" There are certainly principles not worth violating but "It's not my job" probably isn't one of them. Think of it as building a line of credit that you might want to draw on someday, or think of it just as being effective. If it is in the organization's interest for you to figure out what others need to cooperate, then eventually it will also be in your interest.

A Word of Warning: Beware False Advertising

As discussed, the language that you use to describe your offers can increase the chances that those goods or services will meet the needs of the other party, that is, address its desired currency. Careful, thoughtful communication adds needed precision to the imprecise process of equating your offer with another's needs.

Nonconvertible Currencies

The founder-chairman of a high-tech company and the president he had hired five years earlier were growing more and more displeased with each other. The president, a Harvard MBA, was committed to creating maximum shareholder value—the currency most precious to him. He predicted that the company's line of exotic components would soon saturate the market, and risky major research investments would be needed to make the strategic move to end-user products. Accordingly, he concluded that the company was in a perfect position to cash in by squeezing expenses to maximize profits and then going public.

The chairman was unmoved, however, because he valued a different currency, the fun of technological challenges. An independently wealthy man, he wasn't at all interested in the $10 million or more he would get if the company maximized profits by cutting research and selling out. He wanted a place to test his intuitive, creative hunches, not an inert cache of capital.

Their disagreements led first to bickering and then to hostility. But they were able to move beyond this, and, in further exploration, they realized that they would never be able to reach accord. Their currencies just weren't convertible at an acceptable exchange rate. That understanding freed them to agree that the president should leave—on good terms—after a more compatible replacement could be found. And he did leave, moving to another company where he successfully used his skills.

Nevertheless, there are dangers in the process. Having a way with words is useful in any selling activity, but avoid gilding the lily or exaggerating claims. Within your own organization, an impossible promise, a claim that proves to be false, or even too much wishful thinking can damage your credibility and get in the way of future transactions. As we have tried to make abundantly clear, your reputation is a precious commodity in organizational terms. Protect that valuable asset even as you press the boundaries to complete important exchanges.

Last Word: Some Currencies Really Are Not Convertible

Another warning is in order: Not everything can be converted into equivalent currencies. If two people have fundamental differences in what they value, it may not be possible to find common grounds. Open, honest exploration guarantees only that if there is any possibility of mutuality, it will be discovered and the relationship probably won't be damaged by the failure to find a deal. But sometimes, currencies do not convert. Know when to fold 'em—and do it graciously.

Currencies are important, but not always obvious. In Chapter 4, we show you how to figure out what a person's currencies are likely to be when you do not automatically know them or do not have direct access to the person or group you want to influence.

CHAPTER 4

How to Know What They Want: Understanding Their Worlds (and the Forces Acting on Them)

*Do not do unto others as you would that they should do unto you. Their
tastes may not be the same.*

—*George Bernard Shaw, 1903*

You have influence insofar as you can
give people what they need. But how do you know what they need? Knowing the concerns, objectives, and styles of the people you want to influence—all your important stakeholders—is fundamental for determining
what to offer to gain cooperation. The more you know, the better you can
determine valued currencies, the language they speak, and the style in
which they prefer to interact. Some of these things you can perceive automatically, and you can just proceed effectively. But if you're unclear about
what matters to an important person or group, puzzled by resistance,
stymied because "reasonable" approaches aren't working, or angry and beginning to assume the worst about their motives and personality, you may
need to do a careful analysis of their world(s). The greater the number of
stakeholders you have to influence for a given objective or the greater your
anticipated difficulty in figuring out the right approach, the more you
should do in advance. This chapter zooms in on the analytical process for
determining the world of those whose driving forces are not immediately

apparent, so you can figure out how to build present and future win–win relationships.

Continuing to look at a situation only from your own viewpoint makes it easy to stumble into self-defeating repetition of pressure that hasn't worked or slip into tortured silence. The intense desire to do something significant or make an important change has a way of blinding hopeful influencers to what is critical to their potential allies. The resistant ally seems difficult, impossible, or even irrational because his or her behavior does not make sense to the determined influencer. Don't fall into that trap.

Two Forces That Can Explain All Behavior

If you want to figure out an approach for influence, it helps to understand what might be driving the other's behavior. Few social scientists would tell you that all behavior can be explained by only two things, but we do: *personality* and *everything else*. Personality is surely important in understanding what matters to anyone, and if you are confident that you understand the other person's psyche and what makes that individual tick, you can devise your influence approach accordingly. But be careful. Research shows that we usually oversimplify our assessment of others. Personality is not readily accessible if you don't know the party extremely well, and even if you have had extensive contact, personality still can be difficult to fathom. Furthermore, it is not easily subject to change. For both those reasons, we suggest you spend little energy on that territory.

The other forces, however, that drive what people care about are those arising from the situation they operate in. At work, for example, there are numerous factors that might influence behavior. We explore these later, but consider as illustrative one of the most obvious: The way people are measured and rewarded shapes a lot of behavior. Steve Kerr's classic article, "On the Folly of Hoping for A When Rewarding B," makes it clear that the organization's actual rewards are more important than the exhortations of management.[1]

The premise of this chapter is that when you identify the work context (mostly from a distance and without even knowing the individual or group), you will have a good reading on a significant part of what drives the behavior you want to influence. Then you can develop a good working sense of the currencies likely to matter. Occasionally, an important party's personality will override all situational forces operating, but this happens less often than many believe. (One definition of mental health is

Figure 4.1
Contextual Forces That Shape Behavior along with Personality

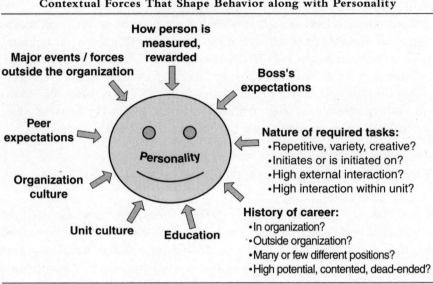

the ability to alter behavior to fit the situation, which suggests that the person who treats everyone exactly the same—his or her boss, mother, lover, child, colleague, and subordinate—is not so healthy.)

With this background, we turn to the most universal factors at work that make up a person's or group's world and usually offer strong clues about what they care about and might be willing to trade for (see Figure 4.1 for a graphic summary of the common forces).

HOW TO KNOW WHAT MIGHT BE IMPORTANT TO THE OTHER PERSON

There are numerous factors that can help determine what might be valued by the person or group you wish to influence.

The Potential Ally's Job Tasks

Understanding a potential ally's duties and responsibilities can be a key to influencing him or her. Think about the impact of the job on these five simple, but basic, organizational factors:

1. Does the person deal with numbers all day or with people?
2. Is the work repetitive or highly varied?
3. Does the person experience demands for careful accuracy and replicability or get rewarded for originality and improvisation?
4. Is the person subject to constant demands from others or the one who makes many demands on them?
5. Is the person in a high-risk, high-visibility position or a secure protected role?

This kind of information can provide a beginning guide to the currencies that the ally values, how he or she sees the world, or the style with which to approach him or her. For example, the tasks of a brand manager, which encompass every aspect of a product's positioning, presentation, price, and so on, are different from those of a market researcher, who works with statistics, validity, scientific method, focus groups, and the like. The brand manager is called on to pull many elements together at once across many parts of the organization; the market researcher usually works alone or with a similar colleague and at a slower pace to discover significant results.

The Potential Ally's Environment

Other factors that shape task demands include degree of contact with:

- The environment outside the organization
- Top management
- Headquarters
- The salesforce
- The factory floor
- Exotic or temperamental equipment
- The media

Each of such contacts, or lack of them, is likely to create pressures that affect the way the person looks at problems and requests. The manager who has to deal with customer complaints on a regular basis may be far more receptive to appeals that involve quality improvement than the manager who never sees customers but is in close contact with the controller's office.

Task Uncertainties

Another indicator of what might be important could be those aspects of the potential ally's job that have the most uncertainties associated with them.

Mismatches Due to Reward System Differences

The bank's mortgage manager, who is furious because her colleague in investments does not recommend that a good customer use the bank for a jumbo mortgage, may not realize that the investment representative gets paid for customer retention. If the bank's mortgage rates are not competitive, the customer might not feel that the investment advisor is impartial and go elsewhere for investments. The investment advisor's response doesn't necessarily arise from a disregard for the mortgage manager or overall bank sales goals, but from what he is measured on.

Similarly, the management information system (MIS) manager who resists the plant manager's pet scheme for automating production costing may be responding to the project backlog measure by which she is judged. Less complex projects that don't require design from scratch may make it far easier to plan and control backlog, so she may be avoiding a desirable but necessarily lengthy project. And, in turn, the chief financial officer who balks at the MIS manager's requests for the latest technology may be judged by certain financial ratios that will be harmed by adding expensive equipment that takes many months before it begins to provide proportionate returns.

In organizational life, control is valued. The bigger the uncertainty, the harder it is to keep control, so it is the areas of greatest uncertainty that receive the most attention. You often can gain an ally by finding a way to help the person get control of a part of his or her job that is currently uncertain.

But the demands of tasks alone do not account for all the pressures and concerns of individuals who are influence targets. Thus, it is useful to think about many other aspects of what might be important to the one you want to influence.

Who's Counting? Measurement and Reward Systems

As suggested earlier, the way people behave is often strongly dictated by the way their performance is measured and rewarded. Those who act "difficult" or negative may only be doing what they have been told will be regarded as good performance in that function.

You need to understand the other people's performance criteria as a means to determine how you might be able to add value or alter your request to fit their requirements. In some instances, it might be possible to raise questions about the reasonableness of the measure because departmental measures designed from the top or left over from the past may have unan-

---

**Two Differing Cultures: Investment
Bank and Insurance Company**

People in investment banking (doing high-risk, high-gain deals) and insurance companies (aiming for low-risk, predictable returns) usually have a different view of how intense to be, how openly to talk about money and ambition, how to dress, how to treat colleagues, what kinds of expertise is respected, and so on. But there are firms in each industry that are unlike the majority, and within each large organization, there may be quite different (and sometimes conflicting) subcultures. Back-office people in both kinds of companies are not as high status, not as money obsessed, possibly more detail oriented, more harassed, and perhaps more direct. They are forced into thinking about very short-term goals—they close books at the end of each day—and they may behave accordingly. In organizations of any kind, colleagues in many units tend to reinforce the cultures of which they are a part because those who do not behave consistently with the assumptions of proper behavior are seen as a threat to the maintenance of whatever the culture is. Thus, when you encounter someone who is brusque, direct, sarcastic, and driving, it may be as much a product of the culture of the organization and function he or she works in as of a type A personality. Similarly, niceness, personal interest, and patience may be by-products of working in a unit that prides itself on many aspects of friendliness or has a strong culture of customer responsiveness.

---

ticipated negative consequences. The organization might eventually want to alter the measures if their negative impact to the company was made clear. But often, in the short run, the other person's way of being judged is a given that has to be worked with or around.

Unit and Organizational Culture

Most people are affected by the culture of the organization where they work and sometimes by the particular subculture of their immediate work group. Culture is the set of automatic assumptions that groups of people have about how the world is supposed to work.

Major Forces Outside the Organization

Outside forces that can drive behavior include:

- The state of the economy
- How threatened people feel about jobs and mobility

- Major competition
- Legal rulings affecting the industry or company

These forces can affect everyone in the organization or differentially among departments. The threat of an SEC action, an injunction about discrimination in hiring and promotion policies, or a falling stock price can induce strong reactions. For example, members of the legal department at a software firm that is being sued for an acquisition of a major competitor may aggressively challenge colleagues' practices that were previously ignored. Conversely, organizations that are geographically isolated or have dominant market positions may behave quite differently from most other organizations at the time.

WHERE ARE THEY HEADED? CAREER ASPIRATIONS AND PERSONAL BACKGROUND

Besides the organizational factors that are part of the potential ally's world, many personal concerns will arise from the person's previous work experience and current goals. You might not know the person well enough to know his or her entire history, but you might gain valuable insight if you happen to know or can easily ask about where the person worked previously and what his or her former jobs involved, Although you don't want to pry for embarrassing revelations, often the person will drop comments about past experience that can provide clues about what is important.

Friendly or antagonistic, familiar or unknown, the potential ally's world will be more transparent if you get the answers to some critical questions:

- Is your ally on the fast track or stuck indefinitely in his or her current position?
- To what extent is that person under pressure to shake up the department and produce internal change or wanting to preserve a calm atmosphere in the department?
- How long will that person be around to live with the consequences of cooperating (or refusing to), or is he or she likely to soon move on and, therefore, not care much about the consequences?

While being careful to avoid stereotyping, you might also examine what you know about the ally's personal history. Was he or she raised in another part of the world? A first-generation citizen? Educational background can

---

Career Backgrounds That Make a Difference

Stan was vice president of human resources for a *Fortune* 500 company. In executive meetings, he spoke very little and never said anything controversial even on issues that directly affected his area. A new member of that team was puzzled. Stan had come to that job from a line position, so his background might have suggested a more assertive, risk-taking stance. The member got some insight when a colleague told him, "The previous CEO one day got mad at what he said and fired him on the spot. Later that day, the CEO revoked that decision, but Stan has been this way ever since even though Bill, the new CEO, is much more accepting of different ideas."

---

be helpful, including what the person studied and where. Managers without a college degree or, in some organizations, without an MBA or other advanced degree, could be sensitive about their perceived deficiency or about possible slights to their intelligence.

The Ivy League liberal arts graduate might care more about high culture and polished manners than would an engineer who graduated from a big state university. In turn, the engineer or accounting major might prefer more careful discussions of data and detail than the marketing major. It would be foolish to base your approach entirely on such preconceptions, but they may give you helpful clues to start a more careful diagnosis:

- How successful was the person in previous jobs?
- Does the person see himself or herself as highly competent or still learning?
- Is the person a fast-track performer brought in to fix things, or did he or she move slowly into each position and remain there a long time?
- Was the person burned (or made successful) by a previous project that was similar to what you are pushing or for other reasons?
- Was the person a victim of arbitrary firing and a bad manager?
- Was the person let down by a subordinate in a crucial situation or back-stabbed after promised support?

The manager who has worked for IBM or GE will look at problems differently from the manager who has spent his or her whole career in the same medium-size, family-owned company. And the manager who has spent some time working at European and Japanese subsidiaries probably will have a different perspective from the one who has never left Detroit.

All of these situations will likely affect how the person will react to new ideas, major changes, or large projects versus more modest ones.

The Potential Ally's Worries

In addition to looking at the environmental forces that affect your potential ally, you could think about what the person's anxieties might be. Ask yourself what work issues make the person you want to influence toss in bed at 2 A.M. At the least, everyone in an organization ought to be able to answer that for his or her boss. If you don't know, think about it. You never will get what you want from your boss if you can't quite pinpoint what it is that worries him or her most:

- Long-term competition from China? Or issues of off-sourcing jobs?
- Meeting next week's payroll?
- Merger rumor mill?
- Fear of boss's wrath for missing a budgeted expense number?
- Impact of exotic new technologies?
- How to confront dug-in resisters on their nasty political games?

The answers to these and similar questions help determine your approach.

How the Potential Ally Defines the World

Although not always easy to detect from a distance, the potential ally's assumptions about key issues such as leadership, motivation, competition, or change, once known, help you determine what that individual values. Often, people have made lots of overt statements about such basic matters, so their views are known. The manager, for example, who believes that people are inherently lazy and need to be closely watched is likely to value control and predictability, while one who believes that most people want to do a good job is more likely to value currencies of challenge and growth. The ally who believes that anything is negotiable operates quite differently from the one who holds fast to a few eternal truths, no matter what the situation.

As a way to make these previous concepts come alive, think of a difficult-to-influence colleague, and fill out the Inquiry Map (Figure 4.2) about that person. After completion, how much did you know, and how confident are you that you are right? Was it enough to determine the person's world and likely currencies? If not, how can you find out more? And based

Figure 4.2
Inquiry Map

Areas of Inquiry	What I Know	Certainty Scale	Best Sources to Confirm
Key responsibilities		High Low ⊢—┼—┼—┼—┼—┼—⊣	
Priority tasks		⊢—┼—┼—┼—┼—┼—⊣	
How the person is measured		⊢—┼—┼—┼—┼—┼—⊣	
How the person measures others		⊢—┼—┼—┼—┼—┼—⊣	
Primary departments and people the person interacts with		⊢—┼—┼—┼—┼—┼—⊣	
Career aspirations		⊢—┼—┼—┼—┼—┼—⊣	
Work and communications styles		⊢—┼—┼—┼—┼—┼—⊣	
Worries, areas of uncertainty, or work pressures		⊢—┼—┼—┼—┼—┼—⊣	
Previous work experience		⊢—┼—┼—┼—┼—┼—⊣	
Education		⊢—┼—┼—┼—┼—┼—⊣	
Outside interests		⊢—┼—┼—┼—┼—┼—⊣	
Values		⊢—┼—┼—┼—┼—┼—⊣	

on your diagnosis, what are the currencies most likely to be valued by the person?

GATHERING REAL-TIME DATA ABOUT THE WORLD OF OTHERS

A warning first: All of the methods described, including directly asking, yield helpful information, but you have to be tentative in coming to firm conclusions before you act. Treat what you learn as working hypotheses that can be tested further, not as final conclusions that let you leap without looking. For anything you discover, ask how certain you are about the validity of this part of the other's world and how you could verify it. It is often in the direct act of influencing that you find out important new currencies of that person, so listen carefully.

What Did You Say? Language as a Clue to Valued Currencies

Because any argument or request is more likely to succeed if it is framed in the currency valued by the person you want to influence, any clues to important currencies will be useful. One of the best ways to rapidly learn currencies is to listen closely to the language the person uses. When you are tuned in, you will be amazed at how often and how repetitively people broadcast their currencies—what matters to them.

Their choice of metaphors often can be revealing of their preoccupations. Does she use military and sports metaphors that are about battle, competition, and destroying the opposition? Does he use gardening metaphors, which show his concern for learning and development of the organization's talent? Does the person refer to everything in impersonal mechanical terms or use rich examples about people's foibles and accomplishments? Technically, the following two phrases about maintaining organizational change refer to the same thing, but the people who choose one or the other see the world differently:

1. "I'm seeking a kind of interlocking gear to lock in each bit of progress and prevent reverting."
2. "We need to capture people's hearts, so they won't backslide."

When a request for help is met immediately with an inquiry about who else will be involved, you know that political concerns are that person's currency. Another might ask directly, "What's in it for me?" which reveals concern for self and suggests that a blunt, direct response will probably work best. Yet another manager will respond with questions about how the request fits in with the company's mission, which indicates that person values corporate over personal goals—and perhaps will welcome the opportunity to be a good citizen.

Expressed Concerns as Clues

It is remarkable how often the hopeful influencer will completely miss obvious clues to the potential ally's hot buttons. Many resistant allies telegraph their core currencies through the concerns that they raise. "What I'd be worried about if we did that . . ." or "I don't think the finance people would buy it" or "My concern here is . . ." It is too easy to read these as signs of stubbornness and intractability, but they can also be heard as statements of what is important to the other person and, therefore, an invitation to further dialog. Instead of asking exploratory questions that might reveal the currencies that they could be paid in, the listener argues, and that puts an end to hoped-for influence.

The style of language used—metaphors, images, jargon—can be revealing, but tone and nonverbals also can be important cues to feelings and attitudes. Tuning in to others' emotions is a communication skill you should practice because it is especially informative when trying to figure out what is important to a potential ally. Whether you just learn to soften your tone when your boss's neck gets red or you watch for the widened eyes that indicate growing interest in the tack you are taking, careful attention to the nonverbal cues can help you determine which currencies to use and how to make your requests in language that will elicit the desired response.

Being sensitive to nonverbal cues is easier said than done. Time and again in our management training workshops, we find participants eager to demonstrate how skilled they are in reading the concerns of others, but then they promptly get sucked right into selling their own views rather than trying to determine the ally's views.

Other Sources of Data

Even when the person whose help you seek is a stranger, he or she may advertise so clearly that it is hard to miss what is important. Who hasn't encountered a fellow employee who manages to mention his or her (high-status) undergraduate college or MBA school within the first five minutes of conversation, no matter what the topic? It doesn't take great psychoanalytic insight to figure out that status is probably an important currency to that person.

Selling Own Views and Missing Cues to Others' Currencies

Mark wants Rajesh to join a task force that can solve the problems that plague the company in recruiting top talent, and Rajesh responds by saying, "Oh sure, and spend hours going round and round about 'better working conditions' when we all know that top management will never agree to signing bonuses and stock awards." Mark, who has frequently heard Raj's claims about the power of monetary incentives, makes one feeble attempt to say how important the task is, then throws up his hands and walks away from what he sees as a money-obsessed engineer. As a result, he doesn't realize that Raj is sending important messages about how he prefers to get rapidly to decisions, his frustration about the difficulty of getting top management approval, possibly his skepticism about the others who are involved—as well as his belief about the power of money to overcome other objections. All of these currencies could be discussed, some accommodated or shown to be not applicable to this situation, if Mark were really listening and not preoccupied with his own challenge to get the right members for the task force he thinks is obviously important.

For those you do not know and who do not make it so easy to learn what currencies they value, other colleagues might be able to supply information. As a communications manager at a large computer company put it, "When I have to approach someone I don't know, I ask someone who knows him what he's like, what he cares about, what his hot buttons are, what I should definitely not say. At the very least, I don't want to step on any land mines."

With a bit of ingenuity, it is often possible to find someone you trust to be a helpful source.

Just Ask Directly

It isn't always easy to gain access to ask what a person values or has concerns about. And if the relationship is troubled already, it can feel too risky, but we do not want to slight the benefits of a direct approach. We later discuss how to overcome relationship problems that get in the way of direct inquiry, but consider the benefits of being willing to say to the person you want to influence: "I'd like to understand better the pressures you are under so that I can try to be helpful or at least not get in your way with what I am asking. Our areas are interdependent, and both of us could benefit if we could be of more help to each other." It is remarkable how much even a tough opponent will say in return, perhaps expecting that once you

---

An Extreme Solution to Understanding the World of Important Stakeholders: Joining for a While

Christopher Panini is a marketing manager who works at a rapidly growing and aggressive *Fortune* 500 high-tech firm. He was told several times that he had to learn better to understand salespeople to be effective. In his words, here is what happened:

> I realized that in order to bring value to marketing, I would have to learn sales. So I interviewed for a transfer to a sales job and was suddenly in a new world. For two and a half years, I was a hunter rep visiting client offices in Philadelphia, Baltimore, and Washington, DC. My job was to track new customers down and poach business from our competitors. This meant cold-calling executives during the dot-com boom, trying to deliver our value proposition to anyone who would listen. Part of the lifestyle as an account manager was winning people over, entertaining executives at dinner, playing golf with them, hosting them at special events—all to build a network of customer and partner relationships in everything that I did. (This would be a wonderful way to function inside any organization!) All of a sudden I was being perceived at the company as someone that played a strategic role in the information infrastructures of my customers. . . . I was learning as I went and winging it half the time.
>
> One day I realized that I was no longer a marketing guy but a salesman. This realization happened after several of the following changes in my life occurred: waking up in cold sweats thinking about my looming and omnipresent quota, spending my first commission check on impulse purchases, scheduling the events of my personal life around each fiscal quarter, the first half-dozen deals that I lost before I won my first, trading my Japanese economy car in for a German sports sedan, my quota getting raised by management every time I was tracking to make it, daily 7 A.M. team meetings with my district manager, two-hour territory inspections in front of a group of 20 managers who were looking for any hole they could find in my business plan, etc. . . . Living these experiences made me truly understand the people that I was to support. These are funny and real, though a bit sad. When I returned to marketing, my opinions and perspective were suddenly validated by what I had learned in the sales organization. I was a different person.

---

understand, you will go away. It is always possible that you might discover that the desired currencies are impossible for you to deliver on, but that is no worse than not knowing—and you might indeed be able to deliver.

Just Because It Waddles and Quacks Like a Duck Doesn't Mean It's a Duck: The Dangers of Stereotyping

Sift through everything you hear and treat it only as clues, not as certain information. Be careful not to assume any one factor determines all currencies;

people respond to many complex pressures. The actuary who cut his teeth on numbers may indeed prefer crisp, statistical reports, but we have worked with high-level actuaries who are eloquent about the limits of numerical analysis and the need for intuition when making important decisions.

We are not suggesting that it is necessary to compile a complete dossier on each potential ally you try to influence. Often, all you need are a few pieces of information to have a good idea of where you should focus. But the more difficult the situation, the more you would be wise to do a careful diagnosis.

BARRIERS TO ACTING ON KNOWLEDGE OF THE WORLDS OF IMPORTANT STAKEHOLDERS

There are several things that can get in the way of using the knowledge you gain from understanding the world of the person or group you want to influence.

The Negative Attribution Cycle

Having a difficult time getting the influence you desire can lead to a self-defeating cycle of negative attributions about the other person's intentions, motives, and even personality.[2] Suppose you are met with resistance you think is unreasonable, and all of your efforts are shrugged off. Because it has been so unpleasant to deal with this person, you start to avoid any interaction. But you need to find some kind of explanation for why he is being so resistant. The tendency is to assume the worst, something like, *he wants to block you,* and then that *he is a selfish, inconsiderate ass.* You are now at a place where it is going to be extremely difficult to influence him. Figure 4.3, the Negative Attribution Cycle, depicts the process by which this occurs.

Distancing Difficult People

People tend to interact more with those they like (and to like most and interact most with those who are like them). In turn, people tend to avoid interaction with those who are dissimilar. While this makes life more pleasant and predictable, because it avoids the discomfort of trying to overcome un-

Figure 4.3
The Negative Attribution Cycle

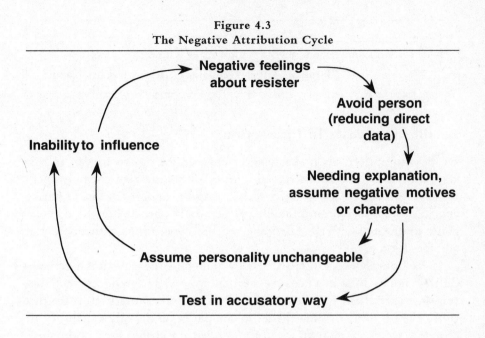

familiarity or belligerence, it tends to cut you off from information about someone whose help you may need.

Thus, the very people about whom it is most important to discover their interests are the least likely to be understood. Difficult potential allies might well value currencies that make exchange possible, but it is difficult to know that if there is little contact or discussion.

Assuming Motives and Intentions: The Presumption of Evil

One of the natural ways that people explain puzzling behavior of other people is to attribute to them motives that make sense of the behavior. They explain the behavior by assuming that it is driven by internal forces, rather than the kinds of organizational factors shown previously (Figure 4.1, Contextual Forces That Shape Behavior along with Personality).

When someone acts in a way you don't like, you tend to demonize that person and label him or her a "jerk" or worse. Although everyone does it, premature negative labeling makes it difficult to gain insight into the potential ally's currencies. And it never matters who started the negative attributions; once begun, they often take on a life of their own.

> Learn to understand others; don't be one of those who says, "He's so bright I don't understand why he doesn't agree with me."
>
> —Pat Hillman, Chief Technology Officer, Fidelity Capital

Further Decreases in Interaction

As the assumptions-about-personality concrete begins to harden in this way, any inclinations to interact diminish. Why waste your time on a person who you believe has negative traits and can't change? Because you have concluded that such an immovable person would only be hurt or angry at being confronted with the offending behavior, you write off that potential ally for all time.

In the unlikely event, however, that you do raise the issue, it is extremely difficult not to do so in a negative, accusatory way. That relieves your frustrations rather than helps the colleague learn something useful. By this time, even if your original belief about the potential ally's inability to change was wrong, your attack just precluded any chance for a positive response, and you walk away from the exchange feeling vindicated in your negative beliefs. While such an outburst provides a momentary release of frustration, it is not exactly a formula for building a trusting relationship where influence can flow both ways.

ALTERNATIVES TO CREATING DISTANCE AND LIMITING INFLUENCE

One of the ways to avoid getting into the kind of negative cycle that limits influence is to recognize the pattern as it develops. Whenever you find yourself assigning negative personality traits to an uncooperative colleague or boss, take it as a warning that needs further investigation. That difficult person may indeed turn out to be a totally immovable object, but until you have thoroughly tested that notion, you can't know if it is true.

You can develop intelligence about another person by asking colleagues whether they see him or her the same way you do. Their views might be more detailed, more detached, and more insightful, and they will protect you from reaching inaccurate conclusions. Be sure they know you aren't fishing for a nasty answer but rather are just trying to understand the person so you can work things out.

Mutual Misinterpretation, Leading to Decreased Interaction and Understanding: Oliver and Mark

For a sad (and not so unusual) example of a downward spiral, take the interaction we observed between Mark Buckley and Oliver Hanson. Mark had recently been promoted from within the company to the position of president of "Vitacorp," the newly acquired life insurance subsidiary of property and casualty company "Magnacomp." Soon after taking office, he became increasingly unhappy with the behavior of Oliver, the Magnacomp group vice president responsible for Vitacorp. Oliver, a meteoric star at Magnacomp but unfamiliar with life insurance, repeatedly went to Mark's subordinates for information. Mark found this maddening, because, on the basis of these apparently casual conversations, Oliver would leap to conclusions and begin asking Mark annoying questions about "the problems" in Vitacorp.

Because Oliver was unfamiliar with Vitacorp's operations, Mark found his questions always slightly askew. They seemed to reflect more about the politics of Magnacomp and the property and casualty business than the real problems facing Vitacorp. After several experiences like this, Mark decided to take action, but his indirect attempts to hint at the issue with Oliver were met with irritation. Oliver would mutter something about needing to have a feel for what was going on.

Mark concluded that Oliver's meteoric rise must be due to the fact that Oliver was an inveterate meddler who wanted to get the dirt on everyone so that he could make himself look good. This made Mark extremely cautious around Oliver, and he made every possible excuse to reduce the contact between them. "The less information I give that power-hungry SOB, the less harm he can do!" he thought. Their relationship became quite strained, and Mark began to wonder why he had ever wanted to be president.

Oliver saw the events quite differently. He had been placed in charge of Vitacorp as a developmental assignment. He had ideas, based on his general knowledge of insurance, about ways to improve Vitacorp's performance, but they were a result of financial expertise rather than in-depth knowledge of Vitacorp's life insurance business. Early on, he sensed Mark's resistance to his conversations with people down in Mark's organization; but since he wasn't an expert on the business, he felt he needed a first-hand feel for the way managers thought. He had no intention of interfering, but he wanted more of a basis for judging how to assess the progress of Vitacorp. Furthermore, because Magnacomp's culture was very political, Oliver assumed that Vitacorp would have the same kind of jockeying for position in the ranks that he had seen at Magnacomp. He believed that only a very naive manager would neglect to develop his own sources for deciphering the political maneuverings in a company he was responsible for.

(Continued)

With this set of assumptions, Oliver was surprised and disquieted by what he perceived as Mark's secrecy and withdrawal. "What's he got to hide?" wondered Oliver. "I'd better spend even more time talking with the troops, or I'll really be flying blind." Thus, Mark's response to Oliver's behavior made the situation worse (see the following figure for a summary of the pattern).

Mutually Reinforcing Actions and Assumptions

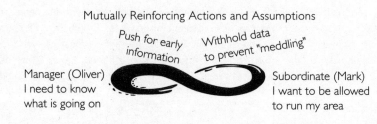

Manager (Oliver)
I need to know
what is going on

Subordinate (Mark)
I want to be allowed
to run my area

Oliver was amenable to changing his style, but Mark never gave him the chance. Once he decided that Oliver was a died-in-the-wool politician and meddler, Mark believed he couldn't broach the subject for fear of having it used against him. Why be open with someone who can't be trusted?

Unfortunately, colleagues are not always the most useful source, although their views, when different from yours, can prevent you from premature hardening of the arbitrary conclusions. There are two potential problems with colleague opinions. First, the people whose opinions you most trust are often those who see the world most similarly. It is the sharing of biases and assumptions that usually makes for trusted colleague relationships, which increases comfort but reinforces distortions.

Second, even when the person you ask for an opinion is not so similar that your prejudices are merely shared and reinforced, often he or she can provide no better evidence than you already have. His or her responses to your queries may be based on a few observations and some rumors rather than on firsthand knowledge. Thus, it is not always as easy to get useful evidence from colleagues as it appears.

I THOUGHT YOU'D NEVER ASK: USING DIRECT INQUIRY AS AN ALTERNATIVE

As suggested earlier in this chapter, a good way to understand others is to take the direct route—to the horse's mouth. Despite the natural fears of

Table 4.1 Sample Questions That Do Not Assume Negative Motives

I'd like to understand more about the forces you are responding to.
Can you help me understand your job and its demands?
What about your job keeps you awake at night?
Tell me more about that.
You seem concerned about _____ ; what makes that a concern?
How can I be helpful at making that less of an issue?

being bitten, when in doubt, just ask. However, your inquiry must be a genuine attempt to solve a problem and not a thinly veiled accusation.

To do that (and not just fake it, which seldom fools anyone), you must set aside any negative judgments you've made and adopt a working assumption that the potential ally does not view his or her behavior as deliberately bad. Most people view their own behavior as reasonable and justified, no matter how it may appear to others.

The trick to unhooking yourself from your negative views is to assume that the potential ally thinks his or her behavior is reasonable, and your job is to understand that reasonable person's rationale so that you can pursue a win-win resolution. In other words, can you see the world through his or her eyes? Try stepping back and (temporarily) taking a novel approach: "Let me assume this is an intelligent, reasonable person who, for some reason that I don't understand, is not cooperating. I am beginning to act as if his motives were intentionally bad. What if that weren't the case? How can I understand better?" What questions can you ask that might open up the discussion? Sample questions that do not assume negative motives are provided in Table 4.1.

Often, a direct question may be all that is needed. But, you get into trouble when you have such a negative view that the only question you can think of would make things worse. Loaded questions only provoke the recipient rather than begin an exploratory discussion.

Once you have reached a negative conclusion about someone, it is difficult to go back to neutral inquiry. Work on understanding an ally's world when you are still puzzled, rather than after you have tried and convicted the person in your mind.

The Benefits of Asking

Despite the natural fear of openly admitting there is something you don't understand (especially to a person who you think might be out to get you), this kind of openness works well for several reasons. First, the potential ally is likely to be surprised by your genuine interest. Because people in organizations rarely bother to ask others exactly how they see the world, those asked are often grateful. They appreciate your willingness to show confusion and, in return, give you the information you need.

Second, most people are grateful for the chance to "tell their story" to explain themselves and their situation. This works, however, only if you are genuinely interested in what the other person has to say and aren't just going through the motions of using a technique you picked up in some book. It is odd that so many organizational members believe they can fool anyone when they want to, but nobody can successfully fool them. (That leaves too many who are nobody's fools.) In general, few are taken in by insincerity, so don't fake interest or confusion if you don't feel it (or can't drop the negative assumptions you've made).

Finally, sincere, direct inquiry builds openness and trust into the relationship, which aids all future transactions. It is easy to get so caught up in influencing potential allies that you fail to learn from them. Asking what is important to them helps keep you in a more open, to-be-influenced posture, which increases their confidence in you.

If You Think You Know the Motive

Sometimes, you are not at a complete loss as to what might be driving the reluctant ally, but you don't want to leap to the kinds of conclusions that will harden opposition. It is possible to test your intuition in an exploratory way.

The more you value the relationship with the person you want to change, the harder it can be to say just what you want. Yet, it often makes things worse to hold back, and it is an enormous relief to get issues out in the open. Often, the ally's irritating position seems far more reasonable when he or she explains it.

BARRIERS TO DIRECTNESS

What keeps people from reaching such mutually satisfying agreements in comparable situations? Why is it so difficult to ask directly what is ultimately crucial to know? If you can explore others' concerns and situations directly, then it is far easier to find exchange possibilities. Even when the relationship is not well developed, it can be useful to inquire. Why doesn't it happen more often?

How to Invite Exploratory Conversation with Difficult or Puzzling Colleagues

Suppose you have a hunch that a potential ally is being pressured by his boss. Something about the way he seems to be constantly looking over his shoulder suggests that the boss's heavy hand is getting in the way. Could you say something like:

> Casper, I have been puzzling about your hesitancy to back this project, especially since I think it has potential benefits for both our areas. I was wondering whether part of the problem is that you think Otto is going to climb all over you if you do anything that could affect your quarterly financials. Is that why we're having trouble connecting?

Even if your hunch is wrong, this kind of direct question is likely to serve as the opening for an interesting conversation. If your question comes across as genuine and does not imply that a negative answer will confirm your conviction that he is a wimp, then, whatever his answer, you have created the likelihood of learning more. If he confirms your suspicion, then you can help him strategize about how to overcome his boss's concerns. And if he responds that his boss has nothing to do with it, consider that an invitation to ask what the problem really is.

Another way to engage allies in direct discussion of their interests, concerns, or currencies is to look for what appear to be mixed messages. Does the person say one thing and do another or say nice things but in a tone fraught with hostility? For example, your boss has been proclaiming that the future of the unit depends on people taking more initiative and being more entrepreneurial, but then she micromanages and requires that you get her approval for every small act. Instead of concluding that she is hypocritical (or that she means it but can't let go) and then giving up, try a direct approach, for example:

> Linda, I'm really confused, and because my confusion is interfering with my ability to do what I think you want me to, I need to understand better what you really want. At our staff meetings, you have been stressing that you'd like us to take more initiative and do what needs to be done. But there are a number of things on which you still insist that I come to you for approval before I can go ahead. These seem to me to be places where I could take action in a responsible, enterprising way; yet, when I do, there isn't much latitude. Can we talk about this because it's puzzling? I could be more effective if we sorted this out.

Accusation, Not Inquiry

Barriers get erected when the other is not behaving as desired and the first few approaches have not produced desired results. Then the negative conclusions begin to form, and they have amazing staying power. Future inquiries turn into statements with strong negative overtones. Just as when a parent "asks" a child, "Why can't you keep your room clean?" inquiry laced with accusation seldom produces useful information.

Confusion between Understanding and Agreement

Although exploration is required when the other's behavior is not quite comprehensible, it is tempting to argue when the other person says something that isn't "correct" from your point of view. If you don't step in, the other person might come to incorrect conclusions—or, heaven forbid, become convincing. The danger of really listening to anyone is that you might have to change your opinion, which is unsettling when you are trying to change his or hers.

Nevertheless, it is possible to work at understanding without conveying agreement. The English language does not afford us the convenient "ah so" of the Japanese, which means that the listener understands but takes no position on the matter, so we have to be more careful to make our position explicit. It can be helpful to say something like, "I don't think I see things the way you do, but if we are going to work well together, it's crucial for me to understand where you're coming from. If I'm silent, it doesn't mean I'm agreeing or disagreeing, just concentrating hard on understanding how

Table 4.2   Summary of Self-Inflicted Barriers to Understanding the Worlds of Others

Factors Requiring Only Your Awareness in Order to Change
Preoccupation with what you want, so you are not tuning in
Assuming all resistance is due to personality, not organizational factors, then demonizing the person's character, motives, or intelligence
Unfamiliarity with the other person's world, so you have little clue or you are filling in with assumptions
Not listening carefully to language of other person, especially about his or her concerns
Not asking

Factors Where You and Your Attitudes Are the Problem
Asking, but in an accusatory way that causes defensiveness or anger
Avoiding the person whose behavior is difficult or resistant to influence
Leaping to conclusions from one piece of information
Disapproving of the world of the other person, rather than understanding it and how it affects behavior

you see this issue—or biting my tongue so I don't jump in to challenge you before I understand properly! Let me know if you think I'm not getting your views." A summary of self-inflicted barriers to understanding the worlds of others is provided in Table 4.2 on the previous page.

The patience to work toward this kind of understanding can make it possible to find opportunities for exchange where at first there appeared to be none. Knowing the world of the potential ally, however, is only part of what is needed. You also need to be clear about your own needs and interests to increase the likelihood that you will find currencies to offer for those valued by the ally. Understanding your world and the power you control is the subject of Chapter 5.

CHAPTER 5

YOU HAVE MORE TO OFFER THAN YOU THINK IF YOU KNOW YOUR GOALS, PRIORITIES, AND RESOURCES (THE DIRTY LITTLE SECRET ABOUT POWER)

. . . [I'm part of a volunteer community organization,] The Columbus Partnership, a group of 16 CEOs. The group picked me as the leader. My inauguration speech was, "I have no authority; you're all here voluntarily—your interest is the community. I'm going to try to lead you, but understand I can only influence you. And I'm very sensitive to that, the fact that you're all presidents, some of you are presidents of businesses larger than ours, so a disparity of interests, but I can only lead from influence. So the notion of an influence model, an authority model, listening skills, organization skills, visioning skills . . . [etc.] it's the things that leaders want to practice, practicing their art and their science. It's a wonderful thing to try these things in communities, let alone your particular skill set. . . . It enriches your career and advances it."

—Les Wexner, CEO of The Limited, Talk at the Kennedy School,
Harvard University, Fall 2003

POWER SOURCES: YOU ARE PLUGGED IN

Our basic premise is that your ability to influence—the power that is due to your skills, as much, if not more than your position—comes from having access to resources that others want. This works because you gain influence by engaging in mutually beneficial exchanges, and the more resources you can supply, the more influence you can get. This insight turns on its head the commonly held concept of what it takes to have influence. Too many people focus only on formal authority and believe that power rests in the ability to say no. Although taking a negative approach is sometimes necessary, overusing it can actually diminish influence. Real power comes from knowing when and how to say yes and from focusing on more ways to be able to say it.

How do you find valuable things to offer so you can say yes and provide needed currencies? Acquiring the power to say yes requires that you know your own world—your interests, capabilities, accomplishments—as well as your potential ally's world. Until this point, we have assumed that your world is perfectly clear to you, but, unfortunately, we often see employees who lack clarity about what they want and what they bring to the table—the resources they command. Although they want influence, they aren't aware that they may be doing certain things inadvertently that diminish their potency.

You probably are more powerful than you think. Careful diagnosis can reveal your untapped resources, which you can then use to gain influence even in difficult situations. We show you in this chapter how to increase your resource pool and influence repertoire by looking carefully at the elements available when you know your own world and the world of your potential ally.

What Do You Want Anyway? Gaining Clarity on Your Objectives

The first step to increase your power is to figure out exactly what you want, which is easier said than done. Most significant influence attempts usually have more than one goal; the problem comes in deciding which goal is most important and which can wait for another day.

In general, it is important to think carefully about what you want from each person or group that you are trying to influence. Decide in advance the minimum you need from each. Because in most cases your wish list will contain more than the potential ally may be willing (or able) to give, it's important to know the difference between what would be nice to have and what is absolutely necessary (see Table 5.1 on page 82).

What Are Your Primary Goals?

Think of Les Charm's goals (see boxed example) when he realized he was not enjoying his job at Prudential. He wanted to meet many people who

Table 5.1   Gain Clarity on Your Objectives

What are your primary goals?
What personal factors get in the way?
Be flexible about achieving goals.
Adjust expectations of your role and your ally's role.

could help him later when he went into business. He wanted experience in complicated, financial deal making. He wanted to be free from the usual company constraints and paperwork. He also wanted to be able to act unconventionally and feel he had not sold his soul to a large company.

Although Les eventually was able to do all of these things, he needed to figure out what his main priorities were. If being unconventional were his

---

Les Charm, a Newcomer at Prudential Insurance, Finds Valuable Currencies to Trade for the Freedom He Wants

To salvage an uncomfortable situation, our friend, Leslie Charm, as a young MBA graduate quickly discovered valuable currencies to trade for the experience he wanted. He was a low-ranked outsider who found a way to achieve influence. Although he was extremely different from those in his organization, he marshaled his skills, ambition, and impatience to achieve amazing opportunities.

Les, now a successful entrepreneur, franchiser, and turnaround expert, has always been full of energy, nerve, and a willingness to take risks. He loves doing complex financial analysis and seeing unusual possibilities. After finishing his undergraduate degree at Babson College, he earned an MBA at Harvard Business School. His first position after Harvard was as an analyst in the five-person private loan placement department for Prudential, which at the time was an old-line, bureaucratic insurance company. The extreme mismatch between his and the company's personality was evident from the beginning.

Les had worked since he was a teenager for his father's leather manufacturing company, and he had always begun his workday early. On his first day at Prudential, Les arrived at 7:30 A.M., raring to go, but no one was there. He hadn't asked, and no one had thought to tell him, about the gentlemanly 9 to 5 workday. Nor was he pleased with the conservative, stiff atmosphere when everyone did show up.

Dick Gill, the senior vice-president of the division and an experienced, long-time Prudential employee, called Les into his office that day and greeted him with,

"Welcome to the Pru. When are you leaving?" Taken aback, Les asked what Gill meant.

Gill replied, "An ambitious, Jewish boy like you isn't planning to make a career at a place like this. So how long do you plan to stay?"

Taken by surprise, Les decided to meet honesty with honesty. "How long do you want?" he asked.

"Two years," was Gill's frank reply, "by which time you'll have learned the business and will have done enough deals to pay me back for letting you learn."

Les thought that a fair-enough arrangement, but within two weeks he was champing at the bit. He hated the required paperwork and the routine-filled, bureaucratic way of life the others seemed to accept. He wanted to meet entrepreneurs all over eastern Massachusetts, create a network of contacts for himself, and be out making complicated loan deals. How could he make the two years bearable or, better yet, enjoyable and educational?

As Les thought about his options, he realized that he was the new kid on the block, an alien in a conservative land. His formal position was two levels below Gill, and he was not in charge of anyone else. The situation did not hold much promise for getting the freedom to do what he wanted in a style that he preferred.

Then Les remembered his only other work experience outside his family's leather business. A week after Les got his bachelor's degree in business administration, his father died. Les took a year off to sell the company before starting on an MBA program. Six months later, the business was sold, and Les found himself without a job. After only one month, the embarrassment of collecting unemployment propelled him into taking a short-term job in the asset-factoring division at the First National Bank of Boston. The interviewer who hired Les sent him to a low-level, credit-approval job.

During his first week at the bank, Les's boss, Richard Ajamian, invited him out for a drink. After some polite conversation, Richard suddenly said to Les, "You must be going off to graduate school in September." When Les didn't protest, Richard continued, "That's fine with me. Don't worry about it. Look, you can do your present job in two days a week. I'm 31, and I want to go places in the bank. I want you to help me, to be my tool for getting ahead. I'm going to get you into our management training program, which will allow you to see every department in the bank. You'll meet lots of people, so it won't waste your time. I'll use the training program as a cover and send you into all the asset-factoring departments. You'll look for every weakness in the system you can find and report back to me every week. That way I can strengthen the division, and you'll find it more interesting."

Les readily agreed, and, as an outsider without preconceptions and with a fresh viewpoint, he was able to spot big holes in the system then in use. Even better, he met many important people in the bank, who served as useful connections in his later ventures.

(Continued)

Best of all, Les learned that it was possible for people to initiate a negotiation for something desirable by offering a win-win proposition that appealed to the interests of the other party. The opportunities Richard Ajamian had provided at the bank could serve Les as a model to get where he wanted at Prudential.

Although Les nominally reported to Dick Gill's subordinate at the Pru, Les's boss preferred to work on his own deals rather than supervise others. Les realized that Gill was the person to influence because he was the company's expert in bringing in new business. He reasoned that Gill might be interested in getting some help finding new accounts, especially the unusual deals that wouldn't ordinarily find their way to the company. If he could work out an arrangement with Gill, Les might free himself from the job constraints he found so irritating, meet all kinds of entrepreneurs and financiers, and, in return, provide valuable business to Gill's area.

Because the department was small and it was easy to approach anyone in it directly, Les spoke to Gill. "Dick, I see you know everybody, but I'm betting you could use help in bringing in new deals. I'll do that for you, but only if you'll meet two conditions: Nobody tells me what hours to work, and you'll have someone take care of all the related paperwork except for the actual deals. I don't want to face office bullshit and spend time filling out forms. If you do that, I'll bring in deals like none you've ever seen. If they look good to you, let me fight the battles upstairs to have them approved."

Gill said he would support Les once Les's efforts proved successful. Until that time, Les was on his own. When Les said he understood the conditions, Gill agreed to the exchange.

Les spent the next five years with Prudential, working the way he liked and producing the highest volume of loans in the division. Although he worked hard, he rarely appeared at the office and conformed not at all to the customary requirements. When he did show up, he was wearing a turtleneck; then he'd casually saunter into the executive dining room for lunch. His expense account, which he used for wining and dining potential and not-so-potential clients, was always the highest in the office. And he delighted in tweaking Gill. One day he strolled in at 9:00 A.M. and answered Gill's, "What are you going to do today?" with, "Oh, I'm done for the day; I've already finished two deals."

Even Les's eventual departure involved important exchanges. After five years, he went to Gill to tell him he was leaving. He didn't know exactly what he was going to do, but he was looking to start his own business. "Have I got a deal for you," Gill replied. "Stay five more months, which will let you finish the big deal you're working on and give you time to train your replacement. In return, I'll give you an extra day off each month to do your own business—one day the first month, two the second, and so forth—at no loss of pay. I'll cover for you." Les agreed. Although this arrangement was not mentioned in the Prudential policy manual, both Les and Gill got what they wanted, and the company benefited.

main goal, Les might have focused on that and created an adversarial relationship with Dick Gill. (Plenty of young hotshots have irritated their
bosses with their failure to catch on to the way things work in the organization.) Then, he would have lost the chance to get out and explore new
deals. By focusing on freeing himself from routine paperwork, he could
get the time to meet people who would be potential loan candidates. The
chance to behave in an unconventional manner would come when he
proved himself, which he soon did.

One of the first requirements in any job is to deliver what is expected
of you. Les would have been just a loud-mouthed, overconfident new MBA
if he hadn't been good at finding financing deals. By combining clarity of
what he wanted with excellent performance, he got to shape the other requirements of his job.

Being willing to hold off your personal needs, even temporarily, isn't
easy. Too often, we have seen people who are consumed by their personal
demands, which drives out task goals and prevents others from hearing
what they want. It isn't a matter of squelching all desires, but of getting
clarity on priorities.

Personal Factors That Get in the Way

At issue here is not just failure to separate out personal issues from the larger
goal, but the problems that can arise from personal needs and desires blocking the ability to obtain influence. Consider the way that Carl Lutz de-
feated himself (see next boxed example).

The lesson learned is not that you should completely set aside personal
needs; doing that is both impossible and counterproductive. You need personal involvement for the processes and changes this book advocates. Without a personal investment, you won't have the drive to set goals and see
them through. Recognize your needs and accept them as legitimate, rather
than drive them underground and beyond your conscious control. But don't
be controlled by them. Decide deliberately how much to work on them
directly rather than let them be a by-product of good performance.

In most situations where people seek major influence, they have needs
above and beyond their task objectives. They may also need visibility for
themselves or their department, association with the project as a way to
"make a name for myself," approval, or respect. These extra, personal needs
not only can provide the energy to stick through the rough spots but also
can serve the organization. To have the time to reach the loan objectives

The Dangers of Being Out of Touch with Your Own Needs and Skills

Carl was an information systems vice-president in a large financial services company. He had steadily moved up through the organization and, being ambitious, coveted the post of senior vice-president.

He was shocked and upset when he was twice bypassed for that promotion. Although Carl was very bright, those who worked with him found him unpolished and single-minded, which made them suspicious of his ability to handle a job that called for considerable political finesse and personal sensitivity.

Carl had little patience with the kind of delicate, indirect style used at the top echelons. He attacked those who used that kind of subtle style as "always currying favor, being concerned with style—not substance—and failing to have the courage of their convictions."

When Carl was passed over the first time, his boss tried to explain why he had not been selected. But Carl was so caught up in wanting status that he couldn't hear. He stubbornly insisted that he had been treated unfairly, and his loud, angry outburst only served to further convince others that he was "impossible" to work with. As a result of his inability to learn, Carl was eventually asked to leave.

Even worse, his failure to think through his priorities prevented him from realizing that he really enjoyed complex, technical tasks, rather than management duties. Ironically, the division would have been happy to give him more responsibility on major system design projects, which he would have enjoyed and excelled at.

he had committed to, Les Charm, for example, needed more freedom from the usual bureaucratic demands and more than the conventional autonomy. Achieving his objectives then justified his being granted that freedom. His personal needs dovetailed with his professional objectives and the true job requirements. By contrast, Carl Lutz's personal needs ranked higher than the job-related tasks, which produced the unnecessary conflict.

Another way that personal and organizational needs can clash or support one another arises when there are interpersonal difficulties with someone whom you personally like and are reluctant to hurt or you have fear of the person and don't want to arouse wrath against you. Does your job require that you address the interpersonal difficulties, or can the work get done while allowing you some slack? Do you have to set aside your feelings to do what's right, or is it absolutely necessary first to raise the delicate issues? If you raise your unhappiness with the person's performance, can you do it in a skilled way (discussed further in Chapter 9 on influencing difficult subordinates), or is it impossible to address without creating a heated response? Careful sorting of priorities is all the more difficult when personal feelings and work are intertwined but is necessary if you are to be effective—or want to avoid making yourself sick with swallowed feelings that you are afraid to get out.

Another personal needs barrier arises when you are driven by the desire for visibility and recognition at times when staying in the background is far more appropriate. For example, you are trying to get high-powered and independent people to cooperate in establishing a new process that is uncomfortable for them. If you are focused on getting them to take a back seat so that you can get credit for the idea, your overriding need could be just what it takes to get them to dig in. Do you need credit so badly that you have to jump into the spotlight? Or can you make suggestions, show benefits, and then step back to let them feel that they have ownership, too?

Another problem occurs when your personal discomfort with one currency or another keeps you from using it. For example, some people are so uncomfortable with conflict that they can't get into anything controversial, no matter how needed that is. "Oh, I can't ask for that; it will make her argumentative and attacking." Similarly, some people are so in need of being liked that they can't discuss anything that might produce anger before the other person has a chance to digest the request. Still others don't like intimacy and, therefore, have trouble dealing with people who want to exchange feelings and closeness.

The last problem is one we have mentioned before: refusing to pay in a particular currency because you don't like or approve of it and don't think anyone should value it. Perhaps you are turned off by people who strive for status because you believe that everyone should treat others equally. Or maybe you see that a colleague craves recognition, but you look down on that kind of preoccupation. Perhaps it is those who want power and domination who get your blood boiling. But influence is about what you have to do to get cooperation, not about imposing your values on others. You are entitled to feel so strongly about some currencies that you refuse to pay in them even though it would get you the influence you want. You can choose to be *right*, rather than effective. Just do it knowing the consequences.

Be Flexible about Achieving Goals

Even when they know their primary goals, people can lose influence by being too inflexible in the way they go about achieving them. Sometimes, people with an exciting idea and high commitment become more single-minded than is necessary. They lock in on a detailed vision they've created and ignore the variations that also could work. Thus, they miss the chance to get half a loaf—or sometimes an improved, though different loaf—through the adaptation of their allies' ideas.

Research found that people who had carried out important changes from the middle of their organizations were both highly persistent and flexible.[1] They stuck to the essence of the desired results they envisioned but were open to change their approach as they dealt with the many stakeholders whose cooperation they needed. Occasionally, even the fundamental vision changed as encounters with reality brought to light new limits and possibilities, but, more often, it was the details and pathways that changed while the vision remained intact.

Les Charm, for example, knew that he wanted to start his own business, and he wanted the skills and contacts to do that. Initially, he thought he would work for Prudential for only two years, but he was clear that experience and connections were important so he stayed more than five because he continued to learn and build his network.

Adjust Expectations of Your Role and Your Ally's Role

People can limit their potential power and cut off options when they arbitrarily define the job boundaries between themselves and their potential allies.

There are several reasons that conventional job descriptions overly constrain people. One is the changing world of work. The historical contract (or exchange) between organizations and individuals was, "Do your job and the company will take care of you." The emphasis was on staying within the lines and boxes of the organizational chart and not interfering with anyone else's carefully limited job. People now have to do more than what is listed in their job descriptions because no single set of rules can anticipate all the changes flowing by. As a result, it is now initiative, rather than conformity, that is required.

Another reason people tend to overly constrain themselves reflects outmoded attitudes toward authority. It is one thing to step over the bounds in dealing with peers, but it is another in dealing with a superior who holds formal power over you. Also, traditionally, there has been an explicit *exchange* between boss and subordinate. "Let me make the important decisions and I, the wise boss, will do them right." Subordinates buy into this exchange because they can delegate the difficult issues upward. Who

---

The Benefit of Loosening Job Definition Boundaries

Arthur's boss, Theo Snelling, although competent in many ways, could never seem to get memos out. This meant that decisions weren't adequately communicated to the organization. Theo was European-born, unsure of his English, and insistent on composing the perfect message, for which there was never enough time.

Arthur felt more and more frustrated about this problem. Complaining to Theo resulted in apologies but no actions. Although memos weren't the most important issue in the department, they were an increasing annoyance.

Arthur finally realized that he was locked into a too-rigid view of roles: "That's Theo's job and he should be doing it." When he realized this, Arthur went to Theo and offered to draft the memos himself. For him, this was no great chore. This positive exchange resulted in multiple wins: Not only were the memos out quickly, helping reinforce departmental decisions, but also Arthur built credit with Theo that was drawn on later as support for controversial projects.

---

doesn't dream of the perfect boss: the manager who is considerate but doesn't forget the work, who can correct you without being harsh, and who is capable of giving autonomy without casting you adrift? But such a wise and omnipotent superior exists only in imagination, which leaves the hope-filled subordinate trapped in an organizational box. If bosses don't "do what they're supposed to do," what can someone lower in the hierarchy possibly do?

You Can Influence Even Your Boss

Although we offer a whole chapter (Chapter 8) on influencing your boss, we briefly explore the topic here as one key area where most people act less influentially than they could. Too often, they limit their focus to "doing quality work on time" or "keeping their noses clean" and ignore the other vital currencies the boss needs. They too seldom do what Les Charm did: learn the boss's critical needs and then figure out how to meet them.

When you are genuinely aligned with your boss's goals and interests, you can push hard for what you want. You can disagree with your boss and be praised for it. In most cases, delivering on what your boss needs, can give you the opportunity to make demands, talk straight, and effect change.

But just what do you have that your boss needs? What currencies do you command? Although every boss has particular interests that are unique, there are some universal currencies beyond those we mentioned in Chapter 3 that most bosses would be delighted to receive. Think of those you control (Table 5.2).

Although the list in Table 5.2 is far from exhaustive, awareness of how to generate these kinds of currencies allows you to move from just "making a request" (which leaves you dependent on the other person's good graces) to linking your requests with the boss's goals and/or creating credits that can be exchanged for your desired outcomes.

KNOW YOUR NEEDS AND DESIRES, BUT DON'T FORGET THE PERSON YOU WANT TO INFLUENCE

In the first section of this chapter, we stressed the importance of knowing your own goals and gaining a clearer picture of what you need. While that is crucial, it serves only as the first step for dealing with the person you want to influence. Focusing only on what you want means that the change will be defined in terms of meeting your needs, rather than the needs of the person you want to influence, which is less likely to be a successful strategy.

If you see clearly what you want (and if these demands are reasonably within what others can deliver), you are free to focus on what they need from the transaction. Then, by examining what resources you command, you can decide how the exchange can meet their needs. Not being able to deliver a valuable currency is a formula for powerlessness.

SELF-TRAPS: POWER OUTAGES IN MAKING EXCHANGES

Not all difficulties in making exchanges are caused by the other person. You may be creating some of the problems yourself, for several possible reasons.

Reluctance to Assert Legitimate Claims

In the boxed example on page 93, Jim set out to create currencies that would be valuable to his boss. Some people, however, experience power failures because they don't know how to collect on obligations others have incurred. When the person who "owes you" doesn't acknowledge it, do you give up in frustration? Are you afraid to harm the relationship by pushing? Have you considered the possibility that the other person doesn't

Table 5.2   Currencies You Control That Are Valuable to Any Boss

Performing above and beyond what is required is a traditional way of building credit with any boss, but it is still fundamental. When Les Charm (see boxed example) asked to work directly at finding unusual, profitable loan opportunities and then delivered, he was given extraordinary latitude by a manager who appreciated the results and was willing to bend the rules to accommodate a star performer who provided more than expected.

Not having to worry about the subordinate's area, knowing he or she will deliver, as Les Charm did when he found new customers.

Knowing the subordinate will take into account political factors in the organization (which, living dangerously, Les Charm refused to do when he thumbed his nose at conventions of dress).

Being able to rely on the subordinate as a sounding board; someone who makes sure the boss doesn't shoot himself or herself in the foot.

Being able to rely on the subordinate as a source of information from other parts of the organization as well as from below.

Keeping the boss informed of problems; making sure there are no surprises. Because so many people distort what they tell their bosses in the belief that bosses want to hear only what will please them, managers are always in the position of wanting and needing reliable information about what is going on in the company. The subordinate who proves to be a reliable source of information, who is good at anticipating others' reactions and can warn the manager about land mines, and who brings potential problems to the boss's attention is likely to be valued and trusted.

Representing the boss (accurately) to other parts of the organization, which frees the boss for other important activities.

Being a source of creativity and new ideas.

Defending and supporting the boss's (and the organization's) decisions to your own subordinates. Since many employees blame any tough decisions on "the boss" or on the invisible "they" at the top, managers are grateful when a subordinate "sells downward," rather than subtly undermining the boss's credibility by implying that all unpopular decisions are forced from above.

Providing support and encouragement, "being on the boss's team." It isn't always lonely at the top, but the person in charge often finds it impossible to explain exactly why he or she had to make certain decisions or how the power to affect others' lives can be a tough burden. Managers often especially appreciate a subordinate's loyalty, encouragement, or general willingness to give the benefit of the doubt. Even bold, strong leaders value having someone around who will stick by them through thick and thin. This works only if you genuinely appreciate the boss, but if you do, it is potent.

Taking initiative with new ideas; preventing problems instead of waiting for them to happen. In an era of rapid change, there is even more need than in the past for subordinates who can take initiative, rather than wait for instructions that inevitably arrive too late. The willingness to jump in to prevent problems is valuable and often dramatically noticeable.

Unusual Initiative by a Low-Level Employee Valued by Her Boss

Betsy Barnes was only 19 when she started work as a receptionist at a management consulting firm. One afternoon during her first week on the job, she discovered that a set of slides for an important client presentation had not been delivered. She called the photo lab and was told that the slides had never been received. When she insisted that they had indeed been hand delivered two days earlier, the lab supervisor replied that was impossible and Betsy would just have to look around her office for the film.

Betsy dug through a pile of unfiled materials and found the receipt from the lab; she called them back to insist that they should look harder. They gave her the runaround again, but she hung in, insisted on talking to the manager and, over the phone, guided him through a search for the missing film. When he had finally located the film, Betsy persisted in pressing the lab to do a special rush job so a courier could pick up the finished slides that afternoon in time for the company president to take them to the presentation.

By chance, the president walked by Betsy's desk as she patiently but very insistently demanded that the lab look harder for the film. He was amazed that on her own, this new, young employee was so conscientiously anticipating the disaster of not having the slides and making sure they would be ready. He not only awarded her an instant bonus but also mentioned to the office manager that Betsy obviously had more potential. Within two months, she was promoted to a more responsible position, managing materials sales.

In this situation, Betsy didn't consciously assess her boss's needs and fulfill them to get what she wanted. But that is how it worked out. Exchange need not be a conscious act for it to be operating and effective.

---

realize all that you have done or knows but isn't focused on it? Maybe your colleague assumed you were just doing your job, and you need to show how much effort has gone into being helpful. And consider the likelihood that you are valuable to your colleague, and he or she is just as concerned about losing your goodwill as you are about harming the relationship. At the minimum, some testing is in order.

You don't have to become a miser, hoarding currency and constantly reminding people what they owe you to stake legitimate claims when others fail to notice your efforts. At the very least, initiate a direct conversation in which you ask straightforwardly but politely if your view that your efforts on their behalf are being ignored matches theirs. Until your colleague understands your side of things, you are tossing away the ball before the

---

Reframing a Personal Need into a Possible Benefit to the Boss

Jim encountered a problem with Wes, his boss, who had a tendency to withhold information. This meant that Jim often first heard about new plans coming down from corporate headquarters from his own subordinates, which wreaked havoc on Jim's credibility and influence with them.

For example, Jim found out from one of his people that corporate was planning major divestiture of another division. The subordinate was clearly surprised, then embarrassed, that Jim hadn't yet heard.

Jim's previous attempts to ask Wes to keep him better informed had produced no results. Jim began to fear that Wes saw him as demanding and insecure. To get better information, Jim needed to provide something Wes valued. Rather than put his request in terms of what he needed for himself, Jim went to Wes and said, "We've talked before about the importance to our department of being seen as knowledgeable and on top of issues. As you've said many times, we get credibility by being 'in the know.' I agree with that and want to deliver, but sometimes I can't. When things are breaking and I don't hear from you, the department looks foolish. Could we set up a 10-minute meeting each Tuesday morning where you can quickly brief me on what's coming down the pike?"

Phrasing his request in terms of Wes's (and the organization's) best interests—rather than just Jim's—finally did the trick. Jim offered Wes currency—departmental reputation—that Wes valued enough to prompt him to hold regular meetings.

---

match has started. Raising the question doesn't guarantee the response you desire, but at least it puts the ball in play.

Reluctance to Demand What You Need

A variation of failing to remind people of legitimate obligations is failing to make clear demands for your primary goals. This happens when you know you can't give orders and you expect the other person to be resistant, so you speak only indirectly about what you want. If your project is important and you are not doing it for your personal glory but for true business reasons, you don't have to hold back and sound mealy-mouthed or try to back into your request. Just asserting that your cause is just may not be enough if you don't help others see how compliance gets them something desired, but requesting with confidence helps.

Reluctance to Collect Debts

Sheila Sheldon, a curator of an important collection at a major art museum, complained that she accommodated many other department heads' needs, but they didn't respond well to her requests. "I'm always going out of my way for people, lending staff members for projects, researching questions, or giving up storage space. But I can't bring myself to remind them when I want something. They should know! That's the least I can expect if they're good colleagues. Why can't they live up to their obligations?"

Sheila's model of influence and relationships depended solely on her colleagues' awareness of what she had done, its value to them, and their goodwill, any of which could be lacking. Did they realize how much she had inconvenienced herself for them? Did they think she was only doing her job? Did they find the usefulness of her gestures far more modest than she had thought? Had the fact that she always suffered in silence made them completely oblivious to her efforts and her need for reciprocity or led them to believe she was happy to be self-sacrificing? Because she wouldn't raise the issue, she had no way of finding out.

Knowing the Appropriate Currency—But Being Uncomfortable Using It

Most people have some currencies they feel uncomfortable trading in. For one, it might be giving praise or appreciation because that feels weak or insincere. For another person, it could be using vision out of discomfort with boldness and ambiguous future goals. Still another reverts to warmth because everything else runs too much risk of rejection. If you have a territory that you always try to skirt, figure out how to overcome your aversion or you will be far less influential than you could be. Practice with a trusted colleague or friend if needed.

Knowing the Appropriate Currency—But Not Wanting to Satisfy the Other Person

This problem arises when you have diagnosed what the other person or group would want but can't stand the idea of giving it to them due to history or bad feelings about them. For example, we worked with a group of scientists who had to deal with government regulators, who were seen as much too intrusive and detail minded. The scientists deduced that giving more information before it was requested would make the jobs of the regulators easier to do, and would probably make them less demanding ("After all, it is their jobs to stay informed"), but they hated the idea. They were so used to thinking of the regulators as the enemy that they had trouble cooperating, even though they knew it was in their own interests.

Paying an attention seeker in recognition is another case where we have seen people balk: "I know that if I gave more recognition, I would get more cooperation, but I can't stand the idea of helping that egomaniac get any glory." As we have said before, that is your choice, but make it a conscious decision and don't complain if the cost is losing influence. Get your priorities straight!

Monitor Your Self-Awareness

To achieve all the power of which you are capable, you need to understand yourself as well as your potential ally. Use the checklist in Table 5.3 to monitor your self-awareness.

The questions on the checklist need careful attention if you are to be as powerful as possible. You will then have the capacity to gain influence by making successful exchanges.

This should help you get the most from your influence capacities. Next, in Chapter 6, we discuss in greater depth how to acquire, build, and repair relationships needed for influence.

Table 5.3   Self-Awareness Checklist

- [ ] What exactly are your task or project goals?
- [ ] Which goals are of primary importance, and which can be set aside if necessary?
- [ ] What are your personal and career goals, and do they help or hinder task success?
- [ ] Are you using all available resources?
- [ ] Do you see the many potential currencies you can earn and have available to trade?
- [ ] Can you be collaborative or confrontational as needed?
- [ ] Are you willing to assert your legitimate claims for collection?
- [ ] Are you reluctant to use some currencies, even when they would work? Do you know what is stopping you?

CHAPTER 6

BUILDING EFFECTIVE
RELATIONSHIPS: THE ART
OF FINDING AND
DEVELOPING YOUR ALLIES

The stranger within my gate,
He may be true and kind,
But he does not talk my talk—
I cannot feel his mind.
I see the face and the eyes and the mouth,
But not the soul behind.
The men of my own stock,
They may do ill or well,
But they tell the lies I am wonted to,
They are used to the lies I tell;
And we do not need interpreters
When we go to buy and sell.
The men of my own stock,
Bitter bad they may be,
But, at least, they hear the things I hear,
And see the things I see;
And whatever I think of them and their likes
They think of the likes of me.

—Rudyard Kipling, "The Stranger"

RELATIONSHIPS MATTER
It's not difficult to build relationships with those you know well and with
whom you share similar goals, values, and tastes. Their assumptions and

ways of viewing the world are familiar. Their behavior, even when disagreeable, is predictable, and they can be influenced by known methods. But organizations are filled with people who are "strangers," who view the world differently because they work for differing functions and managers; are a different sex, age, race, ethnicity, country of origin; or have different training and experiences—all resulting from the requirement to bring diverse expertise to bear on complex organizational problems. A wider range of people, backgrounds, and views is needed than in Kipling's time. Then, members of the British Administrative Services were trained to "think like the Queen" so that they would know what to do when messages and instructions took too long to arrive in the colonies. And, since they were recruited from the same narrow social class and shared the same blinders, they already had a running start toward cohesiveness and ease of dealing with one another. Current conditions require more effort to build effective relationships with the range of people whose cooperation is needed.

In any circumstances, good, open, and trusting relationships have several benefits:

- Communication is more complete, so you are more likely to know the needs and currencies of the other person.
- The other person is more likely to take your word and to be open to being influenced.
- You can pay back later in a wider range of currencies and less exactly.
- Personal currencies where there is connection become more important, which broadens the kinds of currencies you can pay in.

Although transactions occasionally can be so clearly beneficial to both parties that the relationship between them is irrelevant, most of the time there are many ways in which a poor relationship affects the likelihood of influence. For example, a poor relationship:

- Decreases the other person's desire to be influenced.
- Distorts accuracy of perceptions of each other's currencies and intentions.
- Increases burden of proof on:
  —The other person's performance.
  —Delivery of promises.
  —The value of what is offered to you for exchange.
  —Expected timing of repayment.
- Decreases tolerance for the ambiguity inherent in valuing different goods and services for exchange.

- Reduces willingness to engage at all and raises spitefulness: "I'd rather go down in flames than help that rat!"

These are big handicaps when trying to achieve influence. If all relationships started with these disadvantages, organizational life would come to a standstill. Luckily, only the most unfortunate have no relationships that are solid and trusting. Most organizational members know one or more people with whom they can be open and direct and realize the benefits of that kind of relationship. Problems arise with all those colleagues who are not so trusted or trusting. It's bad enough when you deal with strangers who are unknown; complications multiply when you seek to influence someone who has heard you have a negative reputation or with whom you have personally had a bad experience.

What can you do when you are not starting with a good relationship or do not have a great deal in common?

ADAPT TO THE PREFERRED WORK STYLE OF THE OTHER PERSON OR GROUP

One of the most accessible areas for building relationships is work style. All people have a certain work style—a way of solving problems, dealing with others, and getting their jobs done. Some people prefer careful analysis before action; others like to blast through and patch up any holes later. Some managers want subordinates to come to them only with solutions, while others want employees to seek help when the problem is still developing. In building a working relationship, some people like to get to know a colleague first before dealing with the task, while others feel they cannot consider closeness until there has been some successful work interaction.

Preferred styles come from training and experiences, from the demands of jobs, and from individual personality. Cultures create work styles, too. In many Asian and Latin countries, no work can be undertaken until colleagues have consumed many cups of tea or coffee and exchanged pleasantries. In parts of the United States, however, people get impatient if the tasks aren't tackled early and socializing saved for later.

Objectively, there isn't one "right way" to interact, declared in heaven and engraved in stone. Subjectively, however, people often do feel there is one right way—theirs! They often are not aware of their styles; it feels so natural, it must be inherently correct. But, in dealing with others, it is important to be aware of your style and that of the person you want to influence.

Have you ever seen a manager who wants precise written requests but is driven crazy by a subordinate who mentions whatever is on his mind when he sees the boss in the hall? One manager we have observed repeatedly asked for concise formal proposals but usually got the same off-the-cuff requests from one stubbornly casual subordinate. The subordinate thought it was all unnecessary bureaucracy.

Not being fully aware of your style can keep you from considering other possible approaches and unnecessarily limit your ability to connect.

ACTION PLAN

You can use the list of common work style differences (Table 6.1 on page 100) to identify your own preferred style, and contrast that with the preferences of the person you want to influence. Do the differences in style account for some of the difficulties the two of you have working together? If so, then you have a choice. One option is to adopt the style the other person prefers. Alternatively, if the other person is willing, you could initiate a discussion about your differing styles and see if there is a way to proceed that would satisfy both of you.

Although differing work styles are often enough to cause serious problems, sometimes conflict results from genuine differences of substance. Very smart and strong people can have opposing views about, for example, fundamental strategic direction. Because they feel so strongly, they begin to think the problem is the bullheadedness of the other person, rather than legitimate business disagreements, so will be unable to reach agreement. We do not want to minimize these honest disagreements as a source of influence disputes. They shouldn't, however, be compounded by communication problems caused by unrecognized differences in work style. Resolving genuine task disagreements are important enough without adding the extra burden of conflicting work styles.

FOR EVERY SEASON: INCREASING YOUR WORK STYLE REPERTOIRE

Although most people limit their power because of a too-narrow definition of the range of currencies that they can deliver, they also can lose power by overspecializing in only one style of interaction.

We have stressed the importance of an open and collaborative style in dealing with potential allies. Although usually the preferred style (especially

Table 6.1 Work Style Differences

Focus on problems [glass as half-empty, what hasn't been accomplished, what failed]	Focus on successes [what has been accomplished]
Divergent thinking [explores new options; expands what is being considered]	Convergent thinking [reduces options; pushes quickly to solutions]
Want structure [likes rules and routines; predictability, not surprises]	Comfortable with ambiguity [few rules and regulations]
Analysis, then action [studies options before acting]	Action before analysis [acts quickly; collects data from results]
Focus on the big picture	Focus on the details
Logical/rational [wants facts/data, does not trust intuition in self or others]	Intuitive [relies heavily on hunches, own "gut"—places less reliance on facts/data]
Seek risks [likes to take chances, willing to fail, try new approaches]	Avoid risks [tends to be very careful, prefers the "tried and true"]
Respect authority [supports established authority, may defer and not push back]	Discount authority [disagrees, pushes back on authority]
Relationships first [sometimes willing to sacrifice task quality for good feelings]	Task first [greater emphasis on task success than on good relationships]
Seek/value/encourage conflict [and disagreements]	Avoid/suppress conflict [and disagreements]
Competitive [likes to compete, turns situations into personal win-lose tests]	Collaborative [prefers to collaborate; seeks win–win outcomes]
Respond primarily to own needs [and concerns]	Take account first of others [needs and concerns]
Like to be in control [determines direction, nature of activities, wants to approve all decisions]	Like others to take control [determine direction, nature of activities, accept decisions]
Optimistic [about how things will turn out; sees probability of success]	Pessimistic [about how things will turn out; sees likelihood of failure]
Like working alone [on projects]	Prefer working with others

A Complete Mismatch of Work Styles and the Negative Consequences

Like a Greek tragedy, Jack Walters and Alexander Athanas played out that kind of mismatch to its unfortunate end. Jack had recently been named vice-president of marketing. This was a lateral transfer from production, with the twin goals of broadening his experience and using his considerable skills in the crucial (but underdeveloped) marketing area. With his engineering training and production background, Jack was used to solving problems himself and taking them to his boss only when he was stuck. He liked things tidy and wanted to be on top of all issues.

Alex, the company president, had come up through marketing. His experience (and personal style) made him comfortable with messy problems. He wanted to hear about difficulties when they first arose. He didn't necessarily have to solve every problem himself; he was amenable to a subordinate's saying, after they had discussed the various options: "I hear your input and certainly will consider it carefully, but I want to handle this on my own." What Alex needed most was to be kept informed and to feel that he had been listened to.

Jack's and Alex's opposite styles led to polarization, then suspicion, distrust, and even paranoia. When Alex was concerned about something, he would ask Jack if there were any problems. Jack would hear this as "any problems that you can't solve?" and say no. Alex would think that Jack was withholding information and probe even further. Jack would feel his competence was being questioned and become even more circumspect.

From Jack's point of view, the problem was Alex: "Damn it," he thought, "he is paying me good money to be head of marketing; why doesn't he let me manage? I guess he really wants to run marketing himself." Jack's failure to recognize the part that his own style played in this problem meant that the problem grew and grew, until the point that Alex saw Jack as not only disloyal but also sneaky and untrustworthy. The problem "ended" one day when Alex strode into Jack's office and fired him.

with people who will be needed in future interactions), at times it becomes necessary to use distance, as the human resources manager (see box on p. 102) found, or even confrontation and threat (carefully) to set the stage for a mutual exchange. Doing this successfully requires more than a willingness to be tough because threats with no resources behind them are empty and self-defeating. As the boxed example on page 103 illustrates, your own skilled performance powerfully undergirds confrontation. You don't want to get into the position of barking a threat only to hear the snide retort, "Got a quarter? Call someone who gives a damn!"

Manager Who Preferred Close Style Learned More Distant Style to Match New Boss

We observed a warm, expressive human resources manager at Levi Strauss struggle to get along with a new boss, the marketing division general manager. Unlike her previous boss, with whom she had a close working relationship based on a shared vision of making the company a human, caring place, the new one was cool, numbers and bottom-line oriented, didn't easily make small talk to ease interactions, and preferred distance to closeness.

The human resources manager, in contrast, liked working on unstructured, ambiguous problems face to face and informally. The harder she tried to get close, the more her new boss avoided her, which bugged her, both personally and because she believed his style was wrong for the division's needs. After many frustrating brief encounters, she finally realized that sending him crisp memos got more response. She didn't like it and would have preferred a warmer, fuzzier style, but she found she could get a lot done. She chose effectiveness over personal comfort.

The choice between a collaborative and confrontational style is only one set of alternatives for increasing your influence repertoire. Another set involves the time pressure for results. Chris Hammond was under external pressures that forced her to move quickly. However, Paul Wielgus was successful because of his willingness to be patient and his understanding of how to make potential opponents into allies (see boxed example on p. 105).

Unlike Chris Hammond, Paul Wielgus was patient and nonthreatening. Yet, he did not let go of what he was certain would be a beneficial activity for the company. He stuck with it even when being attacked, and he found ways to talk about the program that appealed to the currencies of a hard-nosed cost cutter. He focused on productivity increases, enthusiasm for work, and stronger ideas. In this way, he built a good relationship and created a new currency (helping other departments achieve better performance) that gave him something to trade with his peers.

OTHER APPROACHES WHEN THE RELATIONSHIP IS BAD, YET NEEDS TO IMPROVE

What else can you do if trying to match work style is not enough? Whatever the source of relationship problems—past battles with the person, bad blood between your departments, incompatible personal tastes, or general

Successful Use of a Confrontational
Style to Gain Influence

Chris Hammond told us she was forced to take tough actions because of the intransigence of her boss.* Note the way she marshals resources and uses a confrontational style to achieve mutual gains:

> When I was a sales trainee, I knew that if I didn't make the "Computex" Sales Award, my career at Computex would be ended. Although they wouldn't fire me, I would just be a sales rep, twiddling my thumbs for however long I stayed. You have to make your numbers. So there I was, with a manager who had 20 items that he needed to make to achieve his budget by the end of the quarter and who was trying to make sure that I didn't make the Computex Sales Award. Sales trainees aren't supposed to make the sales award, and if I did, then he should have promoted me to a sales representative. So I asked his secretary what budget numbers he needed. I wasn't being devious; I was really trying to support him. I wanted him to succeed because that was the only way I could succeed. But I had to do it with a power play because he wouldn't treat me seriously.
>
> I read the numbers and said to myself, "Okay, he can't make it in these six areas." As it so happened, I had an account that was going to make the numbers in four of those areas. Then I called up every single open lead on which no one had returned calls, identified the ones that were going to close in a month, and found 15 accounts.
>
> As a sales trainee, that wasn't what I was paid to do; I was paid to learn. But I was tired of being a sales trainee; I was determined to be a sales rep and make the Computex Sales Award—and be the only sales trainee to do it that year.
>
> Furthermore, my manager had a fair-haired boy, the only sales rep he had personally hired, whom he wanted to make the sales award. My manager reasoned that if I made the sales award and was leaving on July 1 to take a job at corporate headquarters, I should give 50 percent of anything I booked to the sales rep. I told my manager that I didn't think that was fair unless he was willing to give me 50 percent of all the sales rep's bookings, since I had done a considerable amount of work and could document it on two large banking orders. I was being asked to give the rep a split so that he would make the sales award, and I was getting nothing for it. A key link in my strategy was knowing that exposing my manager would not be advantageous for either the manager or the sales rep.
>
> I went to the district manager and asked whether I would make the sales award if I closed such and such accounts. He said yes. So I said, "That is not what my manager told me: I would have to give 50 percent to the sales representative." The district manager asked why, and when I answered, he looked at me in total disbelief. I explained that I didn't think it was fair that the sales rep should make the award on behalf of my efforts, and if that was the case, the company would not get any

---

*Excerpted from a teaching case, "Chris Hammond" (A) in Allan R. Cohen, et al., *Effective Behavior in Organizations*, 5th ed. (Homewood, IL: McGraw Hill-Irwin, 1992).

(Continued)

of the business I had found. I would leave the company today, take my vacation pay, and go. The district manager said to go back and talk to my manager. What none of them knew was that I already had the bookings in my drawer. I could make good on any deal I worked with them, and I knew what they needed to make their numbers look good to their bosses.

There were two weeks left in the quarter, and my manager was scared now because he wasn't going to make his numbers. I said to him, "I have a problem. I really want to go back to headquarters, and I need your help. I need to make the sales award. You know that and I know that. I can't go back to corporate as a turkey who hasn't succeeded in making the sales award. I believe I've put forth the sales effort required to do that. I also believe I should go back as a sales rep. I believe I've earned that. I think I can make the budget numbers for you, and I can bring in these two accounts. All that I need from you is the assurance that I will receive the Computex Sales Award if I do it. Otherwise, I'm not going to work another day."

He looked at me and finally said, "If you get those orders in, you can make the sales award, and yes, if you bring in that business, then you're more than qualified to be a sales rep." He never thought I could get the orders. I walked into his office with them two days later.

What motivated me for the most part was realizing that they were not taking me seriously or paying attention to how many accounts were closed as a result of my efforts. I also wanted them to know that I was fully aware of their attempt to use me. That kind of approach is a very strong power play and a high-risk strategy, but if you succeed, you are given much more respect and higher levels of managerial credibility.

Chris followed a high-risk strategy that could have backfired at any of several junctures. In some companies, going over her boss's head to the district manager would have been seen as inappropriate, insubordinate, and possibly even grounds for dismissal. The sales manager she cornered might have retaliated by refusing to recommend her for promotion to sales rep or by spreading negative rumors to others in the organization with whom she would be dealing in the future. Further, she might have made a permanent enemy of the sales rep who had been promised credit for her work. These are all the potential costs to take into account before selecting such a strategy.

Nevertheless, when faced with a situation in which she believed there was little left to lose and everything to gain, Chris correctly diagnosed her boss's most valued currency (his sales quota); stressed the currencies she commanded or could command (sales to customers not yet approached by anyone at Computex, her boss's reputation with the district manager); and made an exchange that got her what she wanted, helped her boss, and was good for the company. (She was not insensitive to the organizational culture; managers at Computex are valued for playing exactly that kind of "guts ball," and Chris has continued to do well there.)

Turning an Attack into Support with a Collaborative, Patient Style at Allied Domecq

Paul Wielgus was head of a specially formed learning and training department at global spirits company Allied Domecq. Paul was supposed to find a way to transform stodgy thinking into greater creativity among managers. Despite this mandate from the CEO to stimulate dramatic change, or perhaps because of it, after two years of success there were still many skeptics who didn't see the value in what Paul's group was doing. For example, a senior executive in the internal audit department, David, called Paul in to chew him out for what David considered unnecessary expenses.

Paul could easily have become defensive; instead he responded in a friendly, collegial way and sold his program in terms David cared about. He explained how the trainers helped trainees align their attitudes and values with the company's strategy. "You wouldn't believe the changes, David," he said, enthusiastically. "People come out of these workshops feeling so much more excited about their work. They find more meaning and purpose in it, and as a consequence are happier and much more productive. They call in sick less often, they come to work earlier in the morning, and the ideas they produce are much stronger." This helped David understand the benefits from the program, which was adopted and became a key part in positively transforming Internal Audit. David became a strong supporter of Paul's work.*

---

*Debra Meyerson, "Radical Change, The Quiet Way," *HBR*, October 2002, 79, 9, pp. 92–101, example from book *Tempered Radicals: How People Use Differences to Inspire Change at Work* (Harvard Business School Press, 2001).

---

distrust of "strangers"—the challenge you face is how to turn difficult people into working allies. How do you lay the important groundwork that will help improve the working relationship? The goal is not to build intimacy, where magically your bitterest enemy is converted into your best friend. Remember, the nature of alliance is for both sides to accept that they may have very different objectives and styles, but can find some common ground on which to conduct limited, mutually beneficial, transactions. Although friendships sometimes grow as a by-product of getting past old wounds and doing business with each other, the goal is only to create working relationships satisfactory enough to get tasks done to help the organization.

There are three areas to focus on:

1. Check your own attitudes and behavior. What are you causing?
2. Make sure you have assessed the causes of the other person's behavior. Do you know their world?
3. Alter your strategy for working on the relationship or task.

Are You Part of the Problem?

As maddening as it can be to deal with someone who isn't relating to you as you would wish and as easy as it is to blame the other person for the difficulties, you need to examine your own attitudes and behavior. Have you prematurely written the other person off, making it impossible to see how to approach? As we have stressed, you need to keep an open mind about the worth of the other person. Making a strong negative conclusion will affect the way you interact and usually radiate negative feelings that turn off the target of your scorn.

Problems usually arise because mistrust has entered the relationship or because one person assumes the other's behavior is caused by bad motives. When that happens, the natural tendency to avoid the mistrusted person reduces the very contact that might inject new, more favorable data into the relationship. The absence of favorable data then becomes a fertile breeding ground for more mistrust and negative assumptions, and so on in a vicious negative cycle. Somehow, the cycle must be broken.

A related problem is that once you make a judgment about someone, it is very human to see only evidence that you are right and ignore everything else. People see what they expect to see and feel vindicated by the "proof" that they were right. You need to monitor yourself closely to be sure that you are not so caught up in self-justification that you prevent improvement in the relationship.

In addition to the problem of locked-in perception, pay attention to the possibility that you are provoking the very behavior that you don't like in the other person. We say more about this later, but don't overlook that possibility in the meantime.

Assess the World of the Other Person to Understand the Causes of the Offending Behavior

If you have read Chapter 4, you know that we advocate looking as closely as you can at the organizational situation of the other person. Doing so helps you not only determine the other person's likely currencies but also understand more about the causes behind the behavior in question. The better you understand what is driving the behavior, the more patient and sympathetic you are likely to be. Instead of feeling indignant, you may be able to feel sympathy or empathy and use that to make a positive connection. Knowing the causes of behavior does not excuse bad behavior, and you are certainly entitled to be disapproving, but that doesn't usually help make a better connection.

Choosing a Task- or Relationship-Centered Improvement Strategy

If you have checked your own behavior and attitudes and made an effort to understand what is driving the other person, yet still need to work on improving the relationship, there are three general approaches:

1. Insofar as there is something that you are doing (not providing information, using an incompatible work style, etc.), you could modify your own behavior.
2. You could discuss directly the nature of your relationship. Would just talking about the difficulties clear the air? Or does there have to be a modification of both of your styles (another form of exchange)?
3. You might want to grit your teeth, plow ahead, and just work on the task. This can be more challenging, so we need to explore the pros and cons of this third approach.

Downplay Personal Feelings and Start to Work

Perhaps the most common attempt to fix poor relationships is to overlook feelings and concentrate on working together at some tasks. Successful joint accomplishment can improve trust and foster a better relationship. When there is a poor relationship and neither party can order the other to engage in a joint effort, often they never do find a cooperative task. The most dissatisfied person usually just avoids the other or stalls. But even when two combatants agree to tackle some task together, there is no guarantee that they will improve their relationship.

Unfortunately, the very problems that created the original difficulties are likely to get in the way of task cooperation. This is similar to a divorcing couple trying to negotiate their own settlement. If they could talk reasonably with one another, the property would not be difficult to divide; but if they could talk reasonably, they probably wouldn't be getting divorced in the first place.

Nevertheless, circumstances sometimes force people to work together, and they find that the task demands are so compelling that they can put aside their differences, and, as a by-product, an improved relationship emerges. When that happens, both parties are pleasantly surprised and can build from there. But the odds are not great that such a happy outcome will result.

Speak Directly about the Relationship Problems

If, by their nature, poor relationships depend for continuation on reduced contact, the obvious solution is to increase the amount of contact and make a direct attempt to patch the difficulties. When this is done well, it can make a very big difference in the way two people deal with each other.

During the course of our work in organizations, we have frequently observed people reluctant to openly discuss their poor relationships. A number of factors determine the appropriateness of dealing directly with relationship problems rather than trying to carry on with the tasks.

When to Proceed with a Task or Initiate a Direct Discussion to Improve a Relationship

Table 6.2 lists the conditions for getting down to business versus those for doing a little relationship work first.

Table 6.2 Improving Relationships through Task or Relationship Approach

Start with Working on Task	Start with Repairing Relationship
Animosity is mild.	Animosity is strong.
Task can be accomplished even with animosities.	Bad feelings block task success.
Task success likely to improve feelings.	Even with task success, feelings won't improve.
Culture represses being explicit.	Culture supports being explicit.
Ally can't handle directness.	Ally welcomes directness.
Your style not suited to directness.	Your style suited to directness.
Task failure would hurt both.	Task failure won't harm the other person.

Degree of Animosity.   When prior animosity is too great between two people, it gets in the way of their working together on any task. The feelings bubble to the surface at the slightest provocation and drive out real work. Any disagreement deadlocks decision making, and both parties look for ways to prove how bad the other is—and how virtuous they are. When animosity is moderate, the pull of a difficult task may carry both parties past their feelings. They "get interested," and the work proceeds despite the reservations of each about the other.

How Difficult Is It to Work Despite Bad Feelings? Impact of Success on Feelings?   Some jobs can get done when neither person likes the other at all, but they both see that they need each other. They either buckle down and deal with the task or manage to divide the work to avoid much contact but still complete it. Where interdependence is low or tasks are easily divisible this approach might work. Many other jobs, however, require so much interdependence and free-flowing information exchange that the task has to be critical enough to overcome the unpleasantness of working together. If it is impossible to get the work done, to make any exchanges because of bad feelings, then it will be necessary to work on repairing the relationship first.

Ironically, if somehow a good job is done, both parties may come to feel better about each other. Despite the conventional wisdom that liking produces successful teamwork, the opposite is more often true: Winning teams end up liking their teammates; losers look bad to each other. That doesn't always happen, but one good cure for a poor relationship is doing a good job together.

Degree of Explicitness Approved by the Culture. Degree Welcomed by Ally?   An increasing number of company cultures foster an open style and encourage the confronting of differences of all kinds, task and interpersonal. Members are expected to let one another know what is on their minds, and anyone who doesn't speak up is considered to be weak and unduly constrained. When someone is unhappy with what a colleague or boss has done or said, he or she takes a direct approach, face to face, using as much heat as is felt. Such organizations are generally expressive and animated; problems are settled quickly and everyone moves on to the next issues. There is often a special name for sessions where people take each other on, such as confrontation meetings, heart-to-hearts, off-line meetings, green-light sessions, shoot-outs, come-to-Jesus meetings, or shirt-sleeve seminars. For example, Intel, Microsoft, and General Electric all

have this kind of directness. Although occasionally such direct discussion can turn harsh and create defensiveness, its frequency and familiarity usually allows for self-correction.

Unfortunately, an open, direct culture is less common than cultures that discourage straight talk. Many traditional organizations such as banks, insurance companies, and service firms reinforce members for being circumspect, holding disagreements down, and avoiding sharp interpersonal confrontation. In these kinds of cultures, disagreements are "managed" so as not to be embarrassing, and it is considered bad form to speak directly to a colleague about your relationship. Thus, even those who would be personally inclined to talk straight learn not to do so. They may learn to send subtly encoded messages that protect the receiver and allow denial by the sender. Because interpersonal communication is difficult under the best of circumstances, great distortions arise, with no direct way to correct them.

Fit between Styles.   Earlier in the chapter, we discussed how matching your work style to the style of your colleague can increase effectiveness. But the way your work style interacts with the style of your potential ally is also an important factor in determining whether to directly address the relationship. Some people are skilled at raising relationship issues, while others are ham-handed and immediately manage to insult the person with whom they are trying to patch things up. Some allies welcome a direct discussion about relationships, while others are too shy or uncomfortable to participate in open discussion of differences. And, as a further difficulty, not everyone is good at figuring out what the other person really prefers; often, he or she assumes reluctance when there is eagerness or assumes eagerness when there is great reticence.

Les Charm, the entrepreneurial MBA you met in Chapter 5, used a very direct approach to create the kind of working relationship he wanted. He was fortunate because the division head he negotiated with was a deal maker by profession, so Les's directness was appreciated. Imagine Les Charm trying to talk that way with a circumspect and rule-bound auditor. He would have been (perhaps politely) shown the door.

Your objective should be to size up what your colleague will receive well, and use that if it fits your inclinations. If you can't get a good read ahead of time on his or her willingness, you could try broaching the subject tentatively and assess the response. Raising it in this fashion can allow you to retreat without causing further damage if you find yourself meeting strong resistance.

Fears of Direct Discussion of Relationship Problems.   There are many reasons other than the listener's resistance that people are reluctant to raise relationship problems directly with a difficult ally. Concern about hurting the other, fear of retaliation, worries about possible embarrassment in future dealings, fear that the initiator is really the one at fault and will be told that in no uncertain terms—or just plain dislike of unpleasant encounters—are all reasons we frequently hear. The question you must answer is whether the potential pain caused by an attempt to tell the ally your concerns is worse than the very real and present pain of continuing on in an unsatisfactory way. In general, we believe that the actual confrontation is seldom as bad as anticipated; therefore, we encourage directness—but only with the kind of skill you can learn in this book, of course!

There is risk in putting everything on the table, but there are also risks in letting tension, mistrust, and animosity build. Unaddressed relationship issues have a way of exploding at the most awkward moments possible. Just because the risk of doing nothing is not immediately visible does not mean that it isn't just as real as the risk you take when you confront the problem. Furthermore, dealing directly with such problems tends to create faster and more complete resolution. Thus, for the remainder of this chapter, we demonstrate how to manage and minimize risk when you tackle problems in your relationships with your boss and colleagues.

USING EXCHANGE PRINCIPLES TO ADDRESS RELATIONSHIP PROBLEMS

We do not want to imply that talk is a complete substitute for action. Talk has to be backed with behavior, both as a way of creating good (or better) will and to follow up on whatever is agreed on. You don't want to be seen by others as someone to whom "talk is cheap."

The process of working directly on the relationship to facilitate task exchange is very similar to the influence process for tasks described previously. It involves:

- Knowing your own world (your goals and intentions) and making it clear to the ally
- Understanding the ally's world, by unhooking from negative assumptions about his or her personality and then exploring what is important to the ally

- Making exchanges that remove the difficulties that have prevented task exchanges in the past

Know Yourself

Start the process of knowing your own goals and intentions with a careful examination of what you want the working relationship to be. Are you looking for a way to discuss mutual work needs in a way that doesn't sound accusatory? Do you want disagreements to be raised sooner (and more directly)? Do discussions tend to drag on, and does it take too long to implement decisions? Knowing just what you want can save considerable aggravation and prevent an approach to the ally that is awkward, confusing, or unnecessarily irritating.

Say What You Want

Once you know your goals and intentions, state them explicitly to your potential ally. By being upfront about your objectives, you try to break the negative mind-set the other person has about you. It helps avoid misunderstandings about what you are up to and increases the possibility that future communications will be more accurately received. You can open with nothing more than, "We don't seem to be working very well together; I would like to see if we could find a way to be more productive and to take the tension out of our dealings." Then when you get into the specific issues, "own" them as your needs and do not phrase them in ways that sound judgmental and accusatory.

Estimate the Cost of the Poor Relationship

It is helpful to be explicit early on about how much the strained relationship costs both you and the ally. What are you prevented from doing, and

---

A Very Direct Request

When Tom Jeeter became upset by something his boss told him that a colleague, Mark Stobb, had said about him, Tom called Mark and said, "Are you free now? I just learned you have a problem with me, and I'd like to get it straightened out. I wish I'd heard it directly from you, Mark, but it sounds as if we should talk. Okay?" Mark quickly agreed to meet with Tom to clear the air, and they did.

what does your colleague lose as a result of the difficulty in working together? What are the costs to the organization? Such an accounting helps lay the groundwork for further discussion and motivates the ally to do something about the problem. After all, if you can total up the costs to the ally of not being able to work together, it is more difficult for him or her to just dismiss the problem as a "personality difference" that isn't worth talking about (see Figure 6.1).

For example, Tom might have also told Mark that he was trying to address quality problems and that Mark's putting him down made it more difficult to move a resistant organization and made Tom unwilling to get Mark's views ahead of time (see preceding boxed example). Tom might have added, "Since my instinctive reaction to avoid you makes it less likely that your views will be included in our work, Mark, I'd guess you might want to iron this out so that you'll have a chance to give proper input."

Figure 6.1
Assessing Costs and Benefits of Behavior

1. Identify the problem behavior.
2. Identify the consequences of the behavior.
   Consider both the costs and the benefits.
3. For the costs, consider which are most critical.
4. For the benefits, which are most important.
   Brainstorm alternative behaviors.
5. Identify the increased benefits of the new behaviors.

Assessing Costs and Benefits		
	Costs	Benefits
Task	What are the costs of this behavior to getting work done?	What are the benefits of this behavior to getting work done?
Work Relationships	What are the costs of this behavior to effective work relationships?	What are the benefits of this behavior to effective work relationships?

Leave Your Negative Assumptions at Home

Specifying costs can be a tricky business. You are on safer ground if you stick with the impact of others' actions on you. ("Tess, when you don't return my phone calls, it sure doesn't make me anxious to respond to yours, and that wastes time for both of us.") However, one trap is assuming something is a cost to your ally when it isn't. Saying, "When you argue every point, it makes me and my people reluctant to go to you for help" might be just fine to the colleague who wants to be left alone. In that case, inquiry (not accusation) might be appropriate ("Jed, I and others experience you starting an argument every time we raise an issue. Can you tell me what's going on, because it's decreasing our willingness to want to go to you for your ideas?").

There is a second trap around costs: making the assumption about why others act the way they do. (For example, Jed behaves that way because he is insecure about the acceptance of his department.) It is crucial to unhook yourself from any negative attributions you are making about the ally's motives. You have to adopt the idea that there is probably a perfectly reasonable explanation for that person's difficult response, even if you can't conceive of what that might be. Again, set aside your conclusion, and try to move into inquiry to discover it so that you can take appropriate action.

We earlier discussed how easy it is to attribute the worst possible motives to someone you are having trouble with. Shirley abruptly walks out of meetings when the conversation gets at all confrontational. This means that the important decisions get put off, and you are finding it increasingly frustrating. Before making the attribute that she is *rude* and *inconsiderate,* ask yourself, "If Shirley were here now and could speak for herself, would she use those labels or does she think she was perfectly justified to act as she has?" Could it be that she is acting as she does because she fears becoming argumentative or doesn't see herself as skilled in open confrontation? Her unceremonious departure may have nothing to do with you, but if you have a deep conviction that people should have their say and always make graceful exits, it can feel like a slap in the face. You don't know, but it will be difficult to find out unless you can unhook from your negative conclusion about the sort of selfish person she is.

Ask the Person the Causes of the Exact Behavior You Don't Like

Setting aside your negative assumptions frees you up to genuinely explore the world of your ally. You can now more objectively begin to diagnose the factors in the situation that might be causing the difficulties and start to make direct (but nonjudgmental) inquiries about that world. Notice the difference between asking Shirley, "Don't you know how rude you are to me when you stomp out of meetings?" and instead inquiring, "I'm puzzled about our relationship. What happens at the end of our meetings? You often turn on your heels and get out fast without saying anything and that is bothering me. What's that about?"

Better still, add an admission of the possibility that you may be part of the problem: "Am I doing something that makes you want to leave?" In general, if you are willing to acknowledge that you could be part of the problem, you reduce the likelihood of defensive denials and make real exploration possible. This doesn't always work; sometimes the other person will be unwilling even to admit that there is a problem. The relationship may feel so strained, the colleague may be so convinced you are incorrigible, or he or she may be so resistant to discussion of negative feelings that even your open admission of possible fault gets nowhere. However, directness remains the best bet for increasing willingness to explore a relationship problem. (For more on direct dialog, see the Feedback as Exchange section in Chapter 9, "Influencing Difficult Subordinates.")

Moving to Joint Problem Solving—But Some Sticky Issues

You have opened up the dialogue with Shirley and perhaps have a better sense of what is behind her behavior. It would be nice if that would automatically lead to joint problem solving (the eventual goal), but there could be some difficulties before then.

"You Are the Problem." She says, "Your voice rises and your tone gets belligerent. You just want to dominate and win." Now the shoe is on the other foot. Whereas earlier you were fighting not to make a negative attribution of her motives, she has now done that to you. And rather than her being "to blame," she is now putting all the onus for the problem on you. The same points made earlier apply here. Can you hold down your defensiveness at these attributions and not get into a mutual accusation brawl?

Instead, can you make your own world visible? What are the forces and assumptions that led you to the behavior or style that this potential ally is not happy about? Can you help her see your framework in the same way that you have seen hers, that is, with understanding, if not acceptance? This is far easier to do if you have first demonstrated your understanding of the other person's position.

There is a danger that you will be perceived as making excuses, which is not your objective. Your objective is to be clear about what has been going on with you so that the ally will have accurate information about the world that is shaping you. That will allow you both to find ways to overcome differences or reach an agreement about how to work together. Acceptable reasons, not evasive excuses, are your goal. They will help the ally see that any negative attributions she has made about your motives may not be correct.

"You Started It."   Even if both of you are partially responsible, don't get trapped into trying to assess "who started it" or "who is more to blame." It might be enough to acknowledge that in many, if not most, cases, *inter*personal difficulties have an *inter*personal cause; both parties bring something to the issues. It also can be useful after the issues are out on the table to say, "Let's not worry about the past; let's try to build for the future." Describing the potential payoffs to both of you from what the interaction could be can help move away from the mutual accusation game.

"I Don't Want to Talk about This."   Another trap is a refusal to discuss this further. There are few things more dangerous than agreeing to disagree, which doesn't resolve the issue but drives it underground where it will only simmer and explode again at an inopportune moment.

Instead, this is a time to talk about currencies. What are the costs that both of you are paying for the present situation, and what are the benefits from a successful resolution? Has Shirley also been complaining about the aggravation of delayed decisions? Are there issues that she has mentioned wanting to deal with but has been hesitant to bring to the table? The objective is to increase the desire to deal with your relationship difficulties. You are describing a new type of exchange where the benefit of resolution outweighs the cost of sticking in and dealing with these difficult interpersonal issues.

REACHING AGREEMENT

Sometimes, it is sufficient just to fully understand the other person. Your knowing that Shirley isn't purposely being rude and doesn't personally dislike you can make you tolerant of her wanting a time out on occasions. And her knowing that you don't want to dominate, but that raising your voice is just a sign of your heightened involvement, might keep her in the room.

Or, it might call for one or both of you to modify your behavior. Can you explore what you can do to alter your behavior so that this ally will allow more of a task relationship to grow? And are there things that you need from Shirley? The objective is to work out your interpersonal relationship so that the two of you can productively engage in trades around task goals.

Self-Traps in Finding and Developing Allies

There are a number of ways in which you may be getting in your own way of creating or enhancing requisite relationships.

Waiting for Problems before Bothering with Relationship Building. It is far more difficult to build a good relationship when there is a problem between you and the other person. Effective influencers use every opportunity—including membership on committees, task forces, needs to gather information, incidental contact, and even sitting down next to strangers at lunch and chatting—to build the connections before they have to ask for anything.

Anticipating That No Approach Will Work, So Holding Back Too Long. Everyone knows some types of people whom they don't expect to be able to connect with, whether it is gruff, intimidating people, seemingly aloof colleagues, very confident and ambitious folks, or some other type. It is tempting to assume that the difficult person is immovable and avoid any approach. But there is almost always a human being with emotions and wants lurking within even the most difficult-appearing person, and avoidance only makes it more difficult to connect later.

Saving up Frustrations and Exploding. Too often, the fear of saying something negative to a difficult person leads to holding back and starting to fume. Then, some small event causes an outburst that can make a distant relationship totally dissolve. Perhaps counting to 10 before saying anything is a good idea when you are hot, but not waiting until you count to 12 million. Fix relationship problems close to their origins.

Reverting to Negative Assumptions When You Find Behavior Puzzling. We can't warn about this often enough: If you have tried to influence another person or group and aren't getting anywhere, resist the temptation to assume that there is something wrong with them. If you hear yourself

Partners Making Exchanges to Improve Their Relationship

Friends since high school, Brian Woods and Dennis Longworth were long-time equal partners in an international, financial services holding company with a dozen subsidiaries.* Each looked after one of the two biggest subsidiaries and shared, to varying degrees, management of the others. Although they were highly successful, recent events had crystallized Brian's dissatisfaction with his relationship to Dennis.

Brian had been feeling for some time that Dennis was unconcerned about the partnership and possibly even avoiding him. Dennis, a lawyer by training, was not available when Brian needed expertise or support. Both Brian and Dennis were traveling to different countries a good bit of the time, serving their international clientele, and were extremely busy. But, in the early years of their partnership, they had found ways to be available to each other when needed. Increasingly, however, Brian felt that Dennis was so involved in his activities that, when Brian wanted help, Dennis was unreachable.

A crisis in Brian's main subsidiary brought matters to a head. Brian needed Dennis's support to deal with a very knotty problem. He had left word for Dennis at his hotel in Denmark to rush home for a key meeting, but Dennis had not showed up and had never even bothered to call. Brian was so upset that he was considering a proposal to end their long partnership via a buyout, but, in a last-ditch attempt to straighten out the relationship, Brian scheduled a weekend meeting with Dennis. They invited an old friend with considerable mediation skills to help them.

It was very difficult for Brian to express just what was bothering him. They went back a long way together, as friends as well as partners. With some prodding, Brian revealed that he felt abandoned by Dennis and finally managed to say how disappointed and angry he had been when Dennis hadn't shown up or called. Dennis responded, astonished, "When I realized that I couldn't possibly get back in time, I tried to call, and when I couldn't reach you, I sent a message to my assistant, Marsha. I assumed she had told you."

This set Brian off even more. Marsha was Dennis's cousin, and Brian didn't trust her at all. He had been upset when Dennis hired her, had complained for some time that she was a schemer who wanted to make trouble, and this was just the "proof" he needed. There must be some sinister reason that Dennis would try to use someone Brian so distrusted to send a message about missing a crucial meeting. Dennis, calm and detached as always, tried to explain again about the mechanics of different time zones, international phone calls, and sending the message.

---

*The names are disguised, but the events and emotions are as reported by the friend of Brian and Dennis who served as informal mediator.

Several rounds followed, with Brian getting no satisfaction. Dennis's detachment exacerbated Brian's upset feelings over what he perceived as Dennis's lack of commitment, which just made Dennis pull back further.

Finally, with some help from their friend, they were able to look at the underlying problem of the relationship. Brian wanted to be certain that he could count on Dennis's support in dealing with particularly knotty problems, and he considered a willingness to be physically present at times of crisis the way that a partner should show support. It wasn't even Dennis's legal expertise that was crucial to Brian; it was Dennis's presence and emotional support that Brian sought.

Dennis was unaware of how important it was to Brian that he demonstrate his commitment at critical times. To Dennis, the 50–50 partnership arrangement, with no controlling vote, showed how much he valued and trusted Brian. As far as he was concerned, the unusual arrangement of an equal partnership with loosely defined and varying responsibilities was positive proof of his support. Furthermore, Dennis believed Brian's reaction to Dennis's absences and Brian's dislike of Marsha were irrational. Why get up in arms over an assistant in light of the enormous financial stake they shared? Dennis had assumed that Brian understood how busy Dennis was with his main subsidiary and would learn to deal with certain problems himself if Dennis could not make it. As a result of these differing assumptions, the costs of the strains in the relationship were so high that Brian was contemplating a split that Dennis didn't want at all.

As they explored their assumptions and feelings, they began to see that it might be possible to accommodate each other. Brian said he was willing to keep an open mind about Marsha, and he accepted the fact that it was convenient for Dennis to use her as a communication channel when he was on the road. He also agreed to be clear about when he had to have a direct, personal response and when it would be nice but wasn't an emergency. Dennis agreed to make phone calls on important issues, even if it meant calling Brian at home in the middle of the night, and to make extra efforts to be present whenever it was important to Brian. The partnership, and friendship, survived.

Because the issue was so emotionally loaded for Brian, he did not find it easy to start by understanding Dennis's world and working to achieve acceptance of its meaning to Dennis before leaping to conclusions about his motives. It took a lot of heat and some help from their friend to get to the point where each side understood enough about the other to figure out what kind of exchange could be made. But they avoided a potentially disastrous outcome when they were able to talk directly with each other, see what needed to be fixed in the relationship, and then trade concessions.

writing someone off as stupid, selfish, not interested in the company, or in some way defective, stop at once, step back, and ask yourself (or the other person!): "What might be going on to explain the behavior, and what currencies haven't I discovered that might give me some small area of common interests to trade with?" What clues can you uncover to the currencies valued by the other person? You may eventually have to conclude that the person or group is indeed defective, but the odds are poor that it is true, and once you do it, it will be extremely difficult to gain a trusting relationship or find a way to make satisfactory trades.

CONCLUSION

The goal is not to make everybody best friends. And it is possible to get work done when there are interpersonal difficulties. But relationship problems can be a serious barrier to effective task success, and it is usually worth the effort to turn those troublesome relationships into at least acceptable working relationships. You can develop the influence approaches to make that happen.

We complete the fleshing out of the influence model by looking at the process of making the trades that achieve influence. Chapter 7 looks closely at the ways to make exchanges that sustain and improve your relationships while attaining influence.

CHAPTER 7

STRATEGIES FOR MAKING MUTUALLY PROFITABLE TRADES

When people feel appreciated, they will help you. You can storm things through once, but never get help again. You definitely catch more flies with honey. Being collaborative takes more time sometimes, but if I'm living here in the company, there's a good chance I will encounter them again, have to live with them sometime in the future.

—*Mary Garrett, Vice President, Marketing, IBM Global Services*

We have examined the steps that lead up to the trading process, which include knowing your ally's world, being clear on your own objectives and resources, building trusting relationships, and matching your resources with your ally's desired currencies. In preceding chapters, we included some examples of the process of exchange. In this chapter, we address in detail the actual strategies to follow in producing a win-win outcome.

Exchanges can take many forms and become complicated because there are many ways to "pay back." The payment can be a simple agreement to go along with a request that is not burdensome and is within job expectations, or it can involve considerable costs in time and resources. Many, if not most, transactions take place in a series, over time, so an exchange is not just one request in return for one payment.

The exchange begins to take place before trading is declared to have started. In fact, it has been going on throughout the previous steps, and it is only because we can't discuss everything at once that we separate the process into different chapters. *Every influence-related contact you have with anyone who eventually becomes an ally is part of the eventual exchange.* Whether it is simply a smile the first time you are introduced or an honest effort to ask about the other person's interests so that you can find something to offer in return for the cooperation you want, each interaction feeds the likelihood of successful exchange.

Not only does your general reputation and relationship with the potential ally affect trading, but also the process of finding out what's important is already shaping the reception you will get when you finally make your request and offer. How and what you ask, whether and how you listen, the kind of interest you show, and the sincerity of your concern for addressing the ally's real interests all become part of the trading process. You smooth the way or make the terrain rough by the way you go about your early diagnosis and relationship development.

As with any kind of negotiation, the most important part is the planning. If you have badly misdiagnosed the situation, clever techniques probably won't save the day. Given their history and constant competitiveness, the Boston Red Sox aren't likely to deal with the archrival New York Yankees no matter how slick the presentation. Thus, you need to plan carefully. But you also need to carry out the actual exchange discussions in a way that takes into account your previous relationship with the other person or group, eases the transaction, and leaves the relationship improved for the future. This can be a complex process, even though the actual transaction may be brief.

PLANNING YOUR STRATEGIES FOR EXCHANGE

Although many of the strategies for approaching trade discussions have been mentioned in earlier chapters, they are worth reviewing now to help you focus carefully on what conditions determine which approach to take. To be an effective influencer requires versatility in selecting among exchange strategies.

The difficulty of making an exchange depends in part on how closely your interests match. It is always easier to start with an exchange strategy that demonstrates to the other person the benefits that will accrue to him or her from your request. We explore this strategy first, but then we move on to ways of addressing the ally's interests when the benefits of cooperation are not as evident. (See Table 7.1 for a summary of strategies and when to use each one.)

Table 7.1   Trading Strategies and When to Use Each

Strategy	*Conditions to Use It*
Straightforward trades (free-market trades)	Each has something other wants Roughly equal value Good existing relationships
Show how cooperation helps achieve ally's goals	Your interests match
Uncover hidden value	You can find unexpected benefits
Compensate for costs	You don't have desired resources You know costs and can pay in some currency

Free-Market Trades: Clear Mutual Gain

If both sides readily see the advantages of the outcome and believe each payment of time, trouble, or resources is approximately the same, the exchange is equivalent to going to the store and exchanging money for a desired item that is fairly priced. And, if there is already a good relationship between the parties, neither has any reason to distrust the motives or integrity of the other. Neither side is doing the other any exceptional favor; value is exchanged for value. Free-market exchanges can work even when a good or longstanding relationship does not exist, and they can involve very different currencies as long as they are seen as equivalent.

A free-market trade may still require good diagnosis and careful planning because it may not be immediately self-evident to the other party how the request meets his or her needs. Thus, it is almost always important to have a good understanding of the other side's world and needs.

Showing How Cooperation Helps the Potential Ally Achieve Goals

There can still be mutual benefit if you show how cooperating with your request will help the potential ally achieve other goals (i.e., pay off in a valued currency). For example, an area manager who wanted more current information from his regional manager but didn't want to appear to be prying or criticizing the regional manager's close-to-the-vest style decided to frame the request in terms of the genuine need for information to help defend the region's decisions to skeptical branch managers. Because this very currency was one of the regional manager's objectives for the year, the suggestion of a regularly scheduled staff meeting was seen as helpful rather than as a time-consuming nuisance. The area manager had known enough about his boss's currencies to frame his request in a way that would be seen positively by the regional manager.

Uncovering—and Trading For—Hidden Value

Sometimes, the mutual benefits are not readily apparent and take some effort to discover. That was the case with an enterprising production manager who wanted to obtain his general manager's approval to introduce automated technology into the plant. Knowing that the standard payback analysis based on labor savings would not be fully convincing, he analyzed the impact of faster turnaround time on preventing lost orders. Using this innovative capital expenditure method, he was able to persuade the general manager that the automation would be in the interest of the division.

Such an approach is becoming increasingly common. Examples of measures that reveal hidden benefits include:

- The cost of employee turnover
- Carrying costs for excess inventory
- The link between satisfied employees and increased sales
- The value of customer loyalty
- The cost of bottlenecks or service delays

Compensated Costs

An alternative strategy calls for acknowledgment that costs will be involved and development of a plan to compensate the potential ally for those costs. Although often more difficult to work out in terms of finding equitable payments, this approach may be the only way to engineer an exchange when it is not possible to show the other person the benefit of your request. For example, a person requesting a special report from an analytical group could offer to compose a rough draft using unanalyzed data that already exist, which would reduce the load on the analysts by providing the approach and format for them.

In any circumstance, it is necessary to determine the potential ally's costs of compliance so that you can determine whether you can help defray the costs. For example, a secretary wants early morning flexibility of arrival time from her boss, who would prefer she be there when he arrives. But she knows that even more important to him is her willingness to stay late when there is an urgent job to complete, so she agrees to stay late when necessary in return for being allowed leeway in the mornings when her day care arrangements require an extra 10 to 15 minutes. Both get what they want by exchanging in the same currency: time available for work. The cost to the boss is compensated by the gain of time in tight situations.

How to Make Hidden Costs Visible

In determining what is an equitable exchange, the other party needs to know how important your request is—what his or her noncooperation will cost you and the organization—just as you need to know what your request costs the other party. The potential ally sees only the inconvenience to him or her, not the costs on your side. This can be especially difficult when you want something from your boss because you do not want to sound whiney or threatening in specifying consequences. Peers need the cost information because they haven't done the diagnostic work that you have and often are unaware of your world and your needs, even those aspects that appear obvious from your vantage point.

If you have been highly responsive in the past, others may not be aware of the complexities in your situation (and extra time you have been putting in). In these circumstances, plan a way to make clear the costs you have been paying and will be paying if you don't get your request. For example, can you prepare a spreadsheet of steps taken to get to this point? Can you casually mention late nights or weekends spent on the ally's work? Can you joke about how you just do things by waving a magic wand? Not all allies will respond to your inconvenience when they become aware of it, but when you have a reasonable relationship, this kind of information can help create more responsiveness.

This idea of making hidden costs visible is especially relevant when others initiate the exchange to make requests of you. While agreeableness is usually a good stance, be careful that it doesn't misrepresent the cost to you. Your response that it was "no trouble" might not be true. Without going through a long litany of how inconvenient the request is, it's important that both parties understand the demands that are being made. You could, for example, "think out loud" about the requisite steps to fill the request, what you would have to juggle or let go, then agree. Otherwise, payback to you might be less than what you think you deserve, which can be damaging to your relationship.

STRATEGIES THAT USE THE TIME VALUE OF CURRENCY

In a good working relationship, there is considerable latitude about when to pay back and the form the eventual payment will take. However, when there is a poor relationship and a difficult history, low trust makes each transaction subject to close scrutiny. An outside observer might be puzzled as to why one person's request for help is responded to with smiles and genuine effort to please, while another's is resisted—politely or otherwise. The history between the parties, or even between the groups of which each party is a member, can very much alter the value and costs of requests and payments. Indeed, often the complex economy of exchanges is so difficult to unravel that people desiring something important assume it will be impossible and give up.

Time can enter exchanges in three ways:

1. *In the immediate present.* For what you ask, you can pay now, either by the direct benefit of your request or in an acceptable compensatory payment.
2. *From the past.* Because of things you have done previously, you have built up credit, so you are collecting on earlier behavior. Alternatively, you are in deficit because of history and have to overcome the past.
3. *Promise for the future.* You agree on a debt—specific or unspecified—you will pay sometime later. Here again, the past may come into how willing the other party is to believe in the likelihood of your future repayment at a satisfactory rate.

Thus, a key set of strategic considerations involves the way to utilize past or future obligations to achieve desired goals. Strategic use of time extends what is possible in alliances.

Building Credit: Saving for a Rainy Day

An old joke about banking says that banks want to lend money only when you can prove that you don't need it. The grain of truth in the joke relates to the need to be able to repay the loan, at least at some date in the future. For this reason, it is often wise to invest current resources so that when there is future need, it will be possible to borrow or draw on savings. The same reasoning applies to exchanges in organizations: *Whenever possible, accumulate obligations from others long before you have any idea of asking for anything in return. Before you get to the actual exchange, it helps to have made payments to the favor bank—investments in future considerations.*

This is easiest when your job puts you in the position of commanding valuable resources that others want so that you can naturally do work favors for many people. The people who decide information system priorities, control the scheduling of production, or provide valuable services to line managers are constantly building credits, especially when they alter priorities or give extra service to help others out. The best way of building credit is by doing useful tasks in return for future obligations to help you do your job better. That keeps the focus on real work, not influence for its own sake.

Although not all jobs have such an advantageous positioning, you can often discover alternative ways to help others. Because different players value different kinds of currencies, many opportunities exist to make an extra effort to be helpful, considerate, or thoughtful in advance of needing the help of others. If you have energy, some ability to determine what might be valuable to others in their work, and an inclination toward creating multiple alliances, you can find daily opportunities to earn credit by being useful.

We can look, for example, at the middle-level manager who inadvertently built credit by clipping and sending "FYI" job-related articles of potential interest to the wide range of organizational members he knew. He was naturally interested in people and ideas, and he took the time to chat with others and remember what they were working on or excited about. As a reader of many magazines and newspapers anyway, he was able to convert his natural interests into an activity that he genuinely enjoyed and that was always appreciated. Although he never cynically sent the clippings just to build support, the result was that he did earn credit from others for his thoughtfulness; and his subsequent requests for his own department and projects always received the benefit of the doubt.

Think about any natural advantages you have—extra knowledge, good humor, a long memory, instinctive empathy, or anything else that might be valuable to others—and spread the wealth early and often.

Sleaze Alert

There are situations in which the ally you want to influence doesn't value any work-related currencies, or you have no access to any that he or she does want. That means you will be forced to find more personal currencies to deposit to your account if you want to build credit. Many personal gifts such as kindness, good humor, or bringing snacks for everyone are good social lubricants and can create goodwill.

There is a danger, however, from seeking non-work-related ways of creating obligation, even though it is sometimes necessary. It is unfortunately tempting for employees who realize the power of having credit in the reciprocity bank to use the process of doing favors in a self-promoting way, currying obligation for its own sake. Even when this works, there are often considerable costs to reputation that cannot be overlooked.

You can easily overdo unrequested favors, especially if the recipients suspect that the favors are being done only to create obligations or if the favors are not valuable to the person receiving them. Many years ago, for example, Dale Carnegie advised people to win friends and influence people by, among other things, learning their names promptly and using the name frequently in early conversations because everyone likes the sound of his or her own name. Anyone who has ever had a newly converted disciple flood a conversation with "Yes, Seymour, it certainly is a swell day, Seymour. Would you, Seymour, be interested in hearing about what a fine fellow you are, Seymour?" knows how readily the currency can be debased. Insincerity can cancel out the benefits of what might otherwise be an effective way of building exchange credits.

This leads to an interesting paradox about "building credits for the future." On the one hand, it is always useful to have "money in the bank" that you can call upon for future needs. But on the other hand, overt deposits can create mistrust and suspicion about your intentions. If others are worried about when you are going to "put the hit" on them to collect, they will be chary of your offers.

What is the way out of this paradox? Two guidelines can help:

1. *Be explicit.* Sometimes, saying, "I would like to help you now because I have some slack and I know that I am going to have to come with requests second quarter when deadlines get tight" can remove suspicion because you are being overt about your intentions. It also signals ahead of time the nature of the exchange so the implied obligation is clear.
2. *Put the organization first.* As we have insisted before, If you are helping others primarily to further organization goals in their eyes, then the fact that there are secondary gains to you and your area is likely to be more acceptable.

Using Resources in a Questionable Way That Backfired

Maintainence Manager, Manipulator

The head of the physical plant in a service organization, not usually a position of great power, volunteered to organize the December holiday party each year. As part of the festivities, he always arranged to have a photographer in attendance taking pictures of managers and their families. A few weeks later, the people who controlled resources or were otherwise central would get an enlarged photo "with compliments" of the physical plant manager.

Because there was some doubt whether this gesture was an act of kindness or a ploy to build obligations, many coworkers acted cautiously toward this manager. His goodwill was valuable for getting office equipment moved or repair work done, so no one confronted him about this game, but many were uncomfortable in dealing with him.

Although he didn't overtly mention the photos when he made subsequent requests for his department, his purpose was to build goodwill that could serve him later. When he needed something during the year, he was seldom refused, although people grumbled because they felt trapped. As a result, he got what he wanted, but he was never fully trusted in the organization and was never promoted.

Robert Moses, Master Manipulator

On a far grander scale, Robert Moses was reported to have used the resources of his position as New York Commissioner of Parks to create subtle obligations among reporters, commissioners, and politicians. When he wanted to push through a project, people to whom he had catered found it difficult to oppose him. Moses used limousine rides, fancy meals, and meetings in spectacular places to court supporters or neutralize detractors before he put the bite on them. As a result, he built roads and parks on an unprecedented scale. At the same time, he rode roughshod over the poor, disrupted neighborhoods and spent vast public sums to further his personal vision of New York.

Moses used many other influence techniques, including covert, indirect ones such as burying clauses into complex legislation that later gave him almost unlimited power, but he also knew how important it was to have relationship savings in the bank to withdraw in tight situations. Apparently, he was also charming enough—and dealing with sufficiently seducible allies—to overcome concerns about the sincerity of his intentions.* It is possible that, in complex public situations, with so many differing constituents and interests, only a skilled manipulator can make anything happen; but the process produces enormous cynicism and public costs that make the enterprise questionable. Any tool can be abused.

---

*For a full and fascinating account of Robert Moses at work, see Robert A. Caro, *The Power Broker* (New York: Knopf, 1974). Caro's volumes on Lyndon Johnson are also revealing of a master manipulator/influencer.

Calling in Past Debts

If the person you want to influence happens to be one for whom you have done things previously and the debt level is sufficient to cover whatever it is that you are asking for, exchange should be relatively easy. This assumes that the colleague recognizes the debt previously incurred and believes it to be at least equivalent in value to the cost of what is being requested. If the relationship is good, you can even collect in excess of the existing debt because, among trusting colleagues, the accounts can swing from surplus to deficit and back again depending on circumstances.

Although the concepts in this book are relevant for any influence attempt, a great deal of organizational exchange happens more or less automatically as a natural part of doing the work. Elaborate exchange discussions take place only when you need something out of the ordinary. Thus, it is useful to signal to your potential ally early on that the transaction at hand is unusual and calls for special attention. It is not just a routine part of your job, and it is important enough to spend time on.

What Can You Do When Others Won't Admit What They Owe?

Interesting problems arise, however, when your signal is ignored. What happens when you make a request of a debtor, but the debtor does not acknowledge that there is any obligation? Confusion can arise in polite or high-allegiance organizations where there are strong norms against making exchanges explicit. The past lender may believe that an obligation is created, while the borrower may see past help as just part of the lender's job and, therefore, perceives no debt. It can be very deflating to suggest that a past favor deserves a current response and be told, "Big deal. You were just doing what you're supposed to do." That is especially discouraging when it comes from your boss, who isn't aware of what it has cost you to deliver on a request.

In some organizations, it may be considered crude to say anything as overt as, "You owe me one," so gentle hints are called for. In other organizations (try many New York-based companies and hospitals), it would be considered naive not to bludgeon colleagues with your expectations about their obligations because all take it as a fact of life that the world works on self-interest and quid pro quo. Be sure to adapt your language to the culture. If you're still new in the culture, stay alert for phrases that clue you about the appropriate level of directness.

If it is not an accepted practice in your organization to discuss such issues, you may find it difficult to resolve these differences without elaborate
talking around the point. Instead of being able to say, "I've knocked myself out for you in ways you don't even know about because I didn't want
to burden you; how about some consideration in return?," influence attempts are approached indirectly, with statements such as, "Well, it's not
technically part of my job, and we do have a lot of other things we are responsible for." Such subtle references tend to have low impact (unless the
other person is very tuned to reading between the lines) and often cause the
influencer to prematurely give up in frustration.

The problem of assuring reciprocal expectations is usually best handled
before the gift is given, not afterwards. Each organization tends to have its
own language for conveying strong expectation of a response. At one consumer goods company, members convey the importance of an issue by saying, "This is a strike issue," even though there is no union involved. At
another organization, people say, "I'll go to the mat for this one." "This is
a biggie," is another way that members of a certain company signal that
they are not making a routine request. Somehow or other, you need to use
the organization's shorthand or jargon to indicate the seriousness of what
you are giving. Don't cry wolf once too often, though; be sure that you
mean it and that the cost to you is as great as you are communicating.

What If Currency Payment Isn't Valued? (I Know You Said You Love Me, but You Never Bring Me Flowers)

Even when direct discussion is sanctioned, there can be very different ideas
about what is owed. Exchange rates are imprecise enough so that even when
you say, "You owe me one," and the potential ally agrees, it is possible for
genuine disagreements to arise. Sometimes, the effort put forth to comply
with a request is invisible to the other person, so the receiving party isn't
proportionately appreciative. We have seen situations in which someone
responded to a request that wasn't particularly urgent as if the organization's future depended on it. The person who moves heaven and earth to
accommodate another may not be fully appreciated if the request was not
that important to the one who made it. In that case, an attempt to call in
a perceived debt could be met with, "Hey, cool it, I was just making a suggestion. I didn't expect you to turn yourself inside-out, so don't try to lay
a guilt trip on me."

Conversely, we have seen organizational members who routinely knock
themselves out on behalf of others, but then downplay their efforts by

saying, "It was nothing," in response to thanks. When the beneficiaries are sensitive, the person who has extended himself or herself is properly appreciated, but not every recipient of favors picks up those subtle cues. As a result, the givers come to feel that they are being taken advantage of, and the recipients go blithely forward, not realizing that resentment is stirring.

If you have made an effort for a potential ally, it requires a certain grace to point it out without sounding too crass. But hiding your light under a bushel may be a waste of a good light. The trick is to let the potential ally see you sweat a bit, without complaining, so that the effort is visible but not flaunted.

However, you don't want to be seen as overly preoccupied with the bookkeeping of obligation. The ability to deliver without calling attention to every last deposit in the obligation bank is a rare, but critical one, so you should cultivate it. One of the most influential organizational members we have ever observed regularly performed miracles for others from his "assistant to" role, but he never acted as if it were a big deal. Because his colleagues knew how difficult it was to move the bureaucracy, they appreciated what he must have been doing, and he accumulated great respect and obligation. When the opportunity to take over as director of an important new division came up, he had many supporters and was selected for the job, despite the fact that he had fewer formal credentials than other candidates.

Borrowing on Credit: Deferred Payment/Collateral

If there has been no chance to build prior obligations and you either cannot immediately command the currencies the potential ally wants or do not have time to mobilize them, it may be necessary to request a loan. If you have a reasonably good reputation, you can offer to repay later, either with specific goods or in an unspecified currency to be named at a later date. Where there is prior mistrust, it is not likely that you will be able to use this approach, at least not without considerable collateral; but if the existing relationship is at least not negative, then it can be possible to obtain cooperation on the basis of a promise to pay later.

Similarly, in her study of successful innovators within organizations, Rosabeth Kanter[1] found many examples of managers who made promises of future payback for current backing, use of resources, or budgetary transfers. They would offer better support services in the future,

---

Paying with a Promise for the Future

Marcia Allen, a consumer goods company product manager, needed a rush order for a special-size packaging to get product in the stores in time for the scheduled advertising campaign. This request could cause difficulties for the purchasing manager whose cooperation she wanted: Rushing her order would slow down other priorities, which the purchasing manager made very clear when Marcia approached him. Eager to see the important promotion succeed, Marcia made her request in return for a later payment: She offered to include the purchasing manager in future planning meetings so that fewer surprise rush orders would be needed. He would get early warnings about plans, which would allow him to make suggestions about timing and alternate materials before plans were finalized. She got her materials, and, subsequently, the purchasing manager was included in meetings where he made significant contributions to decisions about special promotions.

---

recognition when the project was successful, or other forms of payback at a later date. Sometimes, all they asked for was a pledge of resources or backing, to be paid only if others also came through. Then they would parlay the initial pledge commitments into further commitments, since they could demonstrate widespread support and eventually could pay back the initial "investors." The backers who made early loans or pledges not only received particular goods or services they wanted but also gained positive reputation for being able to spot good ideas early and support them.

If what you are pushing is suspected or the person does not fully trust you, you may have to explore whether it is possible to put up a form of "security bond" when trying to borrow. You might, for example, offer to publicly support the potential ally before he or she has to deliver on what you are asking, with the understanding that the support is only a demonstration of good faith, not the repayment for the cooperation. This can be very awkward to discuss, but it is preferable to just being turned down or stalled. It can be very freeing to a poor relationship to say something like, "I see you are not comfortable with me, and I want to turn that around. What can I do to show good faith? Would it be helpful if I did_____?" That kind of direct acknowledgment of the problem can become a wedge to open a discussion of difficulties or a way to make it possible to do business even when the relationship is less than desirable.

OTHER STRATEGIC CONSIDERATIONS: WHO AND WHERE?

There are several other factors that can shape your influence exchanges.

Deciding with Whom to Attempt Exchanges

Many influence attempts involve only one other person, but in complex situations, there are usually multiple stakeholders, each with his or her own currencies. One of the strategic choices in these situations is whom to engage with directly, whom to just touch base with, whom to work gingerly around, and whom to avoid entirely. Influence is hard enough without trying to take on the world. But projects that involve large-scale change cannot be accomplished without judicious exchanges with multiple players.

Considerations for deciding how to exchange directly with a potential ally include:

Centrality of the Ally

- How powerful is the other person? Power means more than hierarchical position: What needed resources does he or she control? How exclusive is the person's control of those resources? How dependent are you on that person for success? To what extent does the person's opinion affect others? If the person gets angry with you, can he or she harm your project?

Amount of Effort/Credits Needed

- Do you already have a relationship with the person, or will you be starting from scratch? Is there any way to quickly establish a working relationship, or is the process inherently slow?
- Is the person likely to insist on trading in currencies you do not command or cannot gain access to? How expensive will it be to you to pay in the desired currencies?
- Will the person be satisfied as long as you at least pay your respects and stay in touch, without asking anything directly?

Alternatives Available

- Do you know anyone whose support will help gain the support of the potential ally? In other words, who can influence the ally if you are not able to directly?

- If you can't influence the person in the right direction, can you find a way to neutralize him or her? Can you reshape your project to take the person's opposition into account or to skirt the person's worst concerns?

In general, the important dimensions are the degree of your actual power relative to the array of potential allies and the degree of your dependence on each. This can be represented, as in Figure 7.1, by a two-by-two table, with four resulting strategies.

When you are relatively powerful compared to your potential ally, you should plan to conduct mutual exchange discussions of the kind we discuss throughout this book.

If, however, you are in a relatively low-power position (even after having explored how to increase your power as described in Chapter 5) but are dependent on the ally's cooperation, you need to either follow a submissive strategy or look for others who will help you and who can influence the person. Submissive strategies are those in which you essentially put yourself at the goodwill of the ally. You may be able to bluff from a low-power strategy; but, when dealing within your own organization, bluffing seldom works for long—and then you reduce the likelihood of a sympathetic hearing.

Figure 7.1
Strategies That Fit Your Power Relative to Your Ally

		Dependence on Your Ally	
		High	Low
Your Power Relative to Your Ally	High	Mutual Exchange	Isolate
	Low	Plead, Get Help	Ignore (Pleasantly)

When your power is relatively high and you aren't especially dependent on the ally's cooperation, work around (isolate) the person and create relatively little need for interaction. Finally, when you have low power but low dependence, you can ignore the potential ally, or better yet, keep a friendly manner and pass along information but spend relatively less effort on influence. As we have stressed, there is never very good justification for being gratuitously unfriendly or nasty because the person may become important later, but your purpose is to allocate your necessarily limited energy.

Your Place or Mine? Choosing a Setting

Another strategic factor is the location of the actual exchange discussions. With good colleagues whom you know well, choice of location is less important. Business can be done on the fly with no loss of impact. Some people are used to quick hallway conversations and prefer that early approaches be brief. Others want to see something written first. Location may also matter very little if what you are requesting is relatively easy to give. But when you do not know the person or there is some history of negative feelings on either side, setting can matter a great deal.

In general, people feel most relaxed on their own turf, at their own pace. Sometimes, however, the ally's office will be a nest of constant interruptions that would make it impossible for the two of you to concentrate. In these circumstances, try to arrange to meet in a neutral conference room, over lunch away from the office, or, if it fits the norms of your organization, after work over a drink. Any of these would be better than asking the potential ally to come to your office. Making an appointment, specifying how much time you think the discussion will take, is another way to keep the relationship on a comfortable and relatively equal footing.

It is almost never appropriate to influence colleagues by using cheap negotiating tactics such as trying to make the other person feel one-down in an uncomfortable chair in your office with the sun in his or her eyes. Remember, you will probably have to work with the person again sometime.

FIVE DILEMMAS TO BE MANAGED DURING EXCHANGES

Five possible dilemmas you may need to manage during your exchanges are:

1. Escalate or back off?
2. Openness or partial truth?
3. Stick to plan or react to the moment?

4. Positive or negative exchange arguments?
5. Stick to task or work the relationship?

Escalate or Back Off?

To try to collect on past debts from people who are not responding reasonably, gradually increase the pressure. Unless the potential ally is deliberately determined to take advantage of you, use the least possible pressure necessary to induce cooperation. If you decide that the potential ally is unwilling, for purely selfish motives, to reciprocate, you can up the ante as far as you are willing to be seen as tough or risk permanent anger toward you.

The first step of one form of escalation is to express explicitly the obligation as you see it and insist that the potential ally respond. The next step is to raise your voice or lose your temper in an attempt to make the potential ally uncomfortable enough to comply. By so doing, you alter the exchange currencies, introducing the control of your temper as a new currency to trade: You become willing to drop your anger for (reasonable) compliance with your request.

This kind of emotional blackmail works only when the potential ally dislikes emotional confrontations; it can easily backfire when improperly applied and cause escalated resistance. You have to decide whether you can risk the whole relationship blowing up. But deciding in advance that you will never use this kind of pressure can put you at a disadvantage if the one you want to influence trades in the currency of toughness. These traders in hot emotions often bank on the expectation that opponents may be too inhibited to make a big fuss; then if you hold back, you are playing into the ally's hands. Turn up the pressure just a notch by making your requests in public, in a friendly way at first or with irritation if that does not work. A smiling accusation in front of colleagues to the effect that the recalcitrant potential ally hasn't learned to give and take or wants to only take and not give can make it very difficult for the game player to keep on refusing. Because this is no way to endear yourself to anyone, it is a method to be used only when you are thoroughly convinced that the potential ally is deliberately trying to grind you down.

Openness or Partial Truth?

The best exchanges are those from which both you and your ally get all that you both want at the lowest cost. Where each side very much wants what the other side has and each is happy to trade, both make a considerable

---

The Three Rules of Being a Diplomat

1. Never tell a lie.
2. Never tell all the truth.
3. When in doubt, go to the bathroom.

—Source Unknown

---

profit from the transaction. You can both go away feeling good about the deal and about the relationship.

However, there is a built-in temptation for you to exaggerate. If you can make your ally think that your cost is higher than it actually is, the ally will think it is an even better deal and feel more future obligation. Thus, the temptation always exists to paint an extreme picture of your own costs (and minimize the ally's) in the interests of getting what you want at the lowest cost.

Furthermore, what if you have more to give than your ally realizes? Why reveal everything you are willing to do, especially those things that are costly to you if you can gain what you want for less? That will leave more to spend on other influence attempts. If you hoard currencies and dole them out only when forced to or get caught exaggerating your costs, however, you may reduce all chances for profitable exchange.

Concealing or altering information can have two negative effects: (1) The potential ally may not know enough about what is important to you to be creative in finding alternative ways to be helpful, or, even worse, (2) he or she may sense that you are not being wholly aboveboard and refuse to deal with you or feel spurred into driving a harder bargain to be sure there isn't more hidden in your treasury. Although there is potential gain from being shrewd, the act of exaggeration or concealment may elicit from your potential ally the exact behavior you do not want.

A few managers are wonderful actors and can conceal from others their true feelings, but far more managers believe in their own acting talents than can possibly be true—since almost all managers are certain they can spot insincerity in others. Indeed, in virtually every organization we have observed, those managers who are consistently covert and unforthcoming are eventually tagged as untrustworthy and slowly frozen out of important transactions. That can be hard to believe when the nastiest person gets a promotion or has the ear of the boss, but, over time, few of these people endure in their organization. *Nice guys don't always finish first, but nasty ones seldom do, at least not in situations where they can hardly get anything done without the cooperation of others. No one wants to be a sucker, yet the process of extreme self-protection may be self-defeating.*

In any particular exchange, however, the temptation to exaggerate costs will be present for both sides. Unfortunately, once either one begins to do that, the other is likely to feel the need to do it also, and mistrust grows. But if one side does it and the other does not, the exaggerator may gain an advantage, so the temptation remains.

Stick to Plan or React to the Moment?

The third dilemma arises from the dual need to prepare for discussions with your ally so that you can fit your case to the ally's interests and style, and, at the same time, be ready to change course if new information emerges during the discussion. There is a real danger of missing important data about the ally during the exchange conversation if you are too focused on carrying out your plan.

Trades often can founder because the person wanting influence fails to do the necessary homework and then blunders past the potential ally's valued currencies or personal preferences about interaction style. But the counter trap is so carefully locking into the predetermined game plan that he or she misses obvious messages about what matters to the ally.

The blindness to the signals being sent by the potential ally can be monumental. The resistant ally may say in 10 different ways what first must be done to obtain his or her support, but the determined influencer persists in the wrong approach because the objective is so important and the game plan said, "Stick to high lobs."

Plan to Drop Your Approach

The challenge is to be so thoroughly prepared that you can dispense with your agenda in a flash and tune into the hints about interests, goals, and concerns that any ally will give during conversation. This means treating objections as clues, not irritants, and staying poised to explore valuable clues whenever they appear. Planning a hike in the country but refusing to detour around giant boulders just because they were not on the map is a good way to spoil a journey. You can still reach your destination if you respond to unexpected barriers as trail markers.

Positive or Negative Exchange Arguments?

The fourth dilemma involves deciding whether to stick with positive arguments for cooperation or use negative arguments about potential costs—and recognizing when to switch. Never using negative exchanges can leave you vulnerable to stubbornly resistant allies, but always using them can create unnecessary enemies or give you a reputation for unpleasantness that can hamper future exchanges. It is hard to walk the line between naiveté and cynicism.

Your relative power and dependence should help shape whether you are willing to threaten the negative consequences of noncooperation. If you have relatively low power, don't make threats. Also, the ally's honesty and responsiveness will help determine whether you need to, and effectively can, focus on negative costs such as withholding your own cooperation in the future. While some allies need to be reminded that they work for the same organization, others would be insulted that you thought it necessary to mention it.

Stick to Task or Work the Relationship?

The fifth dilemma arises when you are dealing with a potential ally with whom you have a troubled relationship. Should you focus on the task about which you want to make an exchange or stop and work directly on the relationship to get it to the point where the task can be more readily addressed? As we suggested in Chapter 6, this can be a difficult choice, and it may call for working back and forth through several rounds.

If you can get the cooperation you need without mentioning the relationship directly, a lot of time is saved, but often the relationship is sufficiently mistrustful to make it impossible to skip the preliminaries. This situation calls for kid gloves; too much time spent on relationship building can make a busy colleague restless and give the impression that you are not seriously interested in work accomplishment. In general, we suggest that relationship difficulties be tackled only when they are getting in the way of direct discussion of valued currencies. Then get on with the task discussions as soon as it is feasible. Several iterations between working on the task and relationship may well be necessary to successfully complete a complex exchange.

We should note vast cultural as well as individual differences in this regard. In many countries, you are considered rude if you don't spend a great deal of time first socializing and getting to know each other. North Americans sometimes miss this and plunge ahead into direct task discussions, to

the great discomfort of their counterparts and with harm to their own rep-
utations. But in other situations, not cutting to the chase and filling time
with personal discussions can feel evasive and hurt the relationship. Pay attention to the setting you are working in.

STARTING AND STOPPING THE EXCHANGE PROCESS

Knowing when to insist on making exchanges and when to back off is an
art, not a science, but it is worth exploring. You need to take into account
the relative power of the other person, the importance of the issue to each
of you, your future interdependence, and your assessment of your own ability not to be suckered into competitive warfare.

It probably isn't wise to engage in heated battle with someone who is far
more powerful and whose future goodwill is important to you. When what
you want is arousing strong negative feelings, you should consider just how
important the ally's cooperation is and examine other possibilities. If there
isn't another reasonable alternative, then going slow, working harder to
understand just why the ally has such strong feelings, and listening re-
spectfully to the ally's concerns—or testing whether it's his or her feelings
about *you* causing the problem rather than the particular issue—are appropriate strategies.

It is also useful to pay attention to your own hot buttons when engaged
in transactions. Experienced negotiators recommend never losing your temper except when you deliberately allow yourself to do it for effect, and, although that kind of advice usually presumes a one-time opponent rather
than a potential ally, it is not entirely off target. If it is easy to get your goat,
a tough ally will instinctively provoke you around sensitive issues.

Thus, it is in your interest to be aware of what tends to make you angry
or drives you to become nasty in a way you later regret and to learn to recognize when you are headed for trouble. Then you can take time out to decide whether you want to go to the mat on this issue, want to raise the
temperature, or calm down so that you don't do anything rash.

Although it is sometimes necessary to be very tough in making exchanges (see Chapter 16, a practical applications chapter on hardball), it is
almost never wise to be nasty or attack the other *person* instead of his or
her *position* on an issue. Walk away and count to 10—or 10,000, if necessary—as soon as you feel yourself wanting to deliberately hurt a potential
ally. You can be tough and honest without trying to be hurtful; pain that
is a by-product of honest exchange doesn't cause the same reaction as pain
from a conscious attempt to maim for revenge.

AFTER THE TRADING: THE COOLING-OUT PROCESS

> I've been able to perpetuate what my dad started. . . . He always told me that in any negotiation to let the other guy feel he won. Don't take the last nickel from the table.
>
> —Brian Roberts, Chairman and CEO, Comcast,
> *New York Times,* Sunday Business Section, August 8, 2004

No one likes to feel one-down, even when the person has brought it on himself or herself. Therefore, when you have survived a successful but difficult exchange negotiation, think about how to leave your ally with some dignity. Personal chitchat is one way, but there are others such as letting the ally teach you something or demonstrate superior knowledge about another topic. As with other tools we have discussed, this need not be done cynically. In fact, unless you are a professional actor or con artist, it cannot be faked, but a dose of human kindness at the end of a complex exchange is a fitting finish.[2]

Even when the ally has not "lost," but there has been intense trading activity around an issue, time spent rebuilding the relationship, creating a feeling of mutual satisfaction and trust, is not at all wasted. At the very least, it will save valuable time when you engage in your next exchange.

(For a detailed account of how a manager, Warren Peters, navigated his way through the complicated shoals of a danger-laden set of exchanges, see the example at our web site, http://influencewithoutauthority.com /warrenpeters.html.)

MAKING SATISFACTORY EXCHANGES AND AVOIDING SELF-TRAPS

Making trades can be very simple when trust and mutual knowledge already exist. It is almost automatic, then, to adjust requests to fit the potential ally, and each of you becomes willing to give the other considerable latitude.

If such prior trust does not exist or the request is unusually costly to the ally, then it is necessary to use other exchange strategies.

Game theorists have found that a negotiating strategy that matches the opponent's response—trusting until you are violated, but then quick retaliation followed by a return to trust if the opponent also returns to acting in a trustworthy way—is the most successful long-run strategy.

Making exchanges with colleagues in an analogous way is probably appropriate.

But, when dealing with someone who is trying to take you to the cleaners, you need to be tough. Gradually raising your voice, going public, or calling the person's bluff are tools you need in your repertoire, preferably so you won't have to use them. Use such tools when absolutely needed, but keep them in cold storage as long as possible.

Finally, your approach should be shaped by how much you depend on that ally, and that ally only, for getting exactly what you have requested with no substitutions accepted and on the ally's continuing goodwill. Your willingness to risk is also an important determinant of strategy, modified by the long-term versus short-term consequences you are willing to live with.

Because the likelihood of making satisfactory exchanges on reasonable terms is so greatly increased by preexisting positive relationships, start as soon as possible to build your network of relationships. Isn't there someone you could be meeting now?

Avoid these traps when making trades:

Self-Traps in Making Trades

- Failure to do your homework on what the other person probably cares about.
- Failure to let go of your previous analysis in the face of new evidence happening in real time.
- Bluffing from a low-power position.
- Being so afraid of negative reactions that you don't use all possible exchange tools.
- Forgetting that you will probably see the other person again and going all out to win at the expense of the relationship.

PART III

PRACTICAL APPLICATIONS OF INFLUENCE

This section of the book is designed to help you quickly locate the kind of influence problem you are currently wrestling with and to give you specific, down-to-earth advice on how to solve it. We take the concepts elaborated in Chapters 2 through 7 and directly apply them to the most common influence challenges we find in organizations. The problems in the chapters toward the end of the section are organizationally more complex, and we frequently cross-reference other chapters that can contribute to the practical solutions offered, as well as the detailed examples on our web site. We wish you the best in working through the influence barriers to your greater effectiveness at work.

CHAPTER 8

INFLUENCING YOUR BOSS

Could you be more effective with your boss so that you are granted more latitude, more support, or more challenging assignments? Or is there something about your boss's management style that you would like to influence, such as his or her being more effective in dealing with higher-ups? The challenge is to gain influence with your boss so that it can build your relationship rather than threaten it. There are too many managers and leaders who are not very good bosses, and those who are good could be even better.

What might surprise you, however, is our belief that your boss's effectiveness is part of your job. It starts with you. You are, in part, responsible for helping your boss be a more effective manager and a better boss to you. Whether you or your boss see it that way, you are partners in making your department or team work well:

- *Your boss has only half the relevant information.* It would be lovely if every boss knew exactly what you needed and provided it without your asking, but that is not likely. Your boss is not a mind reader—you are the one who knows best how you can be managed to achieve your potential.
- *The world is growing so complex that bosses couldn't handle everything even if they wanted to.* They are too overloaded, and subordinates come in too many differing styles. Also, subordinates often have knowledge and special competencies that must be used if excellence is to be achieved.
- *You have expertise about how well your manager's intentions in managing you are being achieved.* He or she might want to provide

clear direction, but only you know how clear it is to you. In other words, your boss needs you.

We are suggesting a change in the basic nature of the manager-employee relationship from the old *superior-subordinate* form of interaction (with all its implications of all-knowing dominance and ignorant submission). Instead, we are advocating more of a *partnership* relationship.[1] While a difference in hierarchy remains, junior and senior partners still form a partnership.

How do junior partners act? Partners don't let their partners:

- Make huge mistakes
- Inadvertently look bad
- Go uninformed when you know things the partner should know

Partners do:

- Stay loyal to the partnership's objectives.
- Place the good of the organization ahead of their own good.
- Value and take advantage of differing skills and perspectives.
- Tolerate each other's foibles.
- Not assume that bad behavior comes from bad intentions but rather from misinformation or misguided views. (They assume that senior partners are trying to do their best for the firm and are basically intelligent and competent, or they wouldn't have been admitted to partnership in the first place.)

No self-respecting partners could stand silently by when other partners, no matter how senior, are about to make a costly blunder, overlook important opportunities, or miss vital information that could affect success. It is the obligation of a partner to be as responsible as possible, even at the risk of personal discomfort or embarrassment.

This obligation asks a lot of you, but wouldn't you want that kind of basic mind-set from the people who report to you? Accept responsibility for the relationship with your boss; both of you have a stake in your being more productive. That is the leverage point for influence with your manager.

Accepting responsibility can get you the kinds of benefits many people want: greater scope to your job, better supervision and coaching, a closer or more open work relationship, or a boss who is more effective in the organization. (Not all managers may, at first, welcome such a partnership relationship, and we deal with that later.)

THE APPROACH

To get the kind of influence with your boss that will pay off, there are four main things to do:

1. See the boss as a potential ally (a partner).
2. Make sure you really understand the boss's world.
3. Be aware of the resources (currencies) you already have or can acquire.
4. Pay attention to how the other wants to be *related to*.

Summary of the Cohen–Bradford Model of Influence without Authority

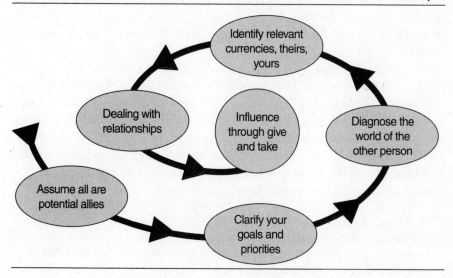

Is your boss as demanding as Donald Trump? Do you experience your boss as highly judgmental, jumping on you when you make the slightest mistake? Would you prefer that your boss begin his or her interactions with you by addressing how you can develop, rather than merely judging every action? Before writing him or her off as totally impossible, assume that your boss might be a potential ally, a partner who is very concerned about success and deeply worried about failure (not a huge leap for the ambitious man or woman that he or she is). If that is your orientation, then maybe you won't just cringe at his or her comments but look for what you can learn from them.

Do you want to influence a person like Trump? If you see that kind of person as a potential ally and partner, wouldn't you want to try to understand his world? It's New York real estate, a rather cutthroat industry in a competitive city, with very large fortunes made—and lost. Isn't that a situation where a manager needs to know that he is working with the best, with somebody who is skilled and savvy in deal making rather than running operating businesses? With those pressures, he probably won't be very patient with subordinates. A real estate tycoon's likely currencies include street smarts, financial acumen, people whom he can rely on, toughness, ability to spot big opportunities, and thoroughness.

Examine what you bring to the party. Let's assume you have the basic financial knowledge. You control how hard you are willing to work, how thoroughly you analyze opportunities, and how tough and tough minded you are. Can you be as nervy as a Trump would like, so that he can feel confident about your bold thinking? Can you actively seek deals and talk to everyone in the industry to hone your opportunity-spotting skills?

Then think of what you have observed in how he interacts with others— clients and business associates (especially those of lower status). Is he usually gruff and blunt? And how does he respond to people who are forceful rather than deferential? (Not infrequently, people who appear dominating respect those who are willing to stand up to them.)

Being aware of the currencies in your arsenal and having a sense of how this kind of boss likes being related to, could you make the following approach (perhaps adapting your language and tone to his)?

> Sir, I am as hungry as you to find great real estate deals and to protect your investments. I work long hours and am always ready to work longer if needed. You have years of hard-won experience in New York. When you see me do something wrong, you would get more for your investment in me if you would go beyond just hitting me as hard as I deserve, but also talk to me about how to do it better. I want to learn, and I can take it, no matter how tough you are with me. But I want to be sure that I am drawing the lessons that will help both of us.

Influence Strategy

We can't guarantee that this way of talking would definitely work with your boss, but it has a chance because it follows three central principles:

1. *You are showing your boss how it is in his or her interest to change his or her behavior.* Notice the difference between saying that you want your boss to help develop you because it will make *you* happy, and wanting development because it emphasizes the return on *the boss's* investment, which he or she cares a lot about.

2. *You are showing your boss that it is in his or her interest for you to be successful and satisfied because it will get the best work from you.* You are acknowledging your interests, but connecting it right back to what your boss (almost certainly) wants.

3. *You are delivering your preference in a compatible style that is preferred by your boss.* You have used a tough, no-nonsense tone, asserting that you can take anything he or she dishes out, but you will be more productive if your boss bothers to think about your learning.

The idea is to always be on the side of your boss, not an antagonist who is just a critic. You are always seeking to help the boss meet his or her goals unless you truly can't stomach the goals, in which case, no technique is likely to work. (If you are that opposed, get out as soon as you can.)

Typical Issues with Bosses

This section takes a series of actual statements about what people want from their bosses and uses the statements as the basis for questions and answers about influencing your boss.[2]

Problem 1: My Boss Resists My Ideas for How to Improve Things in Our Area. "I often have new ideas for how things could be done better around here. Yet, when I raise these ideas with my manager, he resists them and often lists all the reasons that an idea won't work or isn't worth the trouble. I find it very discouraging, especially since my boss is always saying that he wants us to take initiative."

Answer. There could be several issues at play here:

- How well thought out are your ideas?
- How are you presenting them? Do they speak to your manager's concerns?
- Is his response a reflection more of his style than the quality of your ideas? Is he really rejecting your ideas, or is that his way of checking out the quality of your suggestions?

Does your manager like fully developed ideas (rather than wanting to have input early on)? If so, it is probably necessary to do some sorting of your ideas, testing them with colleagues to be sure they are feasible. Because you know from experience that your boss is likely to be resistant to new ideas, don't bring any that you have not worked out or aren't reasonably certain that will be beneficial.

But let's assume that you have already done that and still get his usual response. Why would a boss be so resistant?

- Does your boss really believe that you are on his side? Are you presenting ideas only in ways that help your area, or do they also speak to your boss's concerns?
- Have you understood your boss's world, the forces acting on him that might be inducing resistance? Is your boss already feeling overloaded and out of control, as many are in current conditions? (That may well be why your boss is asking for initiative but not responding well to it.) If your idea would mean more work for your boss, even just for a while, he may be reacting to that, not the idea itself.
- What about the pressures your boss is under? Has he been recently burned with an idea (from somebody else) that went wrong? Or is your boss faced with the same sort of negative challenge from his boss and needs to have all the bases covered?

If your boss is overloaded, what can you do to help? Are there things you could do to ease his burdens, rather than add to them? Can you do more of the homework on your idea, so you can show how it is already fully worked out and how you are prepared to take on more burden to make it easier to implement? Can you do the analysis, the lobbying, or the rounding up of supporters that would make it more attractive for your boss to agree?

Another way to lighten your boss's load is to find a part of his current job that you could help with—an aspect that would be easier for you to do than for him to do because of your skills—or a part that you would like to learn about. That adds to the currencies you have to offer. If you are thinking like an influential partner and not a lowly subordinate, you will want to find ways to help.

Perhaps the problem is in the way you are presenting the ideas. Are you so irritated and frustrated at past responses that you are coming with a bit of a chip on your shoulder, expecting a turndown that proves what a hypocrite your boss is? That isn't likely to be received as a positive suggestion.

The previous diagnosis is an important one, but you are guessing as to what might be bothering your boss and what he might want from you. We always urge you to go to the horse's mouth. Could you, in a nonaccusatory, truly inquiring mode, ask him *why* he responds as he does?

Such a direct approach might not work. In spite of your spirit of really wanting to know (and not as a veiled attack on his competence), your boss might think your question is too presumptuous or forces him into more self-disclosure than he is comfortable with. So you might have to rely on your initial diagnosis.

If asking doesn't work, you could still directly raise the issue with him, but this time framing it in terms of your development: "I really want to take you up on your request to all of us to initiate more, but I have tried several times and you do not seem to be encouraging about my ideas. Can you help me see how to improve them so that they will be acceptable?" That is not antagonistic, and it gives your boss several choices: tell you some things you could do to strengthen your ideas (e.g., calculating payback ahead of time or identifying all the stakeholders who will have to buy in), reassure you to keep trying and to make the ideas bigger or smaller or whatever will help them gain acceptance, tell you more about the reasons he has been so discouraging (which helps you know what currencies to use to alleviate the reasons), or possibly to rethink the way he has been reacting and start to be more welcoming.

Problem 2: *My Boss Doesn't Do His or Her Job Well Enough but Won't Take Help.* "My boss doesn't do the team building and scheduling management that is her job, and she doesn't like my direct attempts at influencing what she does. I have raised the problem with her and tried to use all that you talk about in terms of not seeing her in negative terms, and I have talked with her about how her refusal costs her and harms the department, but she is still unwilling to change. In fact, she gets very uncomfortable when I directly try to talk about these interpersonal matters."

Answer. There are two issues here. One is that your boss has weaknesses but doesn't appear to want help. The second is that she doesn't want to talk about it.

Let's deal with the latter first. Much of what we suggest in this book is the power of being able to directly talk about issues. When the issues can get directly raised, successful resolution is more likely because each party tends to have different, but relevant, information. Only when all the facts and feelings can be put on the table is it likely that a quality solution can be discovered.

However, an open discussion is less likely when:

• Your boss sees you as a critic or even a rival rather than as a junior partner.

- Your boss feels that you really don't understand her world and that you aren't speaking to her concerns.
- There is something in your history or style that makes taking help from you uncomfortable.
- Your boss has a heroic model of leadership, in which she has to know all the answers to avoid looking weak.
- You are approaching your boss in a way that reflects your style but isn't an approach she is comfortable with.

All of these are factors that can interfere with open communication and joint problem solving. But even if these aren't in play, there are some people who can't (or won't) discuss work relationships directly. But all is not lost. Maybe there is a way that you can still speak to your boss's interest in a style that allows you to be influential. The following is a real situation where the junior partner found a way to deal with this sort of challenge:

Helping My Boss (Without Her Direct Assistance)

I've had several managers in my career and have had the good fortune of having supervisors that I could learn from and grow under. In the two years since I transferred into Six Sigma, I have had four managers. The first two were all but nonexistent in terms of providing direction or learning. The third was one of the best managers I've had. He provided me with opportunities that challenged me and allowed me to grow, but most importantly, he encouraged me to challenge his thoughts and opinions. I have had some excellent, energetic discussions with him. When a North American director position opened up, I applied along with one of my peers. After several interviews and discussions, she was chosen for the position over me. Having been peers for several months, we had often spoken of the frustrations we had with the system, process, and leadership, and how we would do things differently. I am a very outspoken person, and the first few months after I started to report to her, conversations were rare and uneasy. When I asked her about changing some of the things we talked about in the past that needed changing, she avoided the question. During the reorganization that happened after her promotion, my territory and staff doubled and included some of her previous direct reports. They were surprised at the camaraderie and productivity of my team. After speaking with them, I realized that team building and communication were weaknesses of hers. This weakness became apparent in her creating scheduling conflicts for many of her direct reports (my new peer group).

Instead of just pushing back on everything, I decided to try to understand what pressures and challenges she was facing. An example of her leadership style was to send out a massive spreadsheet on Wednesday and tell everyone to be on a six-hour conference call on Friday to discuss it. After reading "Managing Your Boss"[3] and the boss chapter from *Influence without Authority* [first edition], I called her to discuss her request. I could tell she was bracing herself for a confrontation, but I asked what end result she needed to get from the spreadsheet. I volunteered to organize the spreadsheet using some pivot tables and send each person a small piece. They would return their pieces to me, I would compile it all, and we could then spend one hour on Friday summarizing the information. She was thrilled. She had the results she needed, and my peers and I had less work and frustration. Fabulous!

Understanding what seen and unseen pressures and goals your boss is facing will help provide you with the freedom and information you need to be successful in your role. I found that my boss had pressures from her managers that were outside her "published" goals. Since I started working with her in a more proactive manner, she has been more helpful and open in sharing some of the rationale behind the decisions being made.

In the preceding example, this manager finally figured out that his boss may have been having difficulty with his aggressive style, especially since he was a former peer who could be difficult to manage. The boss probably felt that she had to resist his aggressive opinions, or she would be overwhelmed by him and his expectations. When he looked at it from her point of view and realized some of the pressure she was under, he was able to offer a genuine service to her that could make her feel supported and look good to her boss and subordinates. In turn, she responded positively, and they were able to develop a good working relationship.

This approach is based on making an accurate diagnosis without being able to check out your assumptions with the other person. In your situation, does your boss's superior pressure her to appear stronger? What have you seen that would help you diagnose the resistance? And despite your efforts to avoid negative interpretations, is there anything in your style of approaching her that implies you don't respect her because of her deficiencies? Are you labeling her as flawed in your mind, then radiating that scorn? Without an accurate diagnosis, repeated approaches to help are likely to be received no better than in the past. You need to know what she values (or fears) in order to pay in the proper currencies.

Problem 3: My Boss Is Distant and Unfriendly. "My boss is unapproachable and negative; I think she is threatened by me. When I get recognition outside the organization (because of my past accomplishments serving on civic task forces), she yells at me for not informing her in advance of my contacts and tries to put me down. When I send her e-mails to inform her, she never responds. She is a recent political appointment, with a great track record in her profession but no managerial experience. She is so impossible; I plan to just lay low and wait her out."

Answer.   While this is unpleasant and objectively inappropriate behavior, before you start to demonize her (because demons aren't human and can't change), take a moment to look at her world. She might not have it as easy as it appears.

First, she comes into a high-visibility job without managerial experience, so she probably feels under great pressure to produce. It is also likely that she is holding a heroic mind-set that says, "I should know and have the answers." Compounding this is that she now encounters and has to supervise a long-term employee who has a lot of the skills that she doesn't have and has great outside contacts that she lacks. Since it is contacts that got her the job, she may worry what that means. She doesn't know if you will be loyal or try to undermine her and talk about her managerial weaknesses to important people on the outside. Unfortunately, your boss doesn't appear to have the confidence to openly discuss the situation. That is a level of vulnerability that most managers won't show—even if it is the very thing that would likely draw you to her. In addition, she is probably overloaded with work, feels alone, and is trying to do it all herself. These kinds of pressures can make anyone behave in an inconsiderate, controlling, and distant way.

But this doesn't mean that there is nothing you can do. In fact, you hold many currencies that your boss might need, including:

- Support, understanding, and acceptance (that she is not inadequate just because she lacks the knowledge you have)
- Loyalty and the fact that you are on her side
- Advance information, heads-up about what is coming
- Introductions to key people that you know
- Your political knowledge and sensitivity
- Ability to tip her off to important happenings in the relevant outside world, to prepare her for public contacts, and to advise her about land mines outside the organization
- Making her look good to her boss

So how could you go about helping her? We usually advise directness because it can sort out issues more quickly and minimize misunderstandings. Could you take the risk of going to her office and saying that you want to help and you are guessing that she is in a tough spot? She is likely to ask, "What do you mean?" Can you, with authentic concern, describe the picture of the pressures you are guessing she is under? Certainly this takes courage, but what is the worst thing that could happen—that she is nonresponsive?

Another option is just to go out of your way to pay her in some of the currencies previously listed, hoping that, over time, she will see that you are helping—not undermining—and will start to include you earlier and trust you more. In some ways, this is the harder option because it does take longer and you might run out of patience.

In fact, the real challenge in this situation is likely to be you. It sounds as if you are angry now about how you are treated. Perhaps the last thing you want to do is to help somebody who yells at you and puts you down. But if that is blocking you from either of these options, you are now aware of what is preventing this situation from improving.

Utilizing Partnership to Gain Responsibility/Greater Scope for Your Job

The next two problems present questions and answers about gaining responsibility and greater job latitude.

Problem 4: How Can I Get What I Want from My Boss in Terms of Improved Job Scope, Challenge, or Autonomy?   "I can do so much more if he will let me. And it would be a lot more interesting, too."

Answer.   The implication of partnership in altering job scope is that you want to be able to share in the responsibility for the success of the unit and take on new tasks to help that happen. That requires having challenging and meaningful tasks; even more, it suggests that you be a partner in deciding how tasks will be allocated. Because you know your own capacities and interests—and know what would be a reasonable stretch versus what would pull you apart—it is reasonable for you to participate in the decision process. Asking for a part in the decision is not a request to displace your boss but a means to include you, the person with important data that can lead to a more informed decision, in the process.

However, your boss may not agree with your assessment of your capacities and readiness, especially if, in his eyes, you have messed up a previous assignment. What do you do then? How can you convince your boss to let you handle more? You will need to learn enough about your boss's concerns to be able to determine exchanges that will address those concerns.

Why is your boss not giving you the challenging assignments? Rare is the manager who wants to *underuse* his or her employee's abilities. So there is a discrepancy between the way you see your performance capabilities and the way your boss sees you.

The key is to initiate a discussion with your boss in which you listen very closely to his concerns about letting you have the kind of responsibility you desire. This is going to be difficult because you will be tempted to rebut. But it's important to keep in mind that the purpose of the conversation is to find out what your boss's concerns are. Are they about something you did (or didn't do) in the past? About how you work with others? Or are the concerns not about you, but about the project's visibility and his own exposure if you fail? You may not agree with your boss's reasons, but you have to start with his concerns—they are real to him, if not to you. This won't be easy to hear, but this approach has a double benefit: You learn the boss's concerns and, therefore, the currencies you will have to deliver, and you relieve the boss of worrying about whether you can take it if he tells you the negative stuff that he has been sitting on all along.

With that understanding, you are now in the position to suggest some win–win exchanges. If your boss has concerns about whether you can do this expanded job, could you ask him how you can improve your performance? If he is worried that you will go off on tangents, can you work out periodic checkpoints with him in exchange for the assignment? You are paying him in the currencies that he is most concerned about in exchange for your acquiring the challenging work you want.

Problem 5: How Do I Change the Quality of Supervision My Boss Provides and Get the Development and Coaching I Want?   This problem has three variations: (1) "I could be much more effective if my boss was willing to give me some coaching, but he appears to operate out of a sink-or-swim philosophy. I am concerned that if I asked him for advice, he would see it as a sign of weakness." (2) "I'm not afraid of my boss; in fact, I like her. But I can hardly get her attention, let alone her help. She is so busy and so preoccupied that I am left to drift. And when she does pay attention, it is only to give a quick criticism. I could use a lot more coaching and direction." (3) "My boss is all too willing to give me advice. In fact, that's the problem; he moves from 'helping me' to 'helping the hell out of me.' I would welcome some general guidelines, but he gets into the details and won't let go."

Earning Your Boss's Confidence Even When in Trouble

The case of Monica Ashley, on our web site at http://www.influencewithoutauthority .com/monicaashley.html describes in detail the complexities of trying to lead a revolutionary product development effort. During the process, problems arise between Monica Ashley and her long-time manager, Dan Stella. As a result of her difficulties in mobilizing support—including his—and in dealing with powerful resisters, Dan Stella removes her as project development manager, and gives her less challenging assignments.

What could Monica Ashley have done to earn her way back into Dan Stella's confidence? Aside from continuing to do excellent work on the assignments she still had, she could have asked him to explain more fully what he meant when he kept telling her to slow down, how he viewed the tradeoff between slowing down to avoid arousing public opposition and possibly missing market opportunities, why he had concluded that it was never productive to fight in public, what signals she sent that made him think she was on the verge of a breakdown, and so on. Because they had a good relationship of 10 years' standing, she might even have asked him what he did with his anger and impatience when the old guard made unreasonable and irrational accusations or how he had changed as he moved up and what he was doing to make himself a more effective executive.

Genuinely listening, she would demonstrate that she is not so emotional that she cannot listen, that she has the interest to learn how to do what he had hinted she should do, that she takes seriously the need to keep learning as she advances, and that she recognizes that the game changes as you get nearer the top.

Furthermore, if Monica Ashley could admit to Dan Stella that she had been caught up in the heat of the project, as she came to realize, that in itself would be a sign of growing maturity that would reassure him. In fact, something like that eventually happened, and she was let out of the penalty box and once again asked to take on mainstream, vital projects. She went on to a very successful career— not a bad comeback for someone who had plummeted so far and so visibly. You can find the fascinating saga at the web site.

Answer. Even though these situations are different, they have in common the requirement that you find a way to talk directly with your boss. Second, while you are seeking coaching so *you* can improve, it's always advantageous to also point out why this is in the best interest of the organization (and even of your manager).

As far as the first scenario, the *sink-or-swim issue,* what stops many people from asking for help is the fear that their bosses will see them as weak, ineffective, confused, or lacking in leadership ability. Perhaps your boss has said outright that no one should ever admit that he or she has anything to learn. Or maybe you have merely inferred this from your boss's behavior, but believe it as gospel. While many bosses sometimes get hung up on looking tough, many subordinates assume that their bosses are so entangled in heroic assumptions that any sign of the subordinate's being merely mortal is the kiss of death.

The first question is: *Do you really know that is the boss's orientation?* You state that your boss *appears* to operate out of a sink-or-swim philosophy. Is that based on definitive evidence, or is that a conclusion drawn from one or two offhand comments? Even if you are convinced that this is your boss's stance, you can still talk to him about this issue. But before doing so, there could be some useful diagnostic work to do to understand *what* might be causing his position:

- Is he already overloaded with a wide span of control so that he could be concerned that if he starts coaching one person, he will be inundated with multiple requests?
- When he took over this operation, were most of the employees passive and he might be afraid that too much coaching would produce the same dependency?
- Is sink-or-swim the approach that his boss uses with him?
- Has he never worked in an organization where development of talent is an active part of being a manager, so he figures if he could swim, others will?

For the sake of discussion, let's assume that you have a hunch that it's the first reason. Could you say:

Ricardo, my sense is that this organization really values people who take initiative for their own development. That's fine with me and I have done that in these and these areas. . . . And I will continue to do that, but I wonder whether, in addition, I could get some advice from you. We are facing a lot of negative reaction to our bold new change plans. I'm not as good as I want to be in my ability to deal with people who are giving me a hard time. You seem to be good at that, and I'd like to learn from you. I know you are busy with multiple tasks, including a lot of us to manage, but would you be willing to talk about my encounter with Ulrich? I didn't defend the department the way I wanted to. Could we discuss that for 15 minutes?

What's the worst that could happen? Ricardo could say, "Figure it out on your own." And you'd smile and say, "Will do." But the odds are that he will agree, and if you don't overdo these requests, they could probably be repeated for special occasions. And if your boss seems to value your development, maybe that could later lead into a lengthier discussion of areas he is willing to coach in and areas he thinks you should do on your own.

Even with tough-as-nails bosses, it may be possible to ask for help in a way that is in itself strong. You can demand to know how you can be an outstanding performer, making your request from a posture of being strong enough to expect tough standards. "I need to know in order to deliver" is not the plea of a wimp. This approach can appeal even to a macho boss and change the assumption of weakness into an impression of strength.

In the second scenario, *the boss is too busy,* analyze whether some of the activities that are consuming her time are less important and/or ones that you think you could accomplish. Would it then be possible to go to her and say:

> Ellen, you really seem to be juggling a lot of balls in the air at the same time. I could be more effective if I could get some coaching, but I realize that all of these activities don't give you any extra time. If I took on some of these like X and Y, would that free enough time for you to occasionally give me some advice on how I could improve? These don't have to be lengthy sessions. For example, in the meeting we had yesterday with cost accounting, I could have used just 10 extra minutes afterward to hear how I could better have handled what seemed like their petty requests.

If she evades the issue, you don't have to give up. You can ask if the subject makes her uncomfortable or if there is a better way to capture her insights. You can stress how much better you think you can do for the department if you learn to be more effective at the particular skill in question. You can offer to make an appointment to discuss it at a later time that would be more convenient. One rebuff does not have to end the possibilities.

In the third scenario, *the boss over helps,* it's the opposite problem: Your boss is only too ready to help and gets too involved. What could be a valuable resource, since any boss probably knows a thing or two, becomes an enormous burden. How can you capture the best of what your boss has to offer without being obligated to take all the advice and "guidance" that comes your way?

The key, once again, is to show your boss that too much "help" hurts his own interests. Being swamped with more advice than you want reduces the challenge in your job and thus reduces your ownership of the problems and your responsibility for solving them. If your boss rides the bike for you instead of just giving you instructions, support, and a gentle push, you'll soon have to call him every time you want to get anywhere.

Even worse, if you feel stifled by this experience, you might not ask for help the next time you need it to preserve your latitude. Ask your boss:

> Do you mean to push me into avoiding asking for help? If not, if you still want me to use my judgment about when to get you involved in tough issues, then you need to give me breathing room. I want to be a responsible partner to you, but when you try to take over for me, I start to back away. I don't want to go passive and let you do everything, and I can't believe that's what you want. You don't want to make it tempting to cut you out, do you?

At the least, these kinds of questions ought to prompt a good discussion about what your boss does want and what you require to be as useful as possible.

In short, if you think of yourself as a partner, you can take the initiative to admit you want help, ask for something specific that is reasonably recent, and respond with interest rather than defensiveness. These all smooth the way for your boss to give you what you want.

All these steps comprise an attempt to redefine the nature of the traditional boss-subordinate contract. Where the exchange used to be, "I'll do what you say if you'll take care of me," it becomes something more like, "I want to perform well, which will be helpful to you, but to do it we both have to take responsibility for helping me learn. I'm willing to do my share; now, will you join me?"

Most managers now realize that continuous learning has become a way of life in organizations; the subordinates who recognize this first and request help to grow are the most likely to be favorably received. They will also achieve the most. Your boss might be the exception, but the risk of failure to try to alter the relationship is at least as great as the risk of continuing to try to outguess your boss and thereby stay out of trouble.

Improving the Superior–Subordinate Work Relationship

Traditionally, any problems in the relationship between superior and subordinate were considered to be the problem of the subordinate, who would have to adapt. That's just the way it was. However, in these days of the knowledgeable workforce, when no single individual has a monopoly on talent and answers, good junior partnership cannot consist only of constant agreement with the boss. Bosses cannot afford to send in the clones; they must create, value, and work with strong individuals who have the knowledge the boss does not have, and both must learn to blend views rather than always fight to win or compromise away strength.

Thus, there are powerful forces pushing everyone in supervisory positions to seek partner-like responses from those they supervise. Bosses need to be able to say, for example, "I am good at seeing the big picture but not good at attending to crucial detail; thank heavens for Junior Partner's conscientious attention to the little things that mean a lot," rather than look at such a difference and proclaim, "I can't be bothered with that midget-mind who can't see the forest for the trees."

Nevertheless, not all bosses are interested in having the kind of work relationship with subordinates that includes openness, full trust, and expression of all feelings or collaborative problem solving. What can you do if your boss is not ready for the kind of partnership you want?

Problem 6: My Boss Doesn't Want a Partnership. "I have tried to use your suggestion of being a junior partner to my boss, but he doesn't seem to want this. In fact, he seems quite annoyed and defensive, as if he thinks I am criticizing him. He even said once, 'You were hired to do your job; I can do mine quite well, thank you.' Should I just give up?"

Answer. It sounds as if your boss has a heroic idea about leadership, where not knowing how to do something is perceived as a terrible flaw. The idea that the job of the subordinate is to stay in place and let the boss be the boss is a very old one, created when work was simple, subordinates weren't highly educated, and they needed to be told what to do. It is possible that this boss isn't movable and that you will have to lump it or leave the position. It could come to that. But don't leap to that conclusion without exploring two other choices:

Option 1: Is there a chance that you could persuade your boss that his model of leader and follower is outmoded and misses opportunities to get help from below and/or increase overall performance by making better use of your resources?

Option 2: Are there opportunities within your role (or a reasonable expansion of your role) that would be helpful and would make you more valuable in the boss's eyes?

Let's take each of these in turn:

1. *How your boss defines leadership.* Many leaders act heroically because they don't have any other model of how to act. They also believe that this style is the only way to gain respect from their subordinates. You can tell your boss that this isn't true for you. Or your boss may be more open to the published word. A book on modern leadership (that we are inordinately fond of) discusses alternatives to heroic leadership, *Power Up: Transforming Organizations through Shared Leadership.*[4] (Try reading Chapter 2.)

   Another possibility is to develop a list of good ideas, specific knowledge, and skills available from you and other subordinates and show your boss what he is missing by insisting that everyone know their place and stick to it.

   In either case, pay attention to the style in which your boss is most comfortable. Often, bosses who have such structured ideas about respective roles have acquired them from the military. If that is the case, then use a more formal and respectful style of raising the questions, emphasizing that the boss always has the right to decide what to listen to, and you do not wish to challenge that—you wish only to add to the boss's resources, and you respect the role of leader deeply. You might want to gently point out that today's military is seeking more input from those below; for example, the Army has instituted After-Action Reviews, where each engagement is analyzed in the field by those who took part and where opinions of all who participated are welcomed. *Fast Company* magazine has several articles available online (http://www.fastcompany.com/guides/bizwar.html) on high-performing military commanders who solicit the views of the troops. But keep emphasizing that none of this is intended to undermine the seniority and ultimate control of the top person.

2. *New opportunities.* If you don't think that a direct discussion will work, then look for ways you can contribute within the role as your boss conceives it. Are there things you can do that the boss doesn't like to do or avoids (e.g., memo writing, speeches, organizing meetings, drafting follow-up notes, checking on milestones of projects)? Can you anticipate needs and have information or reports ready? Is there information the boss would like to know and you can acquire? No matter how your job description is written, there are many possible activities not explicitly spelled out that you can do as a loyal subordinate and gain appreciation and, *possibly,* eventual latitude to be more of a partner.

Keep in mind that, in some ways, you don't need your boss's permission to act like a junior partner. You might not be able to directly influence your boss's style or discuss the nature of your relationship, but "partnership" can be more than that. It is seeing the larger picture and taking the initiative to do more than the minimum your job requires. Doing so can allow you to have the influence you want while building credit.

A Tool for Using a Business Approach: Cost-Benefit Analysis

Some bosses are too uncomfortable to ever directly discuss their relationship with their subordinates, but there are ways to sneak up on a discussion that have a better chance of working. The operating principle is to use language that is more businesslike than relationshiplike, expressing your views in a less personal way.

One set of business concepts involves cost-benefit analysis. Usually used to assess investment or other big decisions, it can be applied to your relationship with your boss. Your analysis could go something like this:

> Boss, can we examine how the way we communicate and make decisions affects our performance? There are many benefits of our current style. You inform me on a need-to-know basis; that saves time and lets you preserve important confidences. You ask my opinion when you think I have a contribution to make; that method is efficient and it lets you control communication from the people who work for you. And you can ignore what I say when you don't agree, which saves hassles for you. It also lets me spend more time on my job.
>
> But we should look at the costs, as well. Things are moving so fast you aren't always aware of what I need to know, so sometimes I find myself going in the wrong direction because I don't have the right data. Other times, I know things that could help you because my training and assignments give me different kinds of data; but if you haven't first talked with me, you sail into mined waters with one eye blindfolded. As a result, it's difficult for me to be fully invested in our departmental decisions. I could have helped navigate around unnecessary blowups, but I was never given the chance.
>
> Are the benefits worth the costs? Would we be more cost effective if you and I found a better way to pass information back and forth?

Notice that relationship-oriented phrases such as "share feelings," "trust," and "openness" are omitted from this approach. Rather, the language is businesslike and hard-headed about the nature of information exchange, which is at least part of what trust and openness are about. There's no guarantee that this way will work, but at least it doesn't wave red flags in the face of a bull-headed boss or one who is made uncomfortable by discussions of relationship issues.

Disagreeing with a Boss Who Wants to Be in Charge

We worked with a manager who was faced with a difficult, and apparently unapproachable, boss. Malcolm Miller, a controller in a large scientific organization, was concerned about how to deal with his new boss. The boss had been a high-ranking military officer before joining the organization. In several early meetings with Malcolm, "the general" had suddenly interrupted Malcolm's attempts to argue a point based on his knowledge of the organization by saying sharply: "Wait a minute, let's get this straight; I'm the boss and you're the subordinate! I don't want to hear any more about this."

Malcolm was extremely frustrated and believed he could not do anything to counter such a hierarchical attitude. We suggested utilizing currencies the boss would value, in language that fits his style. The pushing back would need to be done in a manner that established respect for the power of the boss's office and would need to utilize language that fit the general's experiences, but at the same time demonstrate that it was possible to be respectful while disagreeing. Malcolm's approach went something like this:

> Well, General, I would never want to question that you are the boss, and I fully respect your position. I'm a very loyal person, and I want to be sure that you make the right decision. Part of my job as your subordinate is to protect you from snipers, and in this case I think you are about to walk into a trap. Here's why I'm resisting backing off on this one.... Of course, if you order me to stop, I will, since you're in command, but I'm really concerned about making sure you don't get ambushed on this issue.

Indeed, Malcolm later learned that another colleague—one on Malcolm's level—had refused to back down from the general. The peer insisted on taking the matter to the general's boss and the risk paid off. He won the issue and established a more peer-like relationship with the general as well. So the apparently invulnerable lion had already been bearded in his den, and the challenger had survived to fight another day. Malcolm had overestimated his boss's unassailability.

Disagreeing without Being Insubordinate

It's not so easy, you say? You're right. There are some managers who are highly resistant to any kind of disagreement from subordinates. Even though it is a very costly position to them, since it cuts off news they need to hear, there are some diehards who are still imagining themselves to be ruling by divine right—and to be speaking ex cathedra when they take a stand. At least some of these managers are impermeable; but, if you use the kind of approach we advocate, you may be more likely to influence such a tyrant than you ever assumed.

Malcolm has plenty of company in the world. Many people assume the worst about bosses they think they can't influence, and they never find out that more than they imagined was possible. They decide that the boss is a negative, impossible person, and they decrease interaction just when it is most important to stay in touch. After all, staying in touch not only makes it easier to gather information about just what currencies matter to your boss but also allows you to demonstrate that you are on the boss's side and that you are a true partner who will do everything you can to prevent the boss from making a mistake that would go against his or her own objectives.

It is by no means easy to get that kind of message across, but when you do, you can make a friend for life. Strong bosses who prevent anyone from disagreeing with them are their own worst enemies; they try to dominate everyone, but when they are successful at it, they suffer by cutting themselves off from the kind of information they need. Saving bosses from their own strength is a risky but potentially very rewarding business; the rewards increase when everyone else who deals with that boss is too afraid to test the possibilities.

Problem 7: How Can I Help Develop My Boss?   "My boss really wants to be a good leader, but there are some things that he doesn't do so well, such as lead meetings. He seldom remembers to set agendas in advance, stifles dissent when he means to encourage it, and is less effective than he could be. I want him to succeed, but how do I go about it?"

Answer.   One of the areas in which it is most desirable to influence managers is their ability to do their own jobs better so that, ultimately, you can better perform yours. Many people have good relationships with their bosses, are satisfied with the challenge and autonomy they are granted, and receive the supervision they want, but they find they could improve

---

Helping the Boss Become More Effective

Catherine Weiler, a personnel manager in a manufacturing division of a high-tech company, knew that her boss, the division general manager, was frustrated about the lack of initiative from his direct reports. Yet, he was blind to his own part in creating their passivity. At the meetings he ran, his frequent oscillation between laissez-faire openness and impatiently taking charge when he grew frustrated had led subordinates to believe that he would inevitably do things his way, no matter how many times he requested their ideas. Catherine believed that, if she could get him to see how his own behavior was sending the wrong messages to his people, he would be far more effective and tap the considerable talent of his team.

Catherine initially held back because she was concerned about his pride and whether he could take a suggestion about leadership style from a subordinate. But eventually she decided that, as his loyal supporter, she should try to be helpful. She knew that her boss was an impatient person, so Catherine decided to approach him in terms of a currency he valued: time.

She asked him if he were satisfied with the way the meetings were going, and he confirmed that he was not. Then she said that she thought she knew a way to speed up decision making, and she would be glad to help do that if she could. She caught his attention. He began to discuss the issues with her, which made it easier for her to say that she thought he inadvertently made the problem worse.

Although he never became an outstanding meeting leader, he did work at breaking his self-defeating pattern and at encouraging his people to initiate by making clear requests of them, with deadlines, and then waiting for them to take hold. Most important to Catherine, he was grateful to her; and he became willing to plan with her and then review results after meetings. When other team members saw that the general manager was trying, they invested more effort, and the team became somewhat more effective.

---

performance if they could influence the way their bosses function in their roles. Nothing is more frustrating than to watch your boss do something poorly that you could help with but not know how to assist in a way that won't be resented.

True Grit: Being a Worthy Partner

As your boss's partner, you have an obligation to be forthcoming when you have information that he or she needs. On many issues, you automatically have information that can be useful; for example, you know what impact the boss is having on you and, often, on your peers. You may also know

Table 8.1   Ways You Can Limit Yourself in Influencing Your Boss

Treating your boss like a jerk, instead of as a partner needing help.

Withholding critical information out of fear of the reaction, or because it isn't your job.

Being so focused on what you want that you forget the boss's needs.

Being so afraid that you will displease the boss that you don't say what you know that he or she needs to know.

Trying to show up the boss instead of helping him or her look good.

Being too compliant, even at the expense of the work performance.

how the boss is seen further down in the organization, in other units, and possibly by some of his or her colleagues and superiors. In addition, you may have some skills that your boss does not, like the organization member mentioned in an earlier chapter who was good at writing memos while his boss was not.

Part of what keeps people from doing what Catherine did are their own attitudes toward authority. Overdependence leads to the belief that the manager will know everything without needing help from below and a reluctance to risk offending the manager by presuming to offer help. It may also lead to disappointment when the manager turns out to have feet of clay, as is inevitably the case.

Counterdependence also does not lead to offers of help, except in a sarcastic or punitive way that is difficult for any boss to accept. And the independent subordinates figure that the problem is the boss's and needs no attention from them. Only a subordinate who accepts the idea of genuine interdependence, of full partnership, will be willing to look for supportive ways to help the manager be more effective.

Often, it seems that only great courage would allow you to tell your boss that there is something he or she could do more effectively or offer to be helpful. If your motive is genuine help and not punishment, you really care about the effectiveness of your boss, and you do it in the spirit of partnership, many bosses will be more grateful than resentful. Part of the reason it is lonely at the top is that so few subordinates see that bosses need to learn and grow, too. Good bosses appreciate the person who is willing to be helpful. The exchange of information about performance (or advice on how to improve it), in return for appreciation from the boss (and, with luck, better ability to do your job), is a beneficial exchange that is too seldom executed. Table 8.1 lists ways you might be limiting yourself from influencing your boss.

CHAPTER 9

Influencing Difficult Subordinates

Is a chapter on influencing subordinates necessary? Anyone managing people today knows that not all problems can be solved by giving orders or directly exercising position power. Especially with knowledge workers, but increasingly with all employees, *command and control* have major limitations. Do you know everything your subordinates do? Is their work easily observed? Would you be able to tell easily whether they are giving their all? Can't they covertly undermine you if they decide to resist your leadership? And finally, can you think of every contingency for every issue, so that you can give clear, unambiguous, and appropriate direction in advance? Few leaders have so much knowledge and control.

Furthermore, the greater the talent and creativity of those who work for you, the greater is the likelihood that they will have idiosyncrasies that can be irritating or disruptive to others in the organization. They may not want to keep regular hours, dress like others, come to meetings, stop working on projects that have been killed, do routine tasks or complete paperwork, and so on. They often have a maddening tendency to want to do things *their* way. If they are extremely talented and valuable, this poses a dilemma. You don't want to lose them, but it would be desirable to influence their behavior.

CORE INFLUENCE CONCEPTS

The Cohen-Bradford Influence model still applies to dealing with subordinates, over whom you have *some* power, but not total control. The basis of influence is reciprocity, giving something valued for what the other party values. "An honest day's work for an honest day's pay" is the common state-ment describing boss-subordinate relations. But that is too simplistic to ex-plain the multiple ways that managers can potentially influence their employees. To be as powerful as you need to be, consider two concepts from our model that are especially relevant in dealing with difficult but competent direct reports.

The first concept is the necessity to see those reports as *potentially* use-ful performers. When others annoy us with their behavior, it is all too easy to stereotype and even demonize them. You need to prevent yourself from premature judgments like these: Joe's style of dress and behavior is *clearly* due to his egotistical nature. Jane's demands for help just as *clearly* arise from her basic insecurities. Josh just *needs* to show how smart he is while Jennifer has this basic *need* to dominate, which is causing her to want to win every argument. And Jim is just inherently lazy.

The second concept is the necessity of understanding the world of the person you want to influence. If as a boss you hold these negative attribu-tions, you will have trouble really understanding the situational forces act-ing on the subordinate—their world. What is going on in the organization that may be contributing to the problematic behavior? (See Chapter 4 and Figure 4.1 for more on organizational factors that influence behavior.)

One difficulty is that because of the power differential inherent in your position as boss, subordinates are reluctant to be fully open. They have a hard time trusting that you won't have a long memory and retaliate. This isn't necessarily because of anything that you have done but because of their previous experiences with superiors. If that isn't enough, many organiza-tions have the equivalent of urban myths, which "prove" that no boss can be totally trusted because someone once spoke up and got fired. All of this can restrict upward information flow.

If you also hold negative, blaming assumptions about personality and character defects (which few bosses can completely hide), that makes it even more difficult for subordinates to be fully open about their mistakes and concerns. Likewise, it can interfere with your ability to see clearly. Being convinced of a subordinate's defects shapes what you notice—and that seldom includes disconfirming behavior.

Frequently, the very behavior that is problematic to you is irritating enough to also make it difficult for you to talk openly with subordinates. For example, you can easily feel that the brilliant, but argumentative, per-son will just argue vigorously if you try to talk with him or her about it. Similarly, it's difficult not to think that the subordinate you see as insecure and needy will respond to your feedback with an endless litany of self-pity.

But if you don't know what is important to subordinates, how can you influence them? You have to find a way to understand what they care about and what their concerns are.

Can We See Subordinates as Potential Allies?

Making attributions of personality or character defects is a natural response. It is how we are wired to explain puzzling behavior. Nevertheless, it can have a negative effect on the relationship, reducing your potential influence.

This concept is related to a body of research called "the Pygmalion effect," in which people who are expected to be outstanding performers often live up to the expectations.[1] Similarly, people often work down to negative expectations. This situation is more common than you may think. You might be behaving in ways that cause some of the negative behavior you don't like in the subordinate. For example, if you think a brilliant subordinate is difficult to control and likely to go off and work on whatever he or she feels like, you may be extra firm when giving assignments, refer back to the details often to be sure he or she knows how important the assignment is, and check up frequently. To a subordinate who values independence and challenge and has pride about his or her ability to contribute, this behavior on your part can feel slightly insulting and lead to perverse efforts to work on preferred projects. In turn, you would be confirmed in the need to control the subordinate and do even more of the supervision that is stimulating the defiance.

You can test for this by asking yourself if the person in question has the same interpretation of the behavior that you do. Would the subordinate say he or she is impossible to control and irresponsible about working on important matters? Unlikely. People rarely have negative self-images and self-definition. Keep looking.

Your first task is to look at yourself—your assumptions and behavior. Are you doing anything that is in part the cause of the subordinate's negative behavior? Can you alter what you are doing to break the old pattern? (There may be other forces at work, so your behavior is probably only a part of what needs examining.) The challenge is to build a relationship where you can genuinely and with an open mind inquire about what matters to the subordinate. (An open relationship where your direct report can point out what you might be doing that is causing the problem can also be useful. That person might help you identify your blind spots.) Don't be afraid to learn from below.

Know the Subordinate's World and Currencies

There are several areas to focus on to increase your knowledge of what your subordinates care about.

What Do You Want to Know?   While more information is better because it gives you more options and areas to try to please, there are a few critical areas. Start with each person's career aspirations insofar as they know them. Where do subordinates want to move on to, and where do they eventually want to end up? This insight is helpful because you can always be thinking about what experiences would help each person move in that direction, and it lets you tie what you want to the requirements of each person's set of goals. "I'm glad to know you're interested in becoming a senior scientist in our technical career ladder. To be considered for that, you will have to demonstrate that you understand business imperatives and priorities, so let's talk about those assignments you are ignoring." Or, "You are a great contributor, but you often become so argumentative that everyone backs off. If you want to become a senior manager, you will need to learn to state your positions in more inviting ways." This approach moves what could potentially be a win–lose argument into win–win coaching, which makes it easier and more potent in addressing aberrant behavior.

> The servant knows the master better than the master knows the servant.

It is also helpful to know the style with which your subordinates prefer to be approached. Do they like to have their strengths initially acknowledged, or do they want you to cut to the chase? General directions without much detail or lots of specifics? Inclusion of personal and home life subjects or strictly work subjects? Adapting your style to match preferences will get you much better responses.

Bosses and subordinates vary a great deal in terms of how much knowledge of the subordinate's personal issues (as opposed to work desires) they want to share. Johan Ven Der Werf, as head of Spaarbeleg, a subsidiary of the Dutch insurance company Aegon, was completely intertwined in the lives of his team members.[2] He even did initial job interviews at their homes, with kids and dogs running in and out all day. He wanted to truly understand each person to know what he could count on, to build openness and trust, and to be able to give what they needed. He was extraordinarily successful, and he dramatically increased Spaarbeleg performance, eventually winning promotion to a much higher position at Aegon. There are many managers, however, who fear opening that personal door because they do not want to be swamped with personal problems that might make it difficult for them to be sufficiently demanding. They don't want to know about the sick kid, the dying mother, and other personal problems they can't do anything about. You will have to decide for yourself how much to allow on the table.

When Renn Zaphiropolous was running Versatec (a Xerox subsidiary), the company he founded, he would do all-day performance appraisals to be sure that everything was out in the open and discussed. He felt that he had to know his subordinates that well to be effective as their leader and to get the most from them. He, too, got great results.

How Do You Know What Is Important to Them?   As with Johan and Renn, the best way is to spend enough time with your subordinates so you can freely talk about what they think is important. Asking directly what is important to subordinates, what they care about, what their aspirations are, and so on is the most direct route to information. But if the relationship is not developed, you may have to use less direct methods, especially observation.

What does the person like to talk about in meetings? How does he or she approach ambiguous problems? Is there a theme that is usually followed, such as seeing all solutions starting with higher compensation, or is something else, such as status and respect, more likely to come up? What language does the person tend to use? Scientific or biological metaphors? Militaristic tough talk or more nurturing vocabulary? Feelings or facts? Listening closely can help you identify what seems to be important to the subordinate.

How Do You Build Conditions to Get Accurate Information about What the Subordinate Cares About?   We don't have an exact set of steps—it's not a cookbook—because it depends on your style, the subordinate's style, and situation, but we can give some general guidelines:

- Can you make it psychologically safe for the subordinate? Can you be certain not to instantly disagree with ideas presented, take a scornful tone in response to ideas, or cut the person off in mid-sentence frequently? In some instances, you may have to own your part in the relationship if it has become negative and tense.

- Learn to work in the area of true inquiry, which means that you really want to understand the subordinate by asking lots of exploratory questions, not just try to instantly convert him or her to your view. Beware of asking questions that are really statements ("Don't you think it's important to work well with marketing?") or ones that have a prosecuting attorney tone ("And just *why* did you hand in the Williams report late?"). Inquiry comes from truly not knowing and genuinely wanting to understand them—not from questions that confirm your preconceptions.
- Keep foremost the orientation that your goal is to help your subordinates, asking them to do things in their best interests, not to prove to yourself that you are more powerful. A huge challenge of leadership is to link individual goals with organizational tasks and requirements, not to make subordinates knuckle under to your will.

These guidelines entail knowing well what subordinates care about, being clear about what specifically you want to change to accomplish organizational goals, and offering something valued for that. Subordinates care about many different currencies, including those listed in Chapter 3 on Table 3.1. You can use that list as a starting point for identifying what might be important to the subordinate whose behavior you wish to alter.

But what people care about can come in infinite varieties. For example, many or even most subordinates would hate working in an isolated place where no one else ever showed up and there was no chance for informal conversation. Yet Allan Cohen managed one highly productive person who once joked that an unused guardhouse at the entrance of the campus should be allocated as a reward to him. His idea of work paradise was no interruptions, and he felt tortured when he was in a position requiring constant interaction with colleagues, just as Allan would have if kept in isolation. Think of the people you know who have their own unusual preferences about work. If one of them is the difficult subordinate you have in mind, your knowledge of what the person wants will come in handy. And if you don't know, you have some homework to do.

Influence Strategies

Once you know your subordinates' interests, you can tie your request to helping them get their wishes met. This is a good principle for influencing anyone, but in the case of subordinates, if you know their aspirations—whether it is to become CEO, director of marketing, or just be left alone to do their work—you can tie your requests to that. You can't guarantee a particular promotion, but you can show them what skills they will need to be considered and help them develop those skills.

Remember that you are trying to give valuable currencies in return for some new behavior or performance level. Giving feedback in an individually customized way that provides coaching for improvement has a double payoff. It gets you what you want, and it pays the subordinate in the currencies of learning and development.

All influence conversations can take several forms. Two of the more common are:

1. *What does the new, desired position require?* Not infrequently, the skills, behavior, and attitude that the subordinate will need in that new position are close to what you want now. This allows you to say, "If you are going to be successful as sales manager, you need to learn how to relate to people in other areas with other work styles. You have been having difficulty dealing with Hank in production. Whenever you want some coaching on how to work with people like that, let me know."

2. *Return payment for what you will offer.* Helping somebody advance uses up your time (and credit). An exchange geared to advancement allows you to say, "I'd be glad to help you advance, but this is what I need from you in return." (For a potent example of this kind of offer, see Chapter 5 for the story of Leslie Charm at Prudential and First National Bank of Boston, where his bosses gave him the freedom to learn and work irregular hours in return for staying in his jobs long enough to finish the bosses' critical agendas.) This approach enables more direct discussion than usually occurs with a difficult person.

FEEDBACK AS EXCHANGE

One of the most powerful influence tools available to managers is giving developmental feedback. Yet, many are hesitant to use feedback out of fear that it will cause defensiveness and damage the relationship. While that certainly can happen, feedback frequently fails because the person giving it does not think of it as a form of exchange. This exchange takes several forms. First, most of people's behavior represents their attempts at exchange, and, second, the process of your giving feedback on that behavior is an exchange in that you are providing information that the other person needs in return for better performance.

This notion of *feedback as exchange* is built around the following key assumption:

> Human beings are *purposeful* animals. Except when people act totally impulsively (a relatively rare event), they are acting for a reason: to have an effect. That is, they are engaging in an exchange where they have a goal in mind that they expect will result from their behavior.

This key assumption has a series of important consequences:

- Everybody's behavior is reasonable from *his or her* point of view. It may not be reasonable to the observer—in fact, it might appear to be self-defeating—but from the actor's perspective, he or she has a reason.
- If people do things to have an effect, then you, the recipient of that behavior, have a unique *expertise*. You know the effect of the intended exchange. In other words, you know whether the other person was successful in his or her intentions.
- Not infrequently, a person's behavior has *unintended* consequences. These can be positive, unanticipated benefits, or they can be negative. Again, you often are more aware of these unintended effects than the actor.
- What you *know* is the observable behavior and the effects on you. What you surmise is the *reasons* the other acted as he or she did—that person's intentions, motives, and personality. All of that is a guess. It might be an educated guess, but it is a guess nonetheless.

For example, Sam, one of your subordinates, doesn't immediately tell you when problems arise. In fact, when you ask whether there are any difficulties, his response is, "Everything is under control." You have mentioned that you would like to hear bad news sooner rather than later, but Sam retorted that if he feels in trouble, he will let you know. You are feeling increasingly frustrated and distrustful, but what can you do? You want to accuse him of being deceitful, even lying, and sneaky to boot. But you know that would cause all sorts of damage. Instead, you find yourself starting to ask a lot of pointed, suspicious, detailed questions.

You are now in a bad spot. You are starting to build all sorts of negative attributions as to his motives and personality—you hardly see him as a potential ally. When someone is so annoying, the natural human tendency is to write that person off as defective or worthless—and it is hard to want to help such an individual. Furthermore, you are feeling as though you have little influence, so you are likely to rely on your formal position power. At best, this feeling could lead you to isolate this annoying person with secondary jobs and, at worst, have him seek alternative employment (and possibly lose a potentially productive individual).

But this doesn't have to be if you were to see feedback as exchange:

- First, you don't know what is driving him, causing him to act in this (to you) annoying way. You don't know what his intentions are (e.g., the exchange that he wants to set up). Second, it is unlikely that the labels you are putting on him are ones that he would put on himself. Do you really think he gets up in the morning and says to himself, "I think I will be deceitful, lying, and sneaky?" No, his behavior is probably reasonable from his point of view.
- But how do you find out *why* he acts as he does? Will Sam be honest with you? If you blow up and accuse him of duplicity, he might respond by telling you exactly what is going on with him. But given the difference in position power, it is more likely that he will go silent, grow increasingly resentful, and further dig in his heels.
- What you are forgetting is your basis of influence, which is quite large. *You* know the impact of his behavior. *You* know the costs he is paying. What if you stick with your expertise and inform him about the costly exchange he is presently engaging in?
- But, you will need to shift your mind-set so that your tone will be heard as real inquiry, not accusation. At least for the moment, can you stop seeing Sam as a devious slime-ball and instead take the orientation, "I wonder why this competent, well-intentioned person is acting in ways that are so costly to him?" The actual words you use have to be your own, but they have to support the mind-set that you don't know and want to find out (rather than assume you do know and are a prosecuting attorney trying to get him to admit that your predetermined answer is correct).
- It is likely that Sam will now tell you what is motivating him. Is he acting in this way because:
  —A previous boss told him to solve all problems by himself and that is what Sam thinks a responsible subordinate should do?
  —Sam wants to prove his competence to you and this is his way of doing that?
  —He wants autonomy and is afraid that bringing the problem to you will lead you to solve it for him?

—You have a tendency to solve the problems for him and too easily move from "helping" to "helping the hell out of people"?

—Or a dozen other reasons?

- Now that you know his goals, you are in the position to complete his exchange. Your expertise is knowing: (1) whether Sam is successful or unsuccessful in achieving his goal ("As a matter of fact, Sam, I think responsible subordinates *bring* important problems so that we can jointly solve them.") or (2) that he is paying unnecessary costs ("Sam, you are getting autonomy, but at a high price. Can we work out a way that you can have final say in a decision without paying these costs?").

- Note that in this approach, you are not only treating the other person as a potential ally but also speaking to the other person's best interests—the fact that the behavior is hurting him or her. Furthermore, not only are you completing their exchange, but also your feedback is an exchange ("I will provide you crucial information so that you can be more effective in exchange for your improving your performance."). Such win–win outcomes significantly increase your influence.

We conclude this section with three important points. First, Pogo was correct: "We have met the enemy and they is us." We started with Sam being the problem, but is that really the case? Have you lost influence, not because he is a stubborn, resistant cuss, but because:

- You are treating him as an enemy, not a potential ally?
- You don't use your expertise (the impact on you) but move to your area of ignorance and act as if you actually know his motives and intentions?
- You use questions in an accusatory way rather than for true inquiry?
- You get defensive when he points out that it is your behavior (your intrusiveness) that is the cause of the problem?
- Your refusal to modify your behavior is causing this dysfunctional cycle?

Second, we have applied *feedback as exchange* to Sam the subordinate. But this same approach also works for Sheldon the peer and Susan the boss. Seeing them as potential allies, using inquiry to find out what is really going on, speaking to their best interests, and so on works irrespective of

Table 9.1   Tips on the Feedback Process

Stick with your expertise: What is the behavior, and how it is affecting you.

Beware of concluding (guessing) that you know others' motives and intentions.

Are others' behavior not meeting their goals? (Can you listen carefully for statements about their goals and link their behavior to those statements?)

Even if their behavior does meet their goals, are they paying unnecessary costs?

Have you done something that is causing the dysfunctional behavior in the other?

Rome wasn't built in a day. Keep pointing out to others when their behavior is not in their best interests.

Reward has a more potent and long-lasting impact on behavior than punishment. If you are seeing others trying to change, can you acknowledge that?

your positional relationship to the other. One clue for peers and bosses: Often they "telegraph" their goals. When Susan says, "I don't know why marketing treats us with suspicion," you might know what it is in Susan's behavior that is causing that problem, which allows you to speak to her best interests.

Third, as potent as this way of using exchange thinking to give feedback can be, remember that one conversation is unlikely to change years of habitual behavior. This is only a way to start—and to continue—this conversation. (For more on using feedback as exchange, see "Power Talk: A Hands-On Guide to Supportive Confrontation," in *Power Up: Transforming Organizations Through Shared Leadership*.[3] For more tips on giving feedback, see Table 9.1.)

POTENTIAL PROBLEM SITUATIONS

Here are a series of typical problems in dealing with subordinates, and ideas for dealing with them.

Problem 1: The Competent, but Difficult Subordinate. "I have a really competent but trying subordinate. He seems to want to do things his own way and on his own timetable. When I mention this to him, he either has excuses or promises to do better, but any improvement lasts only a few weeks. He is very smart. In fact, I wonder if his goal is to show off how smart he is. And because he often comes up with some very creative solutions, I don't want to lose him. But his prima donna attitude really annoys his peers. What can I do?"

Answer.   This is a familiar dilemma. As a leader, you do not want to be held hostage by a key, special member, but you don't want to be so rigid in your demands that you drive him or her away. And it is a bit easier to put up with challenging behavior when the individual really is a star and not just a good person wanting star treatment. With the true superstar— the Michael Jordan of your company—you might have to spend a lot of your energy running interference for him or her, reminding others that you are all dependent on the talents of the superstar and telling them that when they can produce accordingly, they can have unusual privileges, too. But true Michael Jordans are few and far between (and even he had to have a complementary set of good players around him to win), so you may have to deal with your difficult person directly.

Remember what we said earlier about attribution. The first question is whether you are attributing "desire to show off his intelligence" as the person's motivation. Is that just your interpretation of behavior such as giving long discourses for answers, dominating meetings (when he is interested), or using esoteric language? You can observe the behavior, but be careful about attributing not-so-desirable motives to it. There can be other explanations for those irritating behaviors. For example, large vocabulary can be a matter of training, and giving long discourses and dominating meetings can reflect a deep thinker who sees complexity clearly. Perhaps the norms of the group are to look only superficially at critical problems, and he is reacting to that. Maybe he is so problem focused that he doesn't notice the reactions of others and has no idea that his meeting behavior is annoying anyone.

The idea is not to dream up alternative explanations and then leap on to one of those as the answer, but to accept that it might take some work to determine what is going on with him. This might involve something as straightforward as asking him *why* he acts that way (but be careful that this is true inquiry and not an accusation). As you gain clarity, you discover whether your initial assumptions misled you. If you are lucky, it might even turn out that the person was totally unaware of the impact of his behavior, and your inquiry is enough to get that person to explore alternative ways to act.

Your goal, then, is to create the conditions where you can talk about his behavior, goals and aspirations, and concerns, and thereby reach a better mutual understanding of the situation. How can you act in a way that is reassuring to him that you are not just looking to get him but genuinely want to find ways to give him what he really cares about? How can you make him comfortable discussing these issues with you?

This is not a matter of fancy technique; rather, it is about your fundamental approach and your willingness to suspend judgment about motives and character while you explore with him. Using inquiry, in which you remain open to discovery rather than determined to "prove" that you were right in your initial diagnosis, is what is needed.

Don't forget, too, that you can learn a lot by examining the situation of this guy—his world at work. For example, what are the demands of his job? Is it challenging enough to him? Does he get to use his training and problem-solving skills? Are his ideas respected by his colleagues, or do they mistrust what he says and tune him out? Is he dependent on other people and departments for the information he needs, and does he know how to get it? Is the physical setting conducive to his work style in terms of equipment, noise level, and distractions? How does his work style compare to the preferred styles of his colleagues? Do his colleagues expect certain ways of problem solving that he finds constraining?

What you learn can help you:

- Clarify to him the cost of his present behavior (the negative exchanges he is presently engaging in), and
- Escalate the costs to him, giving him more reason to want to change.

In the process, you can:

- Talk with him about what the desired future could look like, so he can envision a different way of getting his goals met.

Extending yourself in the ways described can cause you to feel resentful that you have to expend so much energy on behalf of someone you find difficult. If you start to feel resentment, it will probably show through and can negate all the good you are doing. You will have to let go of the notion that a good subordinate is one who requires no attention, even if it can feel that way in an age of overload. If that were the case, managers wouldn't be paid more than the subordinates.

Problem 2: The Problem of Retirement on the Job.   "Nathaniel used to be very important to the department, but with the introduction of new technology, he has become less central. A few years ago, he seemed to have given up and now just goes through the motions. He is 58 and has four more years before he can retire with full benefits. I can't really terminate him now, but at the same time I can't just waste his salary for another four years when our budget is so tight. And since others see him as having retired on the job, their morale is affected. They wonder why they have to cover for his work."

Answer.   A central question is whether Nathaniel is genuinely content to be a drag on the rest of the department or just isn't able to find a way to contribute. It is common to assume that those close to retirement are invulnerable to influence. But pride is a powerful currency likely to be valued by a person who has been with the same organization for a long time. Few people when they retire want others to think, "Thank goodness that deadwood is gone." They mostly would prefer that colleagues say, "We are going to miss what that person contributed." Getting some recognition for past contributions may be another important currency. Thus, the person who has appeared to retire on the job might be more vulnerable to influence than it at first appears.

For starters, does Nathaniel know how the others see him? Does he really not care about being seen that way? You would want to get an idea about whether he feels some vulnerability, doesn't like the position he has gotten into, and wants to turn it around if he can.

It appears that it was the introduction of technology that started his downward slide, so that might be a place to start. Does he have some concerns about his own capacity—about saving face at not knowing as much as some younger people in the department? Old dogs can learn new tricks, but it might take them a bit longer. Has the introduction been so fast that he felt it safer to give up than to constantly show his ignorance? Would a chance to master some aspect of the new technology be attractive to him, especially if he could do it in a way that does not feel embarrassing (e.g., taking a refresher class to polish his skills)? Is there a role where he could be the lead coach in this new technology for others who are also having difficulty?

Second, he has years of experience, not all of which is outdated. Can some of that knowledge still be used? In addition, is there a mentoring role he could play for new employees? Does he have some historic wisdom that shouldn't be lost? Finally, is there something that he is enthusiastic about—even something that is outside his normal tasks that still might be important for the organization?

The challenge is to have an open conversation with Nathaniel, in which you say how much you want to help him get the most from his final years with the company, how concerned you are that he is slowly getting into the position of being seen as a drag by his colleagues, and how bad you would feel if he went out to everyone's relief, rather than with his head held high for what he was able to do in his last years before retirement. Can you agree on a last hurrah that would be mutually satisfying?

You are staying positive, but implicitly you are warning of negative exchanges, where in return for his indifferent performance you apply pressure and will not protect him from the reputation he is acquiring. You certainly don't want to use negative currencies such as pressure and scorn, but as a last resort it is a legitimate part of being a manager.

In a similar case, the manager had a difficult conversation with the long-time employee, in which he listened hard to what the employee cared about. He ended up saying directly, "Look, you can slink out with your tail between your legs, or you can have everyone saying, 'Wow, it was great to see his contributions in these past several years; I guess he managed to keep up his energy and make great contributions.'" The subordinate said he wanted to think about it, and he came back in a few days with new readiness to contribute. They worked together to create an assignment where his talents would be valuable, and he proceeded to amaze everyone.

The big trap here is the fear of embarrassing the subordinate by talking directly about what both know is an issue. If you are afraid of hurting his feelings, you will be unable to have the kind of reality-based discussion that can have an impact. Being willing to talk about the "elephant in the room" is almost always a potent way to open more honest, complete discussion, as long as you stick with it and do not back off when the subordinate shows signs of being uncomfortable. You do have the advantage of being the boss, so you can insist on discussion, even though you can't make the person be honest. But if your focus is on finding a way to give the subordinate payment in a valued currency such as respect, dignity, or recognition—maybe even a last chance to learn and grow—you can live through the discomfort.

Problem 3: The Subordinate Wants Currencies You Do Not Think Are Appropriate. "I have this subordinate who is potentially quite productive, but there are all sorts of personal issues that get in the way. She tends to be ill more than most and has used up her sick leave. Also, she is taking care of a parent. She is asking to be allowed more time off. I sympathize with her situation, but we have work to do and I can't go along with what she wants."

Answer.   There are always times to slightly bend the rules and make exceptions. When employees feel that you are concerned about them as people, they will usually redouble their efforts when the crisis is past. (In other words, they are willing to repay their part of the exchange.) However, there are limits to any accommodation, and this situation may have reached those limits. It is always more difficult when what the subordinate wants is not going to also help the organization or you. And you do not have to give everything your subordinate asks for in order to have influence. There can be times when there is no solution, and you have to insist on what you need. (The subordinate might choose to leave the organization, which will create its own kind of bind, but you might want to take that risk. Just do it knowingly.)

But the first round of requests is not the end of the possibilities. You can engage in mutual problem solving around the time off that might be able to satisfy the needs of both of you. And it has the added benefit of showing you are willing to try really hard to find an accommodation, so if you have to say no, you won't create secondary resentment about your inflexibility and hard-heartedness.

One thing you might want to check is whether the request is driven by genuine personal need or is an excuse for other problems, such as too difficult assignments, lack of perceived opportunity in the company, or even your management style. Direct questioning probably isn't useful; you have to listen hard for hints of other dissatisfaction. At some point, check by casually asking whether there is anything else that needs attention, including the way you are managing her. Again, you have to listen hard to see if these are legitimate or made-up excuses. But if there are other problems, you can encourage discussion, demonstrating that you can take any kind of feedback.

But let's assume that she really has personal, nonwork pressures driving her request. You can start by exploring just when the time off would be and for how long. Is this a limited period that you and your department could accept in exchange for extra work time when she returns? Or is there a way that she could do her job, but not just at the office? Are there valuable tasks she can do at home? Does she have a computer and an e-mail account to stay in touch? If not, can you get a loaner, and would that solve the work issues?

Or could she make an exchange with her coworkers? Does she have ideas about colleagues who could cover for her in return for future favors to them? Are her relationships so good that others would gladly pick up the slack? Is her work the kind that only she can do, or are there others who can help?

Finally, is she willing to take unpaid leave or cut back temporarily to part time?

These are the kind of exploratory questions that might be able to find a satisfactory resolution that doesn't require that you give up work output, yet accommodates her needs. You might not be able to find a way, and you might have to say no, risking losing her altogether (as we have seen happen), but you will make a good impression with her and others who see that you are willing to extend yourself for subordinate interests. Think long-term payoffs as well as short-term needs.

FINAL ADVICE

The best use of power is when you don't have to expend it. You don't want to try to give orders when it will create underground resistance, even if you could get what you want in the moment. Keep position power in reserve, and, most of the time, act as if it doesn't exist. Act as though you are only making requests. Your subordinates will remember your position power anyway.

You increase your power and influence by empowering others and by letting them influence you. They can get more done, which helps you deliver, and if they can influence you, they will be more amenable to being influenced.

Don't underestimate the use of vision as a key currency for leading knowledge workers (and many others). If you can show them what a positive difference their work can make for customers or others, they will willingly dig in. When subordinates give commitment voluntarily, they do more. (Using vision is a kind of payment of a valued currency.)

You have several other valuable currencies: openness, understanding, willingness to run interference for good ideas, efforts to get resources, granting of considerable autonomy, giving challenging assignments, and doing developmental coaching. With talented subordinates, these go a long way, and you can ask for what you need in return.

As a boss, it always pays to know your subordinates well because if you understand their aspirations, you can tie what you ask to the chance to be eligible to gain the skills needed to achieve their dreams. Knowing their preferred work styles is similarly helpful. You can't always give what they want, but you can try, and that will be appreciated.

You will be more effective if you build the kind of trust and openness that lets feelings, fears, aspirations, and preferences be directly discussed without fear of retaliation. This can be difficult because many subordinates are naturally suspicious of and cautious around anyone higher in the hierarchy, but it is worth a lot of effort. If you sense resistance to open discussion, say that, and ask why. Don't be afraid to ask whether there is anything you are doing that makes them wary. And be ready to listen to their answers, even if they are painful to hear. Your reactions to accusations will be the proof of whether you can be leveled with.

Just as we have argued that when you are a subordinate you have the obligation to act like a (junior) partner, don't be hesitant to tell your subordinates you want that obligation from them.

One turnaround of a talented but difficult person can pay for a lot of time spent trying to get the most from everyone. Stick with it.

CHAPTER 10

WORKING CROSS FUNCTIONALLY: LEADING AND INFLUENCING A TEAM, TASK FORCE, OR COMMITTEE

THE CHALLENGE OF GAINING COMMITMENT

One of the places where having only limited authority frustrates many people is in managing task forces and cross-functional teams. Yet, the number of cross-functional groups is growing because the need for more diverse specialties and experts, along with spreading organizational locations driven by more global competition, requires more complicated organizations. Even in situations where you are in charge of your own team of direct reports, it still isn't automatic that you will be able to get full cooperation. As the boss, you can push people hard if they aren't fully engaged, but it can still be challenging to gain full commitment. When the members of the team do not report to you, the challenge is that much greater.

How to gain genuine commitment to the core purposes of the team is the critical question—especially for those groups in which members are not your direct reports. In that case, members can be caught by divided loyalties between their ongoing assignment "home base" (the source of their identity, formal evaluation, and long-term security) and this new temporary grouping (committee, cross-functional team, task force, or project team; see Table 10.1).

In committees, members usually come as *representatives* of their home team. They may try to reach agreement, but all work hard to make sure

188

Table 10.1 Percentage of Commitment between Home Assignment and New Grouping

Home Group: New Team (%)		
70:30	50:50	30:70
Committees	Matrix Teams	Task Forces, Cross-Functional Teams

that their area is fairly represented and gains a fair share of the outcome. (This is one reason that committees can be so annoying and outcomes so often weak compromises rather than creative solutions.)

Matrix organizations work best when members are equally committed to both their home team and to the project team. However, for task forces and cross-functional teams to maximize their performance, a majority of members must be committed to this composite group's purpose. Having that commitment is extremely challenging because members' pay and promotion rests with their home team.

In this chapter, we look at what can be done to build a needed 70 percent commitment to the cross-functional team or task force. We are focusing on those groups because of their greater difficulty, even though the points raised apply as well to matrix teams and committees (and even to your home team).

What do you do when your team members have their central loyalty, supervision, measures, and, often, rewards elsewhere? What would make it attractive for members to be committed to the goals of your team? What is in it for them? Remember, the heart of influence is trading valuable benefits for what you want.

Special Cases When Leading a Team in Your Own Area Requires Special Treatment Similar to Cross-Functional

- You have one or more brilliant members (e.g., scientists) who are interested only in doing their specialized work and not in the team's goals. How do you connect individual interests with overall goals?
- You need deep commitment from all members to do constantly challenging, complex work. Commitment of that kind can't be ordered. How do you get it?

SELECTION OF MEMBERS

To build commitment to the committee or task force, you could start with who the members are. If, as often happens, you have no control over selecting members, you can go right to understanding what they want. But if the team is forming, you can think about what would be the best mix and what criteria you would like to use for choosing—especially basic beliefs— and then work to influence the selectors from other areas. You want to collect a mix of original thinkers, experts, and experienced people who have demonstrated that they can think about the good of the whole organization and not just their own areas. At least some of them should be people who are widely known and respected, so when it comes time to present your findings, they will have helped in preselling and making the recommendations respectable.

If you already have lots of relationships (important for gaining influence about anything), you can use your connections to make your case, either for selection criteria or for particular people. It may take great effort to get specific individuals you want because they are probably already fully engaged and seen as valuable where they are, but use your inquiry skills to find out what the objections are and think about whether you can help reduce the concerns. What does the person's boss need from you to let go? Can you accept less than full-time appointments? Can you loan help on the tasks that the person won't be able to do while working with you? Can you offer early information from task force findings or early access to a new product or process?

If, however, you are assigned too many members to work effectively, think about forming a core team of seven to eight people, and utilize other members by forming them into an advisory group or giving them separate assignments and inviting them only to core team meetings when their particular expertise is needed for the agenda that day.

UNDERSTANDING WHAT MATTERS TO MEMBERS

If you have the option of selecting team members, this process will be closely intertwined with your finding out what they do care about and value—their *currencies*. (See Chapter 3 for a full discussion of currencies.) Each member will have favorite currencies, including preferences for how the team should function. You need to know their currencies so you will see how to make the right trades.

Much of this information can come from understanding their worlds, the work situations they are in, and the pressures from their jobs. Determining the goals, objectives, and concerns of each person's home area helps to know what is likely to be important to each of them or to the bosses who are still involved with them. You can often determine much at a distance, just by looking at the public information about their areas. (See Figure 4.1 for a graphic representation of many aspects of any person's work world.) Their daily tasks, the way they are measured and rewarded, their place in their careers, their educational background, and so on give many clues as to what they are likely to care about.

You can then make a preliminary assessment of likely currencies for each person. You will probably want to have one-on-one discussions to get to know each person and confirm what he or she cares about. Ask a lot of questions. Most people like the chance to tell their story—to talk about their work and their aspirations—so you will be building your relationships while you are gathering information.

You also need to find out team members' interests in and concerns about the project. Do they start with excitement or dread? Is this the chance of a lifetime to finally do something they believe in, or does it feel like a waste of time? Has something similar been tried before and failed? Could the preliminary charter cause conflict with goals of their home team? Do they see political minefields? Do they envision the chance to learn in an important territory? In the process, you will also get to know something about their personalities, which will come in handy, too.

This kind of conversation can also help prevent stereotyping. Not all engineers want everything carried to the third decimal point, and not all marketing people are creative conceptualizers. Your preliminary notions of what each person is likely to care about have to be tentative so that you don't miss the unique talents of anyone. Furthermore, this kind of understanding can help you set norms of valuing differences in the team. You wouldn't be bringing together people from diverse parts of the organization with differing specialties if you didn't understand the potential excellence possible from the creative clash of perspectives. And you wouldn't want to lose that potential because some members do not feel valued or cannot be heard because they have divergent views.

INCREASING THE ATTRACTIVENESS OF THE PROJECT

One of the challenges to gaining commitment is finding a way to make the project seem more attractive to members. There are several possible approaches.

Dealing with the Charter

Part of the payoff from learning members' interests is that it can raise questions about the team's charter. Is it clear? Do you understand the scope intended? Is the scope too narrow to be as exciting as it could be if the goals were enlarged or modified? Or is it so general and amorphous that whatever you come up with won't fit certain people's expectations? Are you clear on the extent of your team's authority to solve, recommend, or present alternatives? Never take these aspects for granted. If the answer to any of these questions is no, then you have work to do. It may be that you only have to go to the manager who formulated the idea of the task force to get the answers, but if determined by the executive committee, you may have to do some one-on-one influencing to get a more reasonable or more inspiring charter.

Find out from the chartering group what the intended parameters are, whether there are sacred cows to be avoided, whether they have a preliminary (or even final) answer in mind and how ready to change their views they are, who they believe should be consulted, and so on. Questions ahead of time are easier than when asked late in the process.

The more exciting the charter, the greater the number of ways to link individual members' needs with the team's purpose and the easier it will be to inspire members with the vision.

However, there are some dangers in having the charter be too grand. Think about the history of the organization. Do task forces or committees often suffer from the problem of being asked to solve "world hunger," and end up being shot down because the solution would be too expensive or take too long? Are they asked to think outside the box; but then when they do, they get criticized for likely resistance and difficulty in implementation? Does the chartering manager already know what solution he or she wants and expect you to deliver it? And what are the probabilities that recommendations will get implemented? Is there a tendency for recommendations to disappear into the top management stratosphere, never to be heard from?

Your best shot at having the proper mandate and backing for it is upfront, before you start. You can credibly express your concerns and negotiate for something different before you come up with specific solutions to be pushed. You can always ask the top manager who evades answering by saying to you, "Oh, don't worry, just go ahead, and if you do a good job, we will back you," by responding, "I'm sure that is true, but my experience tells me that greater clarity upfront is critical. I'm very concerned about not wasting your time and the valuable time of all the good people who will work on this. You don't want us to end up with a report that goes into the round file, do you?" Few managers will say that they don't mind wasting time. Remember, you want to show how your request is in the other person's interest.

Bringing in the Sponsoring Senior Executive

Another way to increase the attractiveness of the project is to have the senior manager who gave the charter come talk with the team. Team members can ask questions directly about the charter, scope of authority, and top management intentions, testing the commitment from above. This not only helps gain clarity but also demonstrates management's interest in the project. If a senior manager can show how the project is vital and will help the company, some natural skepticism will be overcome, and team member commitment is likely to increase. (For that matter, taking a public stance is also likely to increase the manager's commitment to the outcomes, which is useful to you.)

Linking Member Goals with Team Objectives: Paying in Currencies Each Member Cares About

At the start, members will likely have more loyalty to their regular jobs and departments, but once you have a reasonable diagnosis of each member, try to get everyone some of what he or she cares about. For some, that might mean more challenge; for others, greater visibility; others might want greater voice, and so on. (To help you think about a wide range of possibilities, see Table 3.1 for a list of common currencies.) Think about how you can allocate the work to accommodate each person's valued currencies.

For example, the members who are interested in visibility might be the ones to contact senior executives for information or to make presentations to higher-ups. Those interested in challenge can be asked to take on the most complex, ambiguous portions of the work, especially those areas where no known solutions exist. Some might want to do benchmarking visits to expand their experiences of other companies.

Collective discussion can reduce ambiguity and generate excitement. One of the ways to increase attractiveness is to remove resistance. Have members talk about problems that this project might cause in their home group and how the team (or leader) can help to deal with that. This starts to give them a stake in solving the organizational problems that they will be worrying about anyway.

You can increase the value of these currencies by talking about the team's goals in other parts of the company and to the bosses of the potential members. It is never too early to do in-company marketing of the group's mission.

Don't overlook the attractiveness to many of the opportunity to learn. Because cross-functional groups usually have challenging tasks for which the organization does not already have solutions, there should be many chances for people to get into new areas and learn valuable information or skills. Similarly, don't be afraid to sell the benefits of being able to do networking with the team members, often from different areas or specialties. This creates potential new allies who can help in getting future work done, serve as contacts for new assignments, and become advocates for one another.

Tell potential and current members: *Serving on an important task force is a license to learn and to build reputation and contacts.* What better way to build capital for future influence? Often, with some imagination, it is possible to pay everyone in a valued currency or two. The idea is to find links between team members' individual goals and interests and the needs of the team to accomplish its goals.

USING VISION, A VALUABLE COMMON CURRENCY

As suggested, a powerful currency for getting team members to commit is vision, a picture of the wonderful outcomes possible from working together. Because members have a home base that they are likely to consider their real job, without a vision of the payoffs, they will not commit to the team. (If you are managing your ongoing direct report team, they still work best with a clear vision of what the team does that is special and unique above and beyond their assigned jobs.)

You need to think about the team's goals and how to express them in a way that is inspiring. Team members need to believe that the task has meaning and makes a real difference to some group or groups of people—customers, clients, other departments, or society as a whole. If the team's main goal is expressed in that way, it is easier to get buy-in and wholehearted commitment. The inspiring vision can overcome members' natural resistance to taking on new work. Even if they are assigned full time to your team for a substantial period, they will be wondering whether the outcome

Low-Status Person Effectively Leading a Product Development Team

Terry Wheeler is an MBA student who did his summer internship at a growing health food company, Healthy Bites, and found that a classmate's recommendation of *Influence without Authority* (first edition) helped him more than he expected:

> I had related and diverse experience pre-MBA, but to my surprise, I was soon given a critical and high-level product development project to run that required the management and coordination of over 20 individuals throughout all levels and functions of the organization. The product is expected to generate several million dollars in revenue in year one and will provide a critical defensive position against competitive offerings.

Here are some of the ways Terry used influence and reciprocity:

Keeping People in the Loop

Each task had an owner and, as a group, we were the task force that was charged with delivering the new product (in $4\frac{1}{2}$ months). Often, individuals were involved with tasks that were part of the early stages, and then their role diminished. For example, Marcus in finance was charged with creating the costing models early in the process to help determine whether the product could meet the desired contribution margins. At the time, he was working with the best available information. Once the models were done, I took the time to sit down with him and really understand his methodology and the sources of his numbers. As the project progressed, the assumptions upon which he based these costs changed almost daily. I was able to make the adjustments and once every week or two, I would update him on the new cost structure. Although he was ultimately responsible for the task of financial forecasting on the project, he was in the midst of budgeting and couldn't give it the attention it needed. I was able to take this workload off him, yet keep him aligned enough such that when asked, he could speak to the status of the financials. This worked out well as I had the ability to quickly see how decisions were going to influence the numbers without having to continue to bug him for updates, and he got credit for delivering the financials.

Dealing with Ms. Nosy

Anne, one of the key members of our team, was in charge of multiple tasks within the work plan. Unfortunately, she absolutely needs to know everything that's going on or she takes offense to being left out of the loop. Her role was crucial to the project, yet in a fairly narrow scope. I quickly learned that anything she knew became public knowledge very quickly. Additionally, she took offense to learning about project-related decisions secondhand—she needed to be the one who "broke the news." This was made more difficult because she didn't work on Fridays, and many of our decisions seemed to happen at the end of the week.

(Continued)

At first, I found dealing with her very frustrating. But eventually, realizing that I needed her and that she wasn't conniving, I just had to adjust my interactions with both her and others in the company. I learned that she was not someone whom you could bounce ideas off. You could go to her only with final decisions. I also learned that she had a clique from whom she got her information, so I needed to control what I let them know as well. I learned that formally announcing decisions by e-mail, not verbally or in meetings, worked well, because Anne was far behind in her e-mails. So if she took offense to being out of the loop, I could say, "Didn't you get the e-mail?" This turned the situation around to where she now felt guilty for not having kept up with the decisions—it put her on the defensive a bit, without making her feel defensive. Finally, I was sure to give her a scoop from time to time (i.e., let her be the first one to know of a decision) as well as being quick to give her credit for processes and decisions that she was involved in. This paid her in the currency that she valued the most.

Involving All Levels of Authority

When you come in as an intern, your instinct is to impress the management team. As a result, you tend to want to go to them with worldly questions and show them every bit of wisdom that you have. Largely thanks to reading *Influence* before I started, I took a different and much more successful tack. I leaned heavily on the operations-level employees. By going to them for information and to discuss ideas and processes and utilize their experience, I was able to present much more polished process steps to management. As we went along, I was very careful to give credit to those who helped me as both a way of building up their trust in me and as a means of justifying my results. By doing so, I gained the respect and trust of the people who truly got things done in the organization and, therefore, gained their endorsement when management asked them how I was doing. Those endorsements led to further responsibility and autonomy on my project.

Winning the Team Over

Over a few beers with a woman who had recently moved to field sales from the office in which I was working, I learned that there had been initial resentment toward me and my role. As it turns out, the management of my project had been a highly coveted role, desired by several long-time employees. (It was given to me due to the other employees' workloads, my related background, and the fact that I was impartial. The project involved the coordination of many facets of the organization, and I wasn't a "marketing guy" or an "ops guy" so I didn't have any political baggage.) When this project was given to a lowly intern, there was resentment and, unbeknownst to me, I had the deck stacked against me. Luckily, I had anticipated this to some extent and through a combination of these factors, I quickly won over the skeptics. The product is on schedule and on budget to launch next month, I am still involved peripherally, and I have an offer to come back to Healthy Bites after graduation.

is worth the effort. They also could be thinking about what comes next—whether their old job will be held for them. Vision can overcome this pull back to home base.

In this context, members who do not buy into the vision should have a chance to say why. Is it possible to modify or extend the vision (without watering it down) so that everybody feels connected? If their desires cannot be accommodated by your charter or take it too far off course, you should try to find another place for them. There is no shame in saying to a member or higher-ups that the person should not work at a job without commitment to its goals and aspirations.

YOUR MANAGEMENT STYLE

Leading a cross-functional team places special demands on your leadership style. You focus on hands-on control at your peril, and if you are used to steering meetings to predetermined conclusions or stifling disagreements over difficult issues, you run the risk of demotivating members. Every member needs to feel that his or her ideas are valued, there is reasonable autonomy in day-to-day work, and opposing points of view will be taken seriously. You will want to move to collective decision making on the big issues (rather than merely taking their advice) because that helps build commitment. The agreement that you are establishing is that members give their commitment in exchange for having full voice in making the important decisions.

Part of your responsibility will be to legitimize conflict over the work, data, and judgments, but not about personal differences. You need to use conflict to energize, get all the data out, get creative solutions, and allow everyone to contribute. You set the climate: Show that it is okay to disagree, but if discussion is getting into personal attacks, step in and refocus it on work issues. You don't have to create a team where everyone loves working with everyone else, but you do want people to feel open and direct because that is what gets the best results.

At the same time, there will be a lot of work to do behind the scenes outside meetings. You will have to do one-on-one meetings at times to gather information, monitor progress, lobby hard for critical issues being considered, and so on. It is tempting when some members are not fully committed or carrying their loads to jump in and do the work for them or provide your own solutions, and there may be occasions when that is necessary. But if you do it very often, members will quickly work out a negative exchange by delegating work upwards to you, leaving too much on your plate and sacrificing the very reasons they are there. They will also not be committed to the final solutions and may purposely or inadvertently undermine the conclusions when talking to their bosses or other key players.

Don't be a purist about everything being decided by full consensus of the group; you (or other team members) can do many things offline that will be gratefully received because they are facilitative of the team's work. Just be sure you are enabling team members to concentrate on the stuff they know and care most about, rather than taking over.

SELLING SOLUTIONS BEFORE FORMALLY PRESENTING THEM

One common influence mistake of project teams and task forces is to assume that once they come up with a great solution, they will get the best reception by having it completely worked out and presented whole. But especially when the solution will change some existing work arrangements, organization structure, or the power and status of key players, surprising decision makers is not a good idea. You and team members should be testing your ideas with key stakeholders and decision makers all along the way. This testing not only helps improve the plans but also gives those people a chance to get used to new ideas and to signal when taboos are being violated so they won't be uncomfortable with what you are planning. The implicit exchange with the decision makers is: "Our checking with you early means that you will support what we come up with later—no surprises from either party."

This circles back to team membership. One thing you could consider when forming the team is finding at least some members who have influence with important decision makers and opinion leaders. While you will need original thinkers, you won't be taken seriously if you have only rebels and iconoclasts as members. If the team composition was fixed without your input, then you may need to form an advisory group or some kind of collection of organizational members who are widely respected and close to the top. That group can also serve as advance scouts and influencers, carrying the ideas and testing them early.

Pay attention, however, to the problem of divided loyalty of task force members. Although you want their commitment to the findings and recommendations, that sometimes places people in opposition to their own areas or bosses. That is a tough position for anyone to be in, and when there are such loyalty squeezes, work with the members to plan their approaches. In exchange for their continued commitment to the project, you may need to visit their bosses to explain and sell the findings and help buffer the member or get a higher-up to help in that way. You may need to help the boss see the benefits (and not just the costs) of having a valuable subordinate be part of the task force, both for the opportunity to have the department's views in the process and for the subordinate's potential learning that can be brought back. That exchange can help gain support.

In turn, you might encourage the member to work out with the boss (implicitly or explicitly) what the expected exchange is for being released to participate. How will the regular work be covered? What reports of the task force work does the boss expect to hear? Are there particular departmental issues to be brought to the task force proceedings?

What you don't want is for members to feel they are in a bind and suddenly fail to support the recommendations or, even worse, surreptitiously tell their boss that the report is all wrong, thereby helping to create an opponent who helps kill the project.

As complicated as managing cross-functional teams is, they aren't going away. Organizational complexity and change require the coming together of people from different functions, products, and regions to create products, set policies, introduce innovations in process, and attempt to predict the future. If you can demonstrate skill at pulling together such diverse resources, influencing them to cooperate, and discovering good solutions that are implemented, you will greatly increase your future value and influence.

As you practice these skills, don't forget that most are highly relevant to managing your own team, which probably has many of the same features and challenges. Any team would benefit from careful selection of members, determination of what they care about, assignments that give them more of the currencies they want in return for their energy and commitment, a clear vision of what difference the team makes, leadership that taps their best talents and gives them full voice, and thoughtful upward influence to get their ideas supported and implemented. Do you hear opportunity knocking?

CHAPTER 11

INFLUENCING ORGANIZATIONAL GROUPS, DEPARTMENTS, AND DIVISIONS

In many ways, influencing a whole group in your organization is parallel to influencing individuals:

- First, you must not demonize them by characterizing them with all sorts of negative stereotypes, tempting as it might be.
- Second, you need to understand their world, what they value, how they are rewarded, what pressures they are under, and so forth.
- With that information, you now have a sense of the types of currencies you might be able to trade in return for what you want from others.
- But, even more than when you are dealing interpersonally, it is important to pay attention to the nature of your relationship. Just as you may have stereotyped other people, they have probably done the same in return.

Any good diagnosis has many facets, but there are some particular issues that are important to pay attention to in dealing across groups, departments, and divisions. Are the dominant currencies of the group true for all members? How much latitude will individuals have to trade for different currencies? Do you need total compliance with your request from everybody in that unit or just some people to go along?

As organizations grow more complex, there is hardly any group that doesn't need cooperation from other units. Furthermore, often the other group does not have to follow your requests. If you are part of a central staff function such as purchasing, information technology, quality control, finance, auditing, or human resources, even when you are able to set or shape policy, you might not so easily be able to enforce it. Or, you might be in a line operation and spot a terrific opportunity (e.g., to develop a new product or service, implement a new practice, tap a new market), but it needs approval or implementation from another department, which sees your hot new idea as just another demand on their time or as requiring them to change their processes or priorities.

Complicating matters is a common characteristic of intergroup relations: A group often gains its identity and increases its cohesiveness through invidious comparisons with other groups. "We in marketing take the larger picture, not like those pedestrian thinkers in sales." "Being in sales gives us a much better understanding of what the customer needs than those isolated eggheads in product development." "Those bean counters in finance only play with their numbers and don't have the compassion for people that we in human resources have." You need to find a way to get past those feelings.

The group you want cooperation from may be resistant for a variety of reasons. Discovering those reasons—the currencies they care about—is part of the challenge. Then figuring out how you can address their concerns and still get what you need done, without sacrificing the aims of your request, is the other challenge.

HOW TO GO ABOUT GAINING INFLUENCE: APPLYING THE MODEL

There are several ways to approach the groups you want to influence.

Step 1: Seeing the Other Group as a Potential Ally

There may be a history of conflict and even interpersonal animosity between some members of the two units, but that need not stop you. It is the *potential* alliance that you are working for. Furthermore, you don't have to like or become close friends with members in the other group to work out what you need, but you do have to find a way to respect them and their work, accepting that they have a different role and will see things differently from you because of it.

You may well still be in competition with them for some things such as budget or priorities from others but still find a way to form a strategic alliance, in which you each get something you want in a specified, limited area. This kind of "co-opetition" is increasingly common among individuals, groups, and companies, and managing the tension is an important part of organizational life.

Nevertheless, the better you know what is important to another group and why, the likelier you will feel empathy and be able to form a good working relationship. That's why the next step is so important.

Step 2: Understanding Their World

Start with the nature of the work. What do people do all day? What skills are central? What special training do they need to be good at what they do? Are they used to directing others or to reacting to requests or demands? Are they spatially separate or nearby? Does their work belong to a profession (e.g., accounting, law, engineering, science), and does that make them likely to identify more closely with their profession than with the company? The work people do is a powerful shaper of what they are likely to care about. It pulls people toward more or less precision, more or less interaction with other areas, faster or slower pace, greater or fewer challenges and novelty, more or less satisfaction and meaning, and so on. Their attitudes may seem strange to you but is that because your work is so different in nature and, therefore, leads to different views of how to behave and what to care about? If you could truly understand the nature of their work, would that make their actions more reasonable? (For more on how to use the organizational world to understand likely desires and goals, see Chapter 4, "How to Know What They Want").

What sort of people are most likely to have those skills? What are their education, background, and work experience? What are their values? The educational backgrounds of most members of a department can make an enormous difference in their values and goals—their currencies. Engineers are drilled in precision and hard work. Scientists are steeped in the long, slow search for truth. Lawyers are trained to look for vulnerabilities and risks. Liberal arts graduates have often learned to value precision in language but think in broad, sweeping generalizations. Each of these educational backgrounds tends to shape its members, affecting their patterns of thinking, language, and, sometimes, values.

What is the language and jargon of the group? Many organizational groups and departments develop their own vocabulary and language style. Knowing this serves two purposes: It often reveals what is important to the group because it will be elaborated around the things they pay attention to, and it gives you clues about what language to use when talking

Table 11.1   Mini-Translation Guide

Management Development Says	Finance Says
Developing coaching skills	Enhancing return on investment
Building trust	Reducing trading friction
Team building	Maximizing collective returns
Increasing management skills	Raising economic rents

with them. For example, finance people tend to have well-developed language for talking about costs, returns, and ratios because that is how they measure the world, translating all organizational activity into numbers. If you are in management development, for example, instead of seeing an activity as too mechanical and impersonal, can you explain your proposal in terms of cost benefits? If you would like to see an example of a training manager who hired a former CFO to teach him how to make hard-nosed proposals to the finance department that controlled his budget, see the case of William "Will" Wood on our web site (http://www .influencewithoutauthority.com/willwood.html). (For a slightly tongue-in-cheek guide to talking across language borders, see Table 11.1, Mini-Translation Guide.)

Beware of stereotypes. Before we go further with this way of thinking, we need to warn that any conclusions you come to need to be checked out for any of the people you are dealing with from the other group. The analysis we are suggesting can reveal only general tendencies, and there will always be exceptions to the general experiences you can diagnose. Not all financial people think in economic and numbers terms, for example. Recently, we were working with a task force focused on how to keep everyone, not just the currently insured, healthy, when a senior underwriting officer of Massachusetts Blue Cross Blue Shield, a profit-making health care insurer, proclaimed: "Finance is trivial and incidental! We can make the numbers work."[1] Similarly, not all lawyers are deal killers, not all human resources people are sentimental and afraid of delivering tough news to underperformers, and so on. So, use your diagnosis to help you know what to look for before you have too much contact, but verify in each individual case.

Often, the nature of the work and the people who do it lead to some common currencies that can be taken as a working idea and tested. You are looking for what the group you want to influence values, what they care about. We call these *currencies* because they are things that can be traded for. Although there is always danger of overgeneralizing, we have listed

Table 11.2   Sample Common Situations and Currencies of Different Groups (As Seen by Colleagues in Their Organizations)

Sales Representatives

Since 9 out of 10 sales attempts lead to rejection, they:
- Have to be confident to constantly start anew building relations
- Need strong ego
- Constantly need to be convincing

Are very focused on the customer:
- Have to figure out customers' needs/personality/likes
- Talk the language of clients
- Have to figure out micro cues about customers

Much time spent managing their own time; they are independent, so they usually hate bureaucracy

Want acknowledgement of contributions

Competitive

Money oriented

Status important to them

Manufacturing

Have to meet numbers hourly, daily, weekly

For them, the buck stops there

Get it done attitude, very down-to-earth

Come from mixed backgrounds: some up through ranks, some college hires

Predominantly male, therefore often "macho talk"

Speak very directly, bluntly, expect the same

Engineers

Work is detailed

Have to fix things, build for manufacture

Mostly men

Hard-working (from education in challenging engineering programs)

Taught to be risk-avoidant, often rule-bound

Tend to see the world in black and white terms, which can cause them to have a narrower perspective

Drawn to "things" (less concerned and often naive about people)

Like tinkering, endless revisions, so deadlines important

Technically competent, but over-controlling

Impatient with anyone not understanding their knowledge

Possibly less interested in customers

Determined, driving

Love challenge

Table 11.2 *(Continued)*

Finance

Concerned with:
- Market information, growth
- Measurability
- Precision
- Safety, risk averse
- Process clarity
- Clarity of the business case for spending

In problem-solving style, tend to focus on logic and rational arguments
Place value on control, audit readiness, and predictability
Workload is usually in predictable cycles
High needs for inclusion in management team

Human Resources

Want to be known as "caretakers of people"
Value soft skills
Can sometimes be bureaucratic, valuing rules and regulations
Called in to clean up messes (and may resent this)
Often don't fully understand or place high value on the economic side of the business
Don't fully understand the pressures managers are under, how tough their jobs are
Because they are often seen as organizationally impotent, concerned about being
included in management decisions

common situations and resulting currencies of selected organizational
groups (Table 11.2). The list comes from people like you, who were trying to figure out what is important to groups in their own organization.
Take this list with a grain of salt, but use it as a starting point for understanding the group you are interested in.

The list in Table 11.2 is partial and should be seen, at best, as only
the *beginning* of a careful diagnosis. We consistently urge a direct
approach. Getting the facts from the involved players tends to have two
payoffs:

1. It can be more accurate than your own speculation.
2. It is a way to build the relationship.

In terms of relationship building, could you go to the head of another
department and say something like:

Our areas are highly interdependent. We could both be more successful if
we could help each other more. I need some things from you, and I think

that I could do things that you would find useful. To do that, I need to know what you need from me. I have a rough idea, but it would help me if we could talk about it. What are the ways that I could be helpful?

This offer, by itself, isn't enough. But it's the basis for beginning a conversation. You are reaching out to the other group (paying them in the currencies of respect, interest in them, and willingness to help—important currencies in the organizational world). As the conversation develops, it gives you the opportunity to test out some of your assumptions about the other group.

This tactic works only if you are *really* interested in the other area and *truly* want to improve the relationship. As a "technique," it would be quite transparent and could backfire.

Step 3: Understanding What You Need from the Other Group

It helps to be clear about your precise goals. There are numerous questions to help sort out what you really want.

Are you trying to gain agreement/cooperation/implementation on a specific project? Or is your primary goal to improve the working relationship across the two units? It is likely that it was a specific task that has led to your thinking about how to deal with the other group, but wouldn't it be nice to have an improved relationship so the next time you have a request, agreement could be easier? Sometimes it is possible to have *both* task attainment and an improved relationship, but if only one is possible, what is more important to you at this point in time?

What actual behavior do you most care about? Giving you information? Trying a new method? Lending resources? Performing some task? Speeding up their responses? All of the above? Which requests are most crucial, and what is the minimum you will settle for? Will you be satisfied with half a loaf or is it all or nothing?

If you are seeking a change in attitude, for example, a new respect for what your area does, is that more or less important than getting cooperation on a specific task, which could serve as a beginning of forming new attitudes? Or is the attitude change so critical to overcome pervasive problems that specific cooperation won't help?

For example, if you are a central procurement office that sees excellent opportunities to save money by consolidating orders for office supplies from previously autonomous divisions, is it more important that others fill out forms telling you their needs ahead of time or that they now see central

Table 11.3   Guidelines for Setting Your Own Goals and Priorities

The narrower your request, the greater the likelihood of success.

Pilot projects are more likely to gain cooperation than wholesale changes.

Decide importance of meeting *task* goals versus improving the *working relationship*.

Changes of behavior are easier to achieve than of attitude or values; attitudes often change after new (successful) behavior.

Try not to mix your desire for respect or status with specific practices you want to change.

---

procurement as a valuable resource to the company? How will you respond to their inevitable complaints that central purchasing takes too long and that they can often buy cheaper locally? Would you get ahead faster by picking one commonly used product such as copier/printer paper and insisting on buying that product centrally as a demonstration, or do you need to have control of all office products to make a dent?

How many members of the group, team, or department have to buy in for you to accomplish your intent? Do you need everyone or just some opinion leaders or pioneers who will try what you want? Would a cooperating subgroup work well as a start?

These are the kinds of priority questions it helps to think through in advance. You will have to make your own judgments about each influence situation, but, in general, Table 11.3 offers guidelines.

Step 4: Dealing with the Relationship

Certain kinds of relationship issues arise among organizational groups with differing views and may need special attention. We refer to *relationship* in two senses: (1) What is the attitude of each group toward the other one, and (2) to what extent do you have a *personal* relationship marked by trust with a significant member of the other group?

We are making the assumption that, in most cases, you want a positive relationship and are playing for the long haul, but the relationship is presently strained. Because you have likely stereotyped the other group, they have returned the compliment. Do you have a sense of how they see you, especially the negative views they hold?

One issue is whether you attempt to talk about the relationship directly or work on the task as a way of getting to the relationship improvement. Talking about it directly works well when:

- The relationships are clearly getting in the way of successful work.
- There is a desire to resolve the relationship difficulties.

- There is enough trust to begin the dialog without intense recrimination.
- There are conflict resolution skills on both sides (or a consultant engaged to help).
- Sufficient time to work the issues through has been set aside.

When these conditions do not exist, it is more useful to find small tasks to do together, slowly building credibility of intentions and trust that your group wants to be a good partner. This takes much longer but can build a solid foundation for perhaps having a more direct discussion at a later time.

If you do talk about it, you can set a positive tone if you acknowledge what you and you area have done in the past that might have caused problems. Humorously talking about how they likely see you can also decrease defensiveness. In discussing the present negative exchanges going on, make sure you use objective language without blaming the other party (because it is likely that both of you have done things to produce this negative exchange). It is also useful to discuss the costs of the present dysfunctional interaction while holding out a picture of the potential benefits if the working relationship improved. You want to have some vision to work toward and to offer a reason to go through the pain of direct discussion.

Another choice is whether to work on the relationship one to one or to have the groups together in a session, usually offsite, where there are many people interacting. Sometimes, it takes a connection between two peacemakers to get their own groups to be willing to engage with the other.

For one approach to working out intergroup differences, see Table 11.4. This activity was developed to deal with warring groups in a company that had not been able to work together effectively.[2]

Table 11.4   Intergroup Image Exchange

Each group prepares description of other group, how it thinks other group sees them, and how they see themselves.

The data is revealed and discussed.

The groups together identify what they see similarly.

The groups identify where there are differences in perception.

The groups agree on which differences to discuss first.

Each group tells what in the history has lead them to that perception.

Each group has to demonstrate it understands the views of the other group, whether or not they agree.

The groups jointly develop working plans to create agreed-on behavior to alter differing perceptions.

Examples of Problems Among Groups

The Cost of "Writing Off" Headquarters

John Sloan was Canada country manager for a large consumer goods company. He saw headquarters groups such as real estate, acquisitions, corporate human resources, and international as political, bureaucratic, and out of touch with local needs and conditions. Over the years, he had tried to ignore them, but they became increasingly irritated and were talking about him in a way that hurt his reputation in the company. They saw him as building "Fortress Canada" and resented it. John's attitudes and dismissive behavior built resentment in the people at headquarters to the point where they were waiting for the opportunity to get him.

When his boss pushed him about it and said that he had to find a better way to relate to them, he thought more about what was important to them, including being respected, listened to, and taken seriously. He changed his behavior toward them, listening better, and took the help of his direct reports, who felt they had less negative history with headquarters. Although the relationships never became close, he was seen as doing better and ended up with a central office assignment leading corporate reengineering.*

Making a Successful Trade Even with a Strained Relationship

Manny, a manager at a leading high-tech company, wanted to incorporate into a new product a feature controlled by another group that had seen his area as a rival. He knew they would be suspicious and reluctant, so he started by laying out what his team's goals and priorities were and showing he anticipated their concerns and needs. He pointed to how the two groups had worked together successfully in the past on certain solutions and how important it was going to be for them to work together in the future because a key new technology they would have to share was only three years away. Recognizing that the other group had to service a small group of specialty customers who to them were a nuisance, he proposed a solution that would be beneficial to the other department. He would add a price increase for the new feature to his proposed product to prevent it from robbing sales from their existing products. And as a bonus in return for letting his group use the technology, he would get his own group to service the other group's nuisance customers. A deal was done, despite the touchy relationship.

---

* This is a disguised but actual example summarized from *Power Up: Transforming Organizations through Shared Leadership*, David L. Bradford and Allan R. Cohen, New York: Wiley, 1998, pp. 67–99.

BE PERSISTENT: ROME WASN'T BUILT IN A DAY

Individuals have long memories, but groups have longer ones! Even a successful exchange, as illustrated in the boxed examples, won't remove the years of encrusted distrust and even animosity. Many positive interactions are needed to erase the past, and even one slip-up can erase several successful interactions. Also, the first time seldom is as successful as Manny was. So look for some small early wins and build on that.

WAYS PEOPLE SELF-LIMIT THEIR INFLUENCE

When there are difficulties in getting what is wanted from another unit, the natural tendency is to blame them. Sometimes they deserve the blame, but we have observed two significant ways in which people self-impose barriers to their being more influential:

1. *Even when understanding what the other group cares about, the frustrated group refuses to pay them in a reasonable currency.* For example, a technical research group was having ongoing difficulty with a federal agency that oversaw their work. After a careful diagnosis and sheepish recognition of the ways in which their group withheld the exact information that government examiners needed to do their jobs, the research group got stuck trying to decide if they were willing to do what they now saw as necessary to gain better relationships, but would, in their own eyes, "demean" them by focusing on "trivial bookkeeping." Furthermore, the past relationship had been so irritating that they resisted "giving the feds anything that would help them."

   Other people don't do what they know they should because:
   • They believe that the other group is not worthy of the effort. For example, John Sloan, the Canadian country manager, was reluctant to drop in on headquarters groups because he saw informal interaction with them as slimy and playing politics.
   • They would rather be "right" (in their own minds), than effective. They get too much pleasure from feeling superior to the other group.
   • They want to personally "win," and giving the other group what it wants feels like they are losing.

2. They fail to accept that the other group has the right to value differing currencies, even though those currencies are not ones your group approves of and are, therefore, unwilling to give them what they care about.

Similar to the previous barrier, this one is a kind of parochial snobbishness about the other group. "Okay, maybe they have to care about short-term goals, but we are protecting the long-term future of the business, and we can't let them have their petty wins." Conversely, "All they do is talk about some distant future, as if we don't have to meet payroll. We're not supporting their research fantasy land."

You can always refuse to do what you know is needed, but choosing to be "right" rather than effective is costly. Do you really want to let revenge or pride rule your department's effectiveness?

It isn't impossible to overcome strong feelings between your group and another one. For an excellent example of an individual who used the influence concepts to make a difference, see the next boxed example. This is a classic organizational problem: As we saw with John Sloan, people in distant geographical regions don't want to listen to headquarters "experts." A more mutually influential relationship is necessary.

Mike Garcia has instinctively found that if he brings something of value to the regional managers—advocating for their needs at headquarters, providing them with tested ideas that can help them, and respecting them for their expertise—they will allow him to have influence over their marketing practices. None of this is easy; he has to fend off his headquarters colleagues who want to maintain a sense of superiority. But he is helped by being a Latin American himself and by his genuine respect for what they know in the various countries. He also realizes that this can't be turned around in one visit; it's a continuous process with each interaction slightly improving the relationship. He has patience and persistence. No doubt, he would love to have the power to just order them to follow the central marketing department's advice, but he realizes that isn't possible. He has found a way to be highly effective.

Finding and Paying in Valued Currencies;
Overcoming Skepticism in Country Offices about
Headquarters and Marketing People

Miguel (Mike) Garcia is a member of the marketing team for software in Latin America at a *Fortune* 500 computer company. As a member of a headquarters function, he has to gain cooperation from country managers and others who resist anything that comes from the central office and who have their own ideas about what might be valuable to them:

> Our worldwide marketing team has the philosophy of going into an area of the world and working closely with our people there, capitalizing on opportunities. We're like consultants—we create programs and materials, show best practices, and so forth. Unfortunately, we're like consultants no one asked for. I'm lucky because Latin American markets are more open to someone like me because they recognize they may not be doing things in the most sophisticated way. But they don't always take what I say, so I have to sell and influence.
>
> To show you what we are up against, one of my colleagues from the European region had written a composite report of what he'd seen on a visit. The Portuguese people returned his report with notations by each paragraph saying, "Not applicable in Portugal!" That led us to think that maybe we shouldn't issue a report, but just try to influence managers in other countries when we're there, hang out, talk, and subtly influence. We sense they don't want an official stance. I'm from Chile, which helps in these markets. I try to be one of them, be their ambassador in headquarters; of course, in headquarters I am "objective."
>
> One of trickiest things is that the people in the markets don't report to me, but rather to the area president. I'm not involved. I just cross my fingers that I'm influencing them.
>
> I have to deal with different levels of authority in each country: the product manager, then the marketing manager, and above them the country manager. In each case, the higher level person can block any of our ideas. Now I'm having conversations at all levels; with buy-in at all levels, we get better results. Recently in Buenos Aires, we had an important meeting of all marketing directors, who are most often roadblocks. It was a nice opportunity to show what we've already been talking about with their folks.
>
> On the in-country marketing side . . . we sell intellectual property. We try to bring best practices from other countries, not money. Often the in-country people say they want a market study. We're trying to convince them it's not about us having the study money. At first they said, "Who needs you without money?" but I'm slowly convincing them that we add value anyway.
>
> Our company values acting based on market research data, so we bring lots of data to the markets. We want to show that our research is suggesting something useful; it's not just arbitrary. "Here's what data says . . ." is more compelling. Sometimes, we get the response, "That doesn't apply here." Other times, they say,

"Good, but we still don't have to do it locally." As a result, we fill our presentations with what worked in other places, so it's not us headquarters people, it's what's working in Holland or somewhere. In-country people don't want to credit me or Connecticut; it's better if they see it's "like Venezuela." I've learned to let the market be the hero, even though in Connecticut the marketing people want to be the heroes. That's a big issue; in Connecticut many think we need to go tell countries what to do. That makes me think maybe I'm not being strong enough. But by hanging out with the local people, they end up thinking it's good to adopt ideas from elsewhere.

At headquarters, I try to influence our product team that a country group wants something, but I can't always ensure it will happen. I need influence in both directions. Say Mexico says, "We need our study completed," but I may not be able to make that happen. For example, our standards team at headquarters in Connecticut for new methods or ideas has defined standard operating procedures, which delays the completion of studies in other countries. But who am I to tell that expert team to get the Mexican study out the door? I wind up as an ambassador to them. That's tricky, I don't have the answer; they know what has to be accomplished to move forward.

In Buenos Aires they were joking that there are new regional acronyms: for Connecticut headquarters, it's PAYOLA, "Pain in the Ass of Latin America," or it's BEBOLA, "Big Bully over Latin America." I say, "No, I'm not a bully"; they laugh and say they know. It's good that they can joke. I see them now as open, but there's still some baggage. They say, "Europe and Asia are not even close to Latin America." Wow, they're not that open yet. There's still some sense of resentment of headquarters.

Now I'm the triage person in Connecticut for my area of the world. That's not the way other teams work. I say to the country people, "We're partners." They like that a lot.

Our software team focus worldwide is to partner with the biggest markets. Unfortunately, those markets come least to headquarters or want help. Little ones were the neediest, so they called the most, and we spent the most time with them, yet bigger markets have bigger payoffs. We're telling them, "You're big boys and we need to work together." We can't afford big markets like Brazil not being on board. If Costa Rica is not, too bad. We're spending more time with them in the field and setting up meetings across the whole company to see what works. The big difference now is that we spend time with them, so we can influence them.

The U.S. marketing people spend most of their time on the United States. Just spending more time with big markets—Brazil, Mexico, Chile—it's easier not to be seen as a seagull (who flies over from headquarters, eats their food, shits on their heads, then leaves). They love that they have a partner in Connecticut for them. It makes influence easier because of the time devoted.

I'm finally starting to hear that Mexico is very pleased with what we're doing: "They hear us out," rather than, "Connecticut comes once a year, tells us what to do, then leaves." Historically, there was more *tell*, but we would not be available when needed. Now it's better.

FINAL ADVICE

Here are some final words of advice for influencing entire groups:

- *Treat other organizational groups, teams, and departments as customers.* The right frame of mind is to treat colleague groups as customers, who might not initially want your services but whom you have to convince to want those services. If they are customers, you want to know what is important to them, what will make their lives better, and what you can offer to accomplish in return for the payment of cooperation or compliance you need. Further, you will want to identify the key influencers in the group, who have to be influenced first to set the tone so that you will approach effectively.

- *Don't assume they care about what you do. Think from their interests in, not your interests out.* Especially if your group has strong ideas about how people should behave and what would be good for the organization, it is easy to get so caught up in "my way or the highway" mentality that you miss the views of the other groups. As we have mentioned, the more cohesive and united your team, the greater the danger of demeaning those groups that see the world differently. Similarly, watch your language. All groups and departments develop their own jargon, but it can easily turn off those who have a different one. If you want a good reception, learn to speak the language of the natives.

- *To be effective, groups with different goals should be different in the way they function. But the more different they are, the more likely that intergroup stereotyping will arise.* When there are in-groups and out-groups, it is easy to develop strong feelings about who is better, more important, and more powerful. In addition, if there is a history of strained relationships, it is more difficult to talk with and do business with each other. The history and all the feelings that go with it have a way of creeping into conversations. It is seldom useful to try to trace who is "wrong" and who started it, but one side or the other has to be a bit vulnerable first to get constructive dialog going.

- *Interunit issues are usually caused by both groups.* It is, therefore, a good idea to examine what your group has been doing to perpetuate the problems, if you can bring yourself to do that and to admit it first. This can start the reciprocal process because, once your group owns up to its mistakes, the other group will feel some obligation to admit its part. Just as reciprocity drives retaliation, it can drive reconciliation. Remember, no finger pointing.

- *To prepare, determine the minimum cooperation you can live with and the potential from full collaboration.* Within organizations, the kinds of departments and groups we have been discussing are more or less interdependent and cannot totally ignore one another for long. It helps to know just how little connection and cooperation you can live with, so that your initial goals are realistic—and you are clear about how important it is to make some progress. But it is also helpful to figure out all the potential payoff from full collaboration, both to hold it up as an incentive and to keep you moving forward in a positive way if your counterparts don't at first welcome your approaches.
- *Be persistent.* Don't let one failure lead you to give up. History can be overcome; it just takes repeated efforts.

CHAPTER 12

INFLUENCING COLLEAGUES

With very few exceptions, everyone at work is dependent on colleagues to get his or her work done. That's the nature of organizations now, with complex, interdependent tasks, specialized roles, and increasing need for many people across departments working together to deliver complicated products and services. A great deal of the first part of this book, Chapters 1 through 7, addresses how to deal with colleagues who do not have to cooperate.

The core concepts, exchange and reciprocity, are still central to gaining cooperation. Colleagues respond when they see that they will get something they value in return for giving you what you need to complete your work. This payment can be currencies that benefit them personally, benefit their area, or assist in achieving organizational goals. Influence is the process of getting to know them well enough to understand what they care about, being clear about what you need, and making win-win exchanges. In this chapter, however, we add a way of thinking about influencing colleagues that can give you another useful perspective. It is the adaptation of *insights from selling to customers and clients,* which can help you develop better approaches to difficult-to-influence colleagues.

Colleagues can range from the person in the office next to yours, to the person in another area in the building next door, to the person you haven't met who is halfway across the world. Trying to gain cooperation from them can be maddening, because the farther away (in function as well as geography), the more likely they are to have different priorities or ideas about what needs to be done and when. This difference in priorities can make it very difficult to get your work done. In addition, because the backgrounds and styles of people from other areas and disciplines are likely to be highly varied, your colleagues may work in ways that are irritating to you, even if they are not barriers to doing your job. And tasks, especially the important ones, often require the cooperation of colleagues from different areas, making influence that much more complicated.

We begin by briefly reviewing our model and then looking at the problem of getting cooperation from colleagues in your department, but most of this chapter focuses on the more challenging problem of influencing those external to your area. Finally, we examine the problem of changing behavior that bugs you.

KEY CONCEPTS FOR DEALING WITH ANY COLLEAGUES

There are a number of things to keep in mind when trying to influence those you work with.

To influence colleagues:

- *Make sure you really understand colleagues' situations—their worlds.* When you encounter resistance, inquire more deeply as to what the person cares about. Complaints and objections can be hints as to what is important; don't treat them as proof that the other person is deficient. It is tempting to jump to negative assumptions about the personality of your resistant colleague. Instead, it may be true that other people are measured on different criteria, hold different objectives, under different pressures, and any number of other forces that may be affecting their response. Their tasks may be already overwhelming, and they may not know enough to be helpful (even though the knowledge needed seems obvious to you). (For a review of possibilities, see Chapter 4, Figure 4.1, Contextual Forces that Shape Behavior Along with Personality.)
- *Get clear on what you want.* When you are not getting the kind of cooperation you need, it is tempting to begin overloading the requests with peripheral desires such as more respect for what you do, a welcoming tone, information in advance, or faster responses. Getting a better working relationship often starts with something specific. After that successful exchange, other currencies you value can follow.
- *Expand the range of options: Look for multiple areas of exchange, not just single point solutions.* Although you may want to start with a focus on one specific request, a full understanding of the many currencies the other person values and a sense of the range of responses that will help you can make it easier to find trading possibilities. This idea is parallel to the wisdom of any negotiations: When possible, work from interests, not a fixed position.

- *Tie all requests for cooperation to the other person's desires, goals, or aspirations; then you can ask for or say anything about any behavior without being offensive.* Show how the old behavior is not accomplishing what the other person intends and how he or she could better achieve the goals by doing what you ask.
- *Even if you do not succeed, don't burn any bridges. Colleagues come back.* As maddening as it can be to have a clear idea of how important your project is but be unable to move your colleague to cooperation, do not start to think he or she is an idiot (or worse). Keep in mind that you may not yet have found a currency valuable enough to trade with, and it is not always possible to have influence. If everything you try still doesn't work, don't insult him or her or otherwise close the door on future transactions. You never know when you will encounter the person in the future. You want to be remembered as gracious.

INFLUENCING COLLEAGUES FROM YOUR DEPARTMENT

All of the general concepts apply when the colleague works with you in your area. While you may have a common boss, each of you has differing responsibilities and, therefore, differing priorities. To get what you need, you have to accommodate to your colleague's needs.

Friendly Competitors; "Co-Opetition"

One of the great challenges in organizations is how to balance your dependence on peers you have to get along with yet are also in competition with—for resources, attention from the boss and others, rewards, and promotions. The organization does not have to be like GE, with forced rankings among department members, to have some implicit competition; even the flattest, most collaborative organizations have some limitation on resources, advancement, and other opportunities. The difference is one of degree and overtness about differentiation. At the same time, the very nature of differing job assignments in a complex world means that peers need one another. They have information, expertise, resources, connections, and desirable support that all must gain in order to be effective.

The related challenge is between taking care of your own needs and responding to the requests (influence attempts) from others. Being responsive can build status and credit, but it also drains time and resources from achieving your own goals.

The people in the vast middle of organizations can falter if they don't keep these opposite necessities in balance. Act too competitively, and you will create resentment and eventual retaliation. (People have incredibly creative ways of letting colleagues get hung out to dry when they think the colleague is behaving badly.) Likewise, respond only to your own needs and you get isolated. But be too collaborative and selfless, and you may get walked on and unable to meet your obligations. The trick is to be "more collaborative and helpful than everyone else," a subtle way of competing without being competitive. But it can't be done as a trick, or it will come across as phony and underhanded and undermine effectiveness. The second guideline is to be as inventive as you can in creating win–win outcomes where you can achieve your goals while helping others achieve theirs.

Helping your colleagues look good is part of being an effective organizational member and worth learning to do automatically. Don't wait for "big" occasions; there are endless chances to be looking out for your colleagues' interests and helping them as you can.

This concept connects to recent research that found that people who made many exchanges as part of daily work life were higher status and more productive. Their relationships with colleagues were rich and involved, not just occasional and distant.[1]

INFLUENCING EXTERNAL COLLEAGUES BY USING A "SELLING CUSTOMERS" MIND-SET

Colleagues working in other, more distant parts of the organization can pose more difficult problems. Many of the issues are similar to dealing with colleagues in your department but exaggerated by the distance. In addition to the concepts already discussed in this chapter and in the first section of the book, we present a mind-set, a special way of viewing colleagues as if they were customers, that we recently saw in action with a group we advised.

You, too, can adapt a sales mind-set, as if your colleagues are external customers of the company.

One warning: Don't think of selling as a one-way hustle to get people to buy things they don't want or need. Various sales systems exist that start with joining the customer in collaborative problem solving, so you are helping develop solutions to their problems. That's the kind of selling mind-set we mean.

The Power of Thinking about Selling to Colleagues

The training and development department of a large software company was meeting to discuss ways of getting more influence with their line management colleagues. They were frustrated at their ineffectiveness and low status.

"We develop programs and offer consultation, but it is like searching for hens' teeth to get people to come. Line managers give us very little support, and when budgets get tight, ours seems to be the first one cut."

After considerable thrashing around, the head of the department said, "Let's assume that the company had outsourced our function and we were an independent training and development company where each of us was selling on commission. Would we act any differently?"

The others were initially a bit taken aback and then started to comment:
First of all, I would know their business better than I do now. I don't really understand what all the functions do. And I certainly don't know exactly what their key concerns are.

Yes, and I would put effort into finding who the rainmakers were. Who are the key line managers, so that if I got them committed, they would really champion my product?

That's key—that we think of what we do as *products*, not as programs. How can we convince them that our product is superior to anybody else's and would really speak to their needs?

But to do that, we need to speak their language. Now we use training talk about how this helps develop their people, but we don't speak in financial, performance terms. When we use our language, it makes training and development seem like a nice thing to do, not as something necessary.

And we need to feel comfortable with selling. Presently, we act as if that is beneath us, and as professionals we should just turn out the best educational program. Selling would feel like hustling, so we are not very good promoters of our products.

This way of thinking led to a new approach from training and development and gained new respect from line managers.

No matter what the approach to selling products, services, or ideas, to be successful, some kind of trade will happen. The customer (colleague) has to see that he or she will get something of at least equal value in return for giving the order (meeting your request). What he or she receives may be tangible—the product or service—or may be intangible—some kind of feeling such as pride, prestige, or connection. When an executive buys a top-of-the-line BMW, for example, he or she is buying not only a means of transport but also whatever else that person associates with the car. It might be symbolic: "I've arrived." It could be relative status: "I'm ahead of my neighbors, who only have a Chevy." Or it could be self-confirmation of what a wise consumer he or she is: "I've found a fabulously engineered driving machine that others don't appreciate."

In other words, do not focus on how wonderful your project or service is but on the benefits to the colleague as he or she sees them. As obvious and straightforward as this is, remarkably often, enthusiastic people and organizations miss it. Companies started by technical people are prone to fall in love with the features of their products and insist on focusing on how amazing their product is rather than on what it can do for users. Similarly, many people get so excited by how important their project is or how critical it is to their own success that they forget the colleagues' desires.

KNOWING THE CUSTOMER'S WORLD

It isn't always straightforward, however, to determine what customers (and colleagues) want. Sometimes they aren't clear about it, either because they don't know themselves or because they want to keep their needs hidden as a bargaining ploy. They genuinely may not connect what you are offering to their needs as they conceive of them. Even worse, they may not like or trust you. This suspicion may disguise what they really want, or they may fear that if you know it, this information will somehow be used against them.

If you are not clear about what they want, go into inquiry mode. Ask about what core problems they face, what methods they now use to solve the problems, exactly how they use existing tools and methods, how satisfied they are, what features or payoffs they wish were there, and so on. Try to unearth what they care about. Salespeople do this, and you can find it productive in dealing with a distant unit.

You have to inquire in a friendly way that encourages openness if not direct liking. You want to build trust so that information can flow about the range of interests of the colleague, which will give you more to work with. The more you know about the interests, needs, and values (or as we call them, currencies) of the colleague, the better the chance to find ways to satisfy them.

If colleagues don't see how what you offer solves their needs, look closely at how they talk about it to see if you are using the appropriate language. Every organizational area has its own jargon and style of communication, so you are likely to fall into a way of talking that fits your department and not necessarily theirs. For example, the training and development people in the earlier boxed example realized that they were talking in too soft a way for line managers who care about business results.

If you are not getting a positive response, deepen your inquiry. Ask what is missing from your request and explore the answer without becoming defensive. Admit true shortcomings, and use that to explore more about just how the colleague will be affected and what is needed. You not only learn but also establish credibility that will help in the future. But be sure to look for other benefits they may not realize are present. Sometimes, you can trade deficiencies in one area for desirable but little known payoffs in another.

Overcoming Mistrust

If others do not like or trust you (or your department), work on that directly. Start by asking what is bothering them and what their concerns would be if you were to collaborate. Listen carefully to the answer, and don't let your defensiveness turn off the hearing aid. Even when they are reluctant to be specific, you can often sense what is being avoided or read between the lines. If necessary, you can specify what they have done or said that makes you think there is mistrust. You can refer to awkward silences, phone calls not returned, averted glances, or whatever it is that has made you think that they aren't fully trustful. This direct, concrete offer of data can be uncomfortable but edge the colleague toward greater openness. You are putting the cards on the table, so you are more trustworthy.

The other reason for listening closely is that the process of doing so also builds trust. Unless you pounce on what you learn and use it to put the colleague at a disadvantage or look bad, listening intently and demonstrating that you understand and are concerned about what is being said are relationship builders.

Often, people's attitudes are shaped by past events (real or imagined). It is helpful to ask about past experiences that are affecting current perceptions. If you or your department has done something wrong, admit it. Evading responsibility for mistakes will reduce the perception of your trustworthiness, and owning up to them makes you more credible. Besides, vulnerability often creates some reciprocal willingness to be more vulnerable by being open, so it is a way of utilizing reciprocity to make a good exchange.

Be sure to ask a lot of questions about the other person's interests, challenges, and preoccupations; then respond with unfeigned interest. Few people do not want to be understood, and, again, demonstrating real interest and curiosity helps reduce suspicion. Furthermore, it is almost always true that when you really understand what the world is like to someone, you will feel more sympathetic, and that is critical to enhancing the relationship.

Next, think about ways to make a deal that proves worthiness, especially where you take the first risk. Can you offer the equivalent of a free trial, a money-back guarantee, or a pilot project that will not only demonstrate the value of your offering but also prove that you deliver as you claim? Can you go out of your way to be accommodating, whether it is literally traveling a long distance, being available at odd hours (e.g., doing a conference call with an Asian colleague at a time convenient to them, not you), or obtaining requested information? Anything you can do to be at more risk than the colleague will help reduce suspicion of you or your department.

Dealing with Hard Bargainers

If you are dealing with someone who believes in driving a hard bargain, first, do not take it personally. Separate your personal identity from the role you are in. Think of the bargaining from the other person as a kind of sport played, perhaps, for high stakes, but not a personal insult. Some cultures or subcultures believe in bargaining for everything, so depersonalize it and figure out how to negotiate. If you are dealing with someone who is used to operating that way, it isn't about you; it's just about negotiating hard.

If the currency of toughness is valued, you will have to use a similar style, even if it is not your personal preference. Although there are a few people who bargain mercilessly and get pleasure out of double-dealing and dominating (like the entrepreneur we observed who would make an agreement then keep asking for another concession; agree, then ask for another), a tough style isn't necessarily about nastiness. You just need to figure out how best to respond to the colleague's rough exterior (which may require your adopting a similar approach), but always be thinking about finding a way to come to agreement and keep the relationship going. People who use a tough style don't dislike tough opponents; they respect them. (In the ironic words of a friend who went through a difficult divorce, "I want my ex-wife's lawyer to represent me if I ever get divorced again.") And if the colleague is good at bargaining, hanging in there and parrying his or her arguments with strong counterpoints can sometimes result in a positive relationship as well as a win–win task solution.

If you have quick verbal skills, use humor to deflect attacks. A quip instead of a counterattack can ease tension, reduce the impact of the other person's aggression, and help build the relationship. When in doubt, use self-deprecating humor such as, "Oh, I see, all you want me to do is to cave in, go belly up, and hand you everything you want. I guess I must come across as the weakest player in the universe." And with tough bargainers, don't give in too soon, or they will worry that more might have been possible and that they left too much on the table. You have to allow them to feel that they have wrested every last concession from you.

Treat Everybody as a Long-Term Customer

Treating everyone as if he or she is a long-term customer is one of the first principles of selling. This principle is related to the point that you should frame what you sell in terms of what others care about, not its importance to you. You can immediately see the parallel to the general requirement for knowing and valuing the situation of the other person.

Just as a salesperson doesn't want to slip into taking an ongoing customer for granted, so it is useful to think of your colleague as somebody you could lose. In some organizations, colleagues outside your area literally can go elsewhere, in that they can buy their own support services, give priority to other issues, or just shut you out. Even when it is not officially permissible to go outside for services, for example, to buy training services from an outside vendor, it is usually possible to ignore your requests or stall.

Second, as with salespeople who have a stake not only in selling their product or service but also in the success of the customer, you, too, have a stake in the success of your colleagues. Not only do you belong to the same organization, but also your assistance builds credit that you might need to draw on at some future time.

Paying in the Currency of Involvement

When you have an ongoing relationship with an in-company client who uses your services (e.g., the training and development department in the boxed example), there might be something additional required. These "customers" are more like *partners* because they are not just recipients of your service but also coproducers of it. They usually have to give a lot of input into the design of the services and may well be very involved in creating those services along with you. They will at the least expect to have what you provide closely coordinated with whatever else they do.

This close partnerlike relationship assumes a close working relationship where ideas flow back and forth and where the nature of the service you have sold will shift and change as needed. Therefore, you should imagine yourself as joining their organization, just as if you were employed by them. As a loyal employee, you will want to shape what they do and in turn be shaped by their needs.

Just as with any colleagues, but even more so, you need to carefully diagnose the pressures they face and the tensions they are under. Understanding their world will allow you to adjust your expectations and proposals on the fly, and that increased responsiveness is yet another currency you can provide.

Many clients have currencies other than financial ones; don't forget to work to discover those. Some, however, will judge performance in financial terms, and it pays to convert benefits to numbers. You may want to review the case of Mike Garcia, the corporate marketing manager who got better implementation of marketing plans from country managers when he gave them more respect and acted as their advocates with headquarters (Chapter 11). If you want another example, you can read on our website about Will Wood, a training manager who learned to convert training innovations into costs per participant (http://www.influencewithoutauthority.com/willwood.html).

Start with the Client's Definition of the Problem

One of the most important issues for selling clients is to start with the client's definition of the problem to be solved. It could be wrong, since an accurate diagnosis may be just the expertise lacking, but that doesn't matter as much as finding a way to *address the concerns behind the definition or problem*. For example, managers come to the training and development department wanting a program to increase innovation. In some cases, the training professional can convince the client that the reason for low creativity is restrictive leadership practices and that innovation training won't help. But until the training folks have established credibility, such arguments often fall on deaf ears. Instead, it is critical to take the manager's ideas seriously.

Starting where the client is gains credibility. Then you can use your credibility and access to begin to get a better shared diagnosis. If the client is your "partner" and eventually has to be the key implementer of your recommendations, he or she has to share in the diagnosis and buy it. Otherwise, it doesn't matter how insightful you have been; nothing happens. You may indeed know what is good for the client, but just because you claim that doesn't mean he or she will believe it. Many services proposed to clients require a great leap of faith on their part if they do not have experience with the kind of thing you are offering. You may have to devise pilot or demonstration projects to show usefulness and to let them have direct experience. Visits to sites that have implemented your service are another way to make the offer concrete. Referrals from other colleagues in the organization are terrific, but references are probably less convincing.

Relationship *Really* Counts

As any salesperson will attest, a positive relationship is frequently critical in being successful with a client. Technical expertise alone is seldom enough. Chemistry counts. Rather than lament this fact or curse the idiots who can't see what a great thing it would be to have your fine new accounting, information, or training system, work on the relationship. Although the other points we make about knowing the other person, listening to understand their world, and not attributing bad motives or character are important, it is your most human moments that make you interesting and trustworthy. So make your true self available.

Sometimes, it is easy to overlook that everyone in the client organization, including low-level people, might be important to how you are perceived—and received. Experienced salespeople not only try to get in front of the key decision makers but also realize that the receptionist and administrative assistant are important and not just nuisances to get past. When you are selling to client colleagues who will remain collaborators, treat everyone as a key player.

BE AWARE OF THE LARGER SYSTEM

Salespeople anticipate that resistance to what they are selling might be coming from other parts of the organization. If that turns out to be true, they help the "purchaser" plan the arguments or approaches to other key players such as the client's boss, the finance department, sister divisions, and so on.

Organizations are interconnected systems, and a change in one part can have a positive—or negative—impact on another. Thus, in addition to understanding the nature of your client's core activities, it is also wise ahead of time to know how your change effort, product, or service will affect other areas. Even a small change can have unanticipated negative consequences. Know the system's effects ahead of time, not after blundering in.

You Can't Win 'Em All

Salespeople have to be able to live with rejection because even the best efforts can fail. Sometimes, the fit between your department's offering and the client's needs is poor, and nothing you can do will lead to better outcomes. Not all situations allow profitable trades; in those instances, withdraw gracefully and do not blame the client. Your reputation will follow you, so leave in a positive way, trying to keep the door open to future influence.

Problem Example: Colleague Won't Cooperate, So You Can't Get Your Assignment Done. "I'm supposed to serve wealthy clients for all their financial needs, but I can't get the people in other parts of the bank to deliver the right kind of personalized service for their products. They see it as a nuisance, not helping them meet their goals much, and not worth the time. I don't think they really understand the benefits of doing a great job for private banking clients."

Answer. Think about the worlds of the colleagues in different divisions. The mortgage officer, for example, deals all day with people who have to sweat the financing and creditworthiness of the loans they need; their incomes are probably more vulnerable than your clients' income and total assets. The mortgage officer is judged on transactions—how many loans he or she closes, moderate risk with acceptable margins, in a restricted list of places, and not on total volume. They may find that a loan discussion with a private client may be unprofitable, taking up a disproportionate amount of time because it may be something unusual such as a second home requiring a jumbo loan or private yacht registered in a country the bank doesn't like doing business with. In addition, the mortgage officer may be uncomfortable around super rich people or even resentful if they are Ivy League in background and style.

The more you know about the pressures on the person who is not leaping to serve your client, the greater the chance that you can offer to do something to ease some of the pressures, whether by getting directly involved in parts of the process, checking out the nature of the opportunity, finding the right internal resources, buffering interaction with the client, and so on.

If the resistance is largely due to being measured on somewhat incompatible criteria, you still have options for finding valuable currencies. You can do some homework to speed up the process if time is a factor. You can work with the client to make the request less undesirable as the rest of the bank sees it. You can show the great overall benefits to the bank and indirectly to the mortgage officer (or whomever else you are trying to influence) using vision as a currency. You can express your gratitude and willingness to sing the person's praises to higher officials. Probably the least useful currency is one that is important to you but not the colleague such as, "But I really need to satisfy this client to make my bonus." *As with all influence exchanges, sell what the other person values, not just what you care about.*

You might also think through just what you need. Is it a rate quote or the complete deal? Would honest information that your bank isn't the right place to do a jumbo mortgage on a third home in India (or trade stocks, or whatever the service is) be useful? Would you settle for a five-minute conversation that lets you explain why helping this client is so important, for example, in bringing in other business? Know what you want and would accept if you can't get that.

ESCALATING UP THE HIERARCHY

It is always possible, but seldom desirable, to take an unresolved issue to the next level where you have a common boss. If you are desperate and can't make any headway with your colleague, it is tempting to try to get support from above. The problem with this approach is that you are likely to be seen as ineffective as a manager if you do this very often. One of the tests of your potential is whether you can get things done without relying on hierarchy. Second, you might not get support, and then you have spent your ammunition. And if you go above, many colleagues will be resentful, feeling as if you are somehow tattling.

If, however, you have tried everything else and believe that what you are asking is critical to the organization's future, you may want to get some help. But instead of going up the line and making a case for why you should receive authority from the higher-up, use that person as a resource. Ask for advice on how to gain cooperation from your colleague, explaining that perhaps you aren't understanding some aspect of what is important to him or her. Never attack the colleague. And don't ask the higher-up to take direct action, though sometimes that might be offered and appropriate. Instead, focus on your own learning, asking for diagnostic help that will allow you to be more effective. In the process, you will probably have a chance to talk about why what you are working on is so important, but your focus is on how you can obtain needed support.

Dealing with Colleague Behavior That Is Annoying or Worse

So far, we have been addressing the problems with colleagues who do not cooperate as you would like. But the interpersonal style or other behavior of a colleague can also be problematic. Behavioral influence is difficult, but not impossible.

Problem Example: Colleague's Behavior Is Maddening.   "One of my colleagues drives me crazy because he is always stuck on the tiniest details and never sees the bigger picture. Even when I don't need his cooperation, his general attitude is maddening. I put a lot of energy into conceptualizing better ways for us to deliver service to our customers, and it's like he is speaking some other language; he never responds with enthusiasm to any new idea. All he can say is, 'How many man-hours will that mean I have to schedule next year?' or something like that. Sometimes I feel like Moses coming down from the mountain, and all he wants to know is why I didn't use a number 6 chisel!"

Answer.   Maybe the world would be more pleasant if everyone were just like you, but the loss in diverse skills and perspectives would not be good for productivity. If you are a creative conceptualizer, that is extremely valuable, but your ideas are likely to be strengthened or executed better if there is someone like your colleague buttoning down the details, making sure the ideas are practical. (In turn, your soaring imagination is probably a necessary antidote to your earthbound colleague.)

Thus, the starting point for influencing this colleague (and most colleagues) is to look at your own expectations and behavior to see whether there is anything in what you do that is the source of the problem or a contributor to it. In this case, your impatience is as much about you as it is about him. You need to think about your own appreciation of skills complementary to yours and find a way to value them. An understanding of your own limits and the value of people with differing approaches will go a long way.

In addition, look closely at whether your impatience and scorn for the detail orientation of your colleague is prompting him to be even more finicky. Sure, he is naturally detail conscious, but you may be so extreme in your insistence on staying in the clouds that you tempt him into even greater delight in sticking to the concrete. And that stimulates you to be even more soaring, which goads him, and on and on. (This reciprocal role relationship is depicted in its most general form in Figure 12.1 on page 230 and explained in more detail in the section in Chapter 9 on Feedback as exchange. See also Chapter 6, "Building Effective Relationships," for more on dealing with colleagues.)

Figure 12.1
Reciprocal Role Relationship

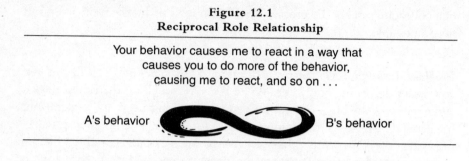

Your behavior causes me to react in a way that
causes you to do more of the behavior,
causing me to react, and so on . . .

A's behavior   B's behavior

The implications of the interconnection between your attitudes and his behavior are that either or both of you might have to change some behavior to improve the relationship. It isn't necessarily just him. But if there is a connection between what he does and your reaction, then either of you can break the pattern by taking initiative. Because you are the one who is bugged and can control your own behavior most easily, think about how you can break into the mutually reinforcing behavior.

One way to start is to test the pattern out on the other person. Draw the pattern, and ask him if he sees the two of you that way. Often, just recognizing the pattern can be freeing and alter the relationship with no other intervention.

If you are uncomfortable doing that, you could initiate a conversation in which you admit that you have sometimes been irritated by his focus on detail (with a few examples), and ask whether there is anything you are doing that provokes it. You could explain why it is so irritating, which could open up a discussion about your fear that he will never get on board (and, probably, his fear that you will never come down to earth). Once something like that is on the table, it isn't too difficult to begin offering exchanges, for example:

> Oh, I certainly don't want to just be pie in the sky, but if I can't get on a roll, it really blocks my ideas. If you could wait a bit before shooting me down with the details, I would be glad to go over all of the ideas for practical details and drop any that haven't a prayer. I can give them up as easily as they trip off my tongue, so you can be sure I won't go on and on, insisting on something totally impractical.

Or perhaps, "I will promise to stop after each idea and give you a chance to respond if you will agree to give your practical objections in a way that we can come back and visit, rather than as pronouncements of doom." Or possibly, "I would prefer to stay on a roll once I get going, so I will agree to take up any points you like if you will list them as I am going. I promise to consider each one. And by the way, I will be happy if you build on something once in a while—and maybe I will even provide some critique of my own ideas if I don't think you will do all of it." The possibilities are great once you both see what the difficulty is. A bit of poking fun at yourself humor doesn't hurt, as some of the dialog suggests.

The Interconnection of Job-Related and Interpersonal Issues

For illustration, we have separated the problem of influencing a colleague about a task from the problem of an interpersonal issue. But sometimes these two areas intertwine. Task disagreements—inability to gain cooperation—create frustration. Then the person desiring influence begins to see the colleague negatively, and soon the issues are entangled. Quite often, the source of personality or interpersonal problems is a failure to agree on whether the colleague will cooperate, but that gets lost in the hard feelings.

For that reason, we suggest that when you have negative perceptions of the colleague, you try to figure out whether there are job-related reasons at the heart of the difficulties or whether it is purely the person's style. It

Table 12.1   Personal Issues That Get in the Way of Resolving Influence Problems with Colleagues

Hard to let go of the past, insisting on determining who was "right" at the start of a disagreement

Reluctance to admit your part in the problem

Fearing you will be vulnerable

Piling on; responding to a colleague's admission with another accusation

Feeling only competition with the colleague, despite talking of collaboration

Perceiving that working out a solution, especially of a relationship problem, might require giving up your sense of personal righteousness

Lapsing back to good versus bad thinking about motivation, rather than seeing genuine complexity

Preferring to feel "right' (about how idiotic or wrong the colleague is) rather than be effective

Worrying too much about looking good in front of the boss

Locking into a position, then focusing on saving face in front of others is easier to work on job-related disagreements using currencies and exchanges, so if you can, start there. If there really are style issues, then remember, you are the other half of interpersonal relations, and don't treat the colleague as impossible. If nothing works, you can always conclude that, but starting with that assumption blocks possible progress.

Working on influencing colleagues raises many traps, especially ones that have to do with who you are and how you are seeing the world. It is probably less a matter of skills in using currencies and exchange and more about not being so self-protective that you spoil the chances of altering the relationship. In organizational life, effective influence is seldom one way; without mutuality, many organizational members will dig in and become more resistant or wait for the chance to right the balance (by upsetting yours). Especially when dealing with colleagues, mutuality is critical, which can be difficult if the organization tends to reinforce competitive views. The many ways that the personal baggage you bring, or cling to, can prevent you from being influential are listed in Table 12.1 on page 231.

CHAPTER 13

INITIATING OR LEADING
MAJOR CHANGE

All influence is about making change.
Whether you are in charge of a new product development process, a change
in organization structure, the implementation of a new compensation system—or have a great idea for a new and different business or a change such
as altering your supply chain to save millions—there will be many people
and groups to influence. But there are some special aspects to leading a major
change effort or to initiating one on behalf of a goal you care about.

Because influence requires giving something of value in return for what
you need, there are key challenges in acquiring the needed influence to
make a major change happen. You will have to influence people above or
to the side of you in the hierarchy, getting them to provide resources, information, support, or approval. You will have to cope with and master
organizational politics. You will have to assemble a working team that believes in what you are trying to do. And you will need an incredible combination of patience and persistence, drive, and flexibility to keep your
ultimate goal in mind while adjusting along the way.

Change encompasses many different aspects of influence, so we urge you
to read the conceptual Chapters 2 through 7 and Practical Application chapters titled "Influencing Colleagues (12)," "Influencing Your Boss (8)," and
"Understanding and Overcoming Organizational Politics (15)." In addition,
you can gain great insights from two extended examples and their analyses on
our website. There you will find the experience of Monica Ashley, struggling
to overcome many barriers to developing and introducing an important but
controversial new product, and the experience of Will Wood, trying to obtain the funds and support to introduce online training into his organization

(http:www.influencewithoutauthority.com/monicaashley.html, and http://www.influencewithoutauthority.com/willwood.html).

While all of this material is relevant to producing major change, we explore a half-dozen concepts that are especially relevant to this area. Then you can see on our website how we apply these concepts to Will Wood's actual situation of introducing a major innovation to show how careful planning and persistent effort can produce successful change.

THE IMPORTANCE OF VISION

Develop a clear vision of what the change is to accomplish, in terms of its effect on customers and clients of the change. Vision is an important currency for attracting support for your change. Many people will respond more favorably if they can see how what you are pushing will make a difference—to the company, customers, or the public. It isn't the only currency you can use, but it is a good starter, and it appeals to many different people. If they can see the eventual good that will come from implementing the change, they are more likely to want to help, be more forgiving of mistakes, and be more inventive at thinking how they can support the effort.

A powerful vision paints a graphic picture of how its successful accomplishment changes the lives of some important group(s). It isn't just *what* will occur, but *why* it's important. It usually won't be as effective if all you can say is that it will make or save a lot of money, although for some high-level managers that might be an initial attention grabber (in all cases, adjust the currencies offered to the audience). At best, vision can help people see important meaning to their work—the sense that what they do matters to people. It grabs them and appeals to their best instincts, paying them in these good feelings.

This means you have to develop a good story (not a fictional one!) that you can tell at a moment's notice. Venture capital experts talk about "rocket pitches" or "elevator speeches" for entrepreneurs—the condensed, potent version of their business plan that they can complete in an elevator ride. They need to be able to differentiate their plan from others and quickly capture attention. You may not always have so little time to tell someone whose cooperation you need what your change is about, but important people are likely to be busy, so be prepared. If you have a compelling vision, but no good idea of how to make it happen, the vision won't be much help, but you can't execute a terrific plan if you can't get anyone's attention long enough to believe in it.

And remember that vision is basically about passion. So it has to be something that you feel passionate about.[1]

Link vision of change with the organization's core values, objectives, strategies, and present dilemmas. Though by definition any change you are trying to accomplish does something different from the way it is done now, you will make people less uncomfortable and, therefore, less likely to automatically resist if you show the connections to tradition and culture. Sometimes that is difficult, especially if you are convinced that the culture itself is what needs to change—for example, from inward looking and comfortable to customer focused and aggressive—but there usually are some connections that can be made. You may have to go back to a much earlier stage of the organization's history to remind people of a time when the company was some other way, but it is worth the effort. That helps to take the strangeness out of the new idea and help people stay open to it.

MANAGE TENSION

Vision not only lays out direction but also can create useful tension about the distance to go to realize the vision. Without some tension between the way things are now and the way they could be, there will be no movement. If the vision is compelling, it helps make clear the distance between the present and the desirable future state. If the vision is inspiring, but not impossible of ever being achieved, it creates a healthy tension about the gap. (If the vision is attractive, but your listeners don't think it achievable, you need to either show them that you see how to get there or reexamine your own assumptions about viability.) People are most ready to learn or change when they are experiencing moderate tension. Too much and they freeze (as with math anxiety); too little and they don't see the need to change.

You can use this insight not only to adjust your vision but also to create greater readiness to change in those you want to cooperate. You can make them more or less uncomfortable, either by stressing the gap between the present state and the desired future one or by focusing on all that is wrong with the present. Either can work, but telling colleagues about how bad things are risks making at least some of them more defensive, especially if they helped create present conditions. So use vision to create moderate discomfort when you can.

One of the interesting complexities about change is that some people are highly resistant, some eager to join, and many quite ambivalent, both fearful and curious. You may not be able to influence the extremes very well, but you want to pay a lot of attention to those who have mixed feelings and, therefore, mixed readiness. They are the ones who will respond best to moderate tension. You can increase tension by emphasizing the gap between the present and the future, going faster, making the dissatisfaction of customers or others more visible, and so on. And you can ease tension by slowing down, encouraging more reaction and thinking through the issues, honoring the past and present practices, spending more time educating people in whatever the new skills will be, and so on. Pay close attention to the people who are in the middle, and manage the tension to maximize their readiness.

IDENTIFY KEY STAKEHOLDERS WHO MUST BE INFLUENCED

For any change project, there will be many people with an interest in it—as recipients, those who implement it, managers, planners, those likely to be affected indirectly, and so on—who can have an impact on its eventual acceptance. This also includes those who will be the beneficiaries, those who will be negatively affected, and some outside groups such as the financial community or the press. From among this list, try to select all who will have to make important decisions to make your dream into a reality. These stakeholders should be identified as early as possible by systematically looking inside and outside the organization.

For each stakeholder (individual or group), decide which ones you absolutely have to influence, which would be nice to influence and win over, and any who can be ignored even though they may not be happy with the changes. Then focus on those who are must-wins.

For each stakeholder, try to determine the currencies they value, using any information you can get: first-hand knowledge and observation, what they say that can give clues as to what they care about, the situations they are in that might shape what they care about, and knowledge that you can get from colleagues. The concerns they raise about the change effort are good clues as to what is important to them. (See Chapters 3 and 4 for more information on identifying currencies and diagnosing the worlds of others when you don't know them.)

HOW TO INFLUENCE DISTANT STAKEHOLDERS WHO ARE DECISION MAKERS

The complications arise when you do not have direct personal knowledge of the decision makers whose support or approval you need. Here are some ways to make progress.

Table 13.1   Conditions Likely to Affect Decision Makers

Rate of growth in the economy
Rate of growth in the industry
Competition—domestic and foreign
Price trends
Dependence on raw materials, their availability, and process
Consumer trends
Interest rates
Legal climate
Dependence on unusual talent
Wall Street expectations

Does your list of decision makers include the CEO or someone reporting directly to him or her? How about the chief financial officer or equivalent? A technology guru? One or more division heads or country managers? The board? The organization's bankers? The earlier in the process you can identify them, the more time you have to do the homework needed to figure out what they care about and how you can provide them with what they would need to give you the decisions you want. For example, in the case of Monica Ashley, the product developer featured in the example on our website mentioned earlier, she had to influence the CEO, Gary Dorr; the senior management staff that worked with Dorr; an old-timer vice president, Ralph Parker, who was dug in against the technology she believed necessary; Ed Kane, Parker's nasty direct report assigned to the project; her boss, Dan Stella; senior scientist, Phil Edison; the board; and others. Some she knew well, and others she had to get to know and learn to deal with.

Once you have your list of decision makers, you can begin to understand their situations (their worlds) and determine the currencies they value. What will they need to know or have happen to gain their support?

Based on what you know, what are the likely pressures on them in their roles? Pressures will vary by the industry or sector the organization is in, its competitors, and context, but decision makers will also usually be affected by well-known forces in the economy and political world. Some of the common conditions likely to affect decision makers are listed in Table 13.1.

Which of these conditions are the decision makers likely to be thinking and worrying about? What keeps them up at night? The higher the position of the decision maker, the more long-term issues are likely to be in the forefront of his or her thinking and the greater the expectations and influence of the external financial community. What will your change do to share price (or bond rating), and how will it be received? Will the press respond in some way, and does the decision maker think about organizational reputation? (As this is being written, many well-known executives are being tried and some convicted for some form of financial manipulation or fraud; is that an issue for the company or industry?) Again, the higher the position, the more considerations of overall organizational benefit are likely to be important.

The decision maker's role and scope of responsibility will also shape what the person pays attention to. Is the person automatically focusing on supply chain issues and possible disruptions or on customer preferences and shifting demand? Is a particular region on the radar screen, or does the role call for only domestic focus—or constant global scanning?

A rich source of what might be important to the decision maker is anything that the person has been quoted as saying, whether in the annual report, a speech, internal memos, or articles about the organization. Discounting for the caution and public relations' sanitizing of public statements, a great deal still can be inferred. Even if what the executives are saying is a reflection of what they want you to think, that still reveals much that is important to them. Just try to notice whether they are talking about growth and innovation or cost cutting. And beware the executive who "doth protest too much" that things are going beautifully; it can be difficult to distinguish clear signaling from whistling in the dark, but if you listen closely and know the company, you can probably tell.

This background checking will help you come up with an appeal that might speak to decision makers' concerns. Then you can try to tie what you need to supplying some of what they might need or want. In this vein, can you sense what information they might not have that they would find useful? If you have a sense of their likely concerns, you may be able to deduce what you know that would be helpful or otherwise inaccessible to them.

Is Your Elevator Pitch Ready?

Since these key decision makers may not be easily available to you, you have to be ready to tell them your vision and how they can help in a condensed way, at a moment's notice. This is where you can use your change vision—the 30-second "rocket pitch" or elevator speech that you can pull out in an instant if you happen to be on the elevator or walking down the corridor with one of the decision makers. At Montefiore Hospital some time ago, a number of executives sheepishly confessed that they had discovered that one of the few ways to get ideas to the world-famous and notoriously busy director of the hospital complex was to study his schedule and then be casually reading the bulletin board outside his office, "accidentally" bumping into him when he came out to go somewhere, and quickly mentioning their current project or requests. Whether he ever caught on to this mild deception or just played along, everyone benefited. If you were lucky enough to be on a flight with one of your key decision makers, would you be ready to capture his or her attention in a few sentences and then get the chance to make your case?

Influence the Influencers They Listen To

If you do not have easy direct access, can you find out to whom they listen and how to get to those people? If you identify the influencers of the people you want to influence, you still have to do an influence job, but it may be with someone who is easier to talk with or to get information to. You will have to find valuable currencies for the influencers, utilizing the same kind of reasoning explained throughout this book.

There are some other external methods for getting to key decision makers, but they are definitely difficult. You can find more information on indirect influence methods in Chapter 14, but here are a few ideas. Can you get to the press or write an article extolling the merits of the change idea you are working on and the benefits to the company? That can help shape opinion. (For an inspiring example of using a press relationship to help promote change, see the description of raising interest in wind power on our website, http://www.influencewithoutauthority.com/montanamiracle .html.) Are there customer or employee groups you can be placing ideas with? Would a customer survey yield useful information about potential demand or an employee survey be available that can be interpreted in a favorable way? You have to be very careful not to be seen as doing anything that can be interpreted as illegitimate for your role or as undermining the company, but if you keep it positive and in celebration of the organization and its accomplishments, it is less risky.

WHAT DO YOU HAVE TO OFFER?

Do a careful diagnosis of what currencies you have that could be valuable to each of the key stakeholders. Some of the currencies you command are obvious going in, such as your reputation for hard work, expertise on the change, track record in getting things done, and, as we have suggested, vision of the benefits. But some may be recognizable only when you see what stakeholders care about. For example, one key stakeholder may feel strongly about fair treatment of employees, and you may be able to see that your plan (or an adjusted version of it) could protect employees from layoffs.

You constantly should be looking for what you can offer as a payment to each stakeholder. Remember, these payments can be explicit, such as promising his or her division early input on the design of the new product, or implicit, such as the feeling of pride that he or she was able to help move the organization in a positive way. What will be received as valuable can be quite different for different stakeholders, who may care a lot about doing good or far more about getting bonuses or the chance to gain visibility to top management. The same project can have differing payoffs to different people; in fact, the same payoff may have different meanings to people. Your praise to the stakeholder's boss can be seen as helping a promotion opportunity or a form of appreciation that reinforces feelings of professionalism. Stay open to the possibilities.

For stakeholders to whom you have little to offer, is there someone else with valuable resources who can be in a three-way deal? For example, a skeptical department is holding you back. You have nothing to offer directly, but you might be able to make a trade with another group—such as, "Loan me two analysts, and your division will get first crack at the final product"—then use that people commitment to demonstrate the value of the project to the doubting department and gain grudging support.

When you are stuck, treat those who are not cooperating as temporarily mismatched with the currencies you can muster, not as enemies. You may not change their minds, but the way you respond to those who disagree will determine whether they only disagree or dig in because they are not being treated well. One cause for resistance is enough!

In his book on influence, Bellman says there are four important ways to influence upwards:[2]

1. Respect your superiors.
2. Treat them with the charity you would like toward you.
3. Deliver what they want.
4. Understand the wider organizational pressures they are under.

These all make sense; use the concepts we have added to learn more about what others are likely to care about so that you can deliver what they truly want or help them to see that cooperation will get them what they want even though at first blush they may not have seen the connection.

DIAGNOSE AND ENHANCE THE RELATIONSHIP

As with anyone you want to influence, starting with a good, trusting relationship will make it easier. (That's why the most influential people in organizations often have the most relationships long before they need anything in particular.) But not all important stakeholders will turn out to be close colleagues. You may have to work on establishing at least a minimum of trust to gain their willingness to work with you.

Although we have personally encountered a handful of people in organizations who were truly inept at making relationships, most people can do it if they are focused on it, rather than thinking they are too busy to bother. It starts with tuning in to others and their interests and can be done by social conversation or by doing small trades where you take the initiative to give first, thereby establishing your worthiness.

One important way to enhance a relationship is to listen closely to each stakeholder you don't already know. Not only are you likely to learn a lot about what matters to him or her, but also being listened to and taken seriously is a valuable currency to almost everyone. If you are responsive and demonstrate that you have thoroughly understood the other person, you do not need to make spectacular comments to be seen positively. However, asking another's opinion with no intention of seriously considering it, is usually transparent and doesn't buy you anything but tends to backfire by building mistrust.

How you approach the person or group is another aspect of building relationships. Some people are happy to directly discuss any bad history between you, while others just won't engage in that kind of conversation. If you perceive that they aren't going to be comfortable with such directness, do not wade in just because you are willing or prefer it that way. Go slow, test a bit, and if you get signals to back off, try another less direct path. Can you find common business topics or outside interests to chat about? Do you have any mutual friends who can casually arrange a get-together or common meeting or, as in Japan, intercede on your behalf? It might be that you have to first build a relationship with someone they trust, who can eventually serve as a door opener.

If you have no way of forming enough of a relationship to be able to make exchanges or have no mutual valued currencies to trade—and the stakeholder is critical to your project's success—you may have to slow down or even find another change to pursue. But don't give up too quickly. If you use the influence approaches we have been discussing, it is often possible to find a way to connect with apparently impossible stakeholders.

One further important aspect of dealing with relationships: Everyone has stylistic preferences as to how he or she wants to be interacted with. When selling a change project, you need to figure out whether stakeholders want to be in on early thinking or see well-developed plans. Would they be insulted by anything less than several years of financial projections in spreadsheet form, or do they like early back-of-the-envelope estimates to get a feel for the magnitude of the payoff? Will the lack of endorsement from a key technical person or department kill the discussion, or does the person like to proceed as if technology perfection can come later? Does the person like to hear the big picture concept first or a lot of details showing thoroughness? These kinds of stylistic preferences can be a huge barrier or enabler, so it is worth doing your homework. Someone you have a good relationship with will know the person's preferences if you don't and would be willing to tell you.

DEVELOP YOUR EXCHANGE STRATEGY

Before you move forward, think about whether there is still information you need or assumptions you need to check out. The same concept of listening closely applies here.

Next, think about the sequence of whom to approach. There are three variables to juggle as you think about how to proceed:

1. Your relative power.
2. The likeliness of a positive response.
3. How critical the other's support is.

Are there some key people who are likely to be early supporters, so you want to get them lined up? Early wins help. Are there stakeholders whose support will bring along many others? What are your chances with them? Do you need to work through issues first with some less prominent people to be sure that when you approach the opinion leaders, you have a strongly developed case? Are there stakeholders who have necessary expertise to improve your idea? You may want to get to them early. Is there anyone who is likely to be negative if he or she is not in on the ideas from the beginning? Are there important stakeholders who are so busy that you get only one short shot, so they should be held until near the end when you have many other pieces in place?

Finally, are there some stakeholders who will cooperate only if you shape the concept to fit their interests? Do you want to see them early so that you can more easily accommodate their views? Or wait until you have enough in place to narrow the territory for discussion? It is important to reflect on these questions early; you may not get it right, but plunging in may get you too far down the road to retrace your steps with some critical players. Some answers may become clear only when you start to produce change. Be open to new information and modify your approach accordingly.

CHANGE ROLES: MOVING AMONG DIFFERENT-SIZE GROUPS

For any major change project, in addition to the change champion (you) and a sponsor (individual or team) at higher levels, you will need to have a small working team to manage the process (the core team) and occasions when greater numbers of people will be included, individually or at large meetings.

How many to involve, and at what times, is another aspect of strategy. Too restrictive an in-group can let you go much faster but leave out critical stakeholders whose support or opposition will determine ultimate success. Involving too many stakeholders or involving them too early can be wonderfully inclusive, generating lots of ideas and feedback, but it can be so unmanageable and difficult to shape toward final decisions that the project gets paralyzed.

The solution? Use the *accordion method*. There are times for large, many stakeholder meetings and times to squeeze down to small, core group meetings. Don't stick to only one. Small groups can develop a first cut at the change, and then large groups can give reactions and ideas to pursue. Then go back to a small group for homework, back out to a larger group for reaction and suggestions, and then have the small core group do the plan, which finally rolls out to the larger group. Don't try to make decisions in large, multiconstituent groups or hide them in the small core group.[3]

PLANNING VERSUS CALCULATION

Because you have to do comprehensive planning for change, you need to be careful that in executing your plans you do not become mechanical or manipulative, which can backfire. For example, there is definitely a difference between (a) taking stakeholders to lunch to get to know them, using the conversation to better understand them, and in the process feeling closer; and (b) being totally instrumental in the conversation, mechanically feigning interest but only going through the motions. Occasionally you will encounter someone so hungry for attention that they are easily fooled, but much more often, the recipients of phony interest sense it and are turned off. Once they suspect that they are being courted just to get them to do something, they become more resistant.

Here's an example we witnessed firsthand. A rather inept manager who was trying to get independent professionals to collaborate had developed almost no support. She couldn't proceed without allies, but wasn't making progress. Her manager advised her of the key players with whom she would have to form at least cordial working relationships. A few days later, he ran into one of the people he had identified, who exclaimed, "I just had the strangest visit from Hannah. She came to my office unexpectedly, and I couldn't figure out what she wanted. It was so strange; I felt like I was being checked off some kind of list!"

No one wants to feel so depersonalized, or made into an object. Thus, while compliments, friendly small talk, little gifts, various favors, or even valuable resources may be offered, unless there is sincerity behind them, they can readily backfire. It is like giving a fake Rolex; it may look nice at first, but after a few minutes, the glitter fades. You can hardly expect deep gratitude.

But if you are genuinely interested in the colleagues you approach, that will come through, and you will receive a fair degree of latitude in the transactions that follow. In fact, once you have a good relationship, you can sometimes be more tough-minded in your requests for cooperation. *As long as you can show that your overt offer is in the other person's best interests, you can go straight to the point.* With a good colleague, it is possible to say something as direct as, "Listen, I need help, and I know it will be a pain for you to do it. So I'm going to tell you how much I need you, and how terrific you are, and ask you to help me in return, because this will make a difference to our customers." That kind of statement would be deadly with someone who is a stranger, or who you were just hustling for a one-time favor, but a friend would smile and try to respond if possible. You would be trying to do something worthwhile by trading on the good history, and your friend would presume that he or she could do the same with you when in need.

For an example that illustrates the principles discussed in this chapter, see the extended case study of a training manager figuring out how to get financial and organizational support for an innovative online training system at http://www.influencewithoutauthority.com/willwood.html.

FURTHER IDEAS ABOUT CHANGE

Because organizational change can be so complicated, there are related issues that require separate (but relevant) chapters. Sometimes the decision makers are hard to reach, or unlikely to pay much attention to what you want without considerable ingenuity. For more on ways of coping with this challenge, see Chapter 14, "Indirect Influence." In larger organizations, there can be many complexities of introducing change that arise from the varied interests and power of different groups, departments, divisions, and geographies. A victory from one point of view can cause other stakeholders to become opponents. To go deeper into this complex territory, see Chapter 15, "Understanding and Overcoming Organizational Politics."

CHAPTER 14

INDIRECT INFLUENCE

There are times when you can't directly influence a key stakeholder. You may be too far away in the hierarchy, in a position or location where there is no access to important line managers, representing an unpopular or radically new point of view, or even outside the organization (a supplier, customer, or community member). The basic approach is similar to the one on influencing decision makers spelled out in Chapter 13, "Initiating or Leading Major Change," but there are a few additional things you can do to, in effect, make exchanges when you aren't present. You want to change someone's mind or get the person into a more receptive mode so that he or she will move in the direction you desire.

In addition to figuring out what might be important to the person or group you wish to influence, you want to see whether you can influence the person or organizational systems that influence your stakeholder. You may also be able to find ways to mobilize outside forces of some kind that will have an impact.

UNDERSTANDING THEIR WORLD FOR LIKELY CONCERNS, SENSITIVITIES

How can you figure out what might be important to distant stakeholders?

Collecting Information from a Distance

Let's assume you are far away from that stakeholder (outside the organization, far down the organization, or in a division that has a totally different purpose or product). You can start with what you know about the indus-

246

try and the socioeconomic forces acting on it. If you know the growth rate of the industry, its competitors, issues of the economy, supplies vulnerabilities, customer and employee trends, and the like, you can often narrow the likely concerns of the people you want to influence, depending on their positions in the organization.

This knowledge can be supplemented with what the business press and the financial analysts have written about the organization. Has the organization been under attack for anything? For example, even well-regarded companies such as Nike and Donna Karan have been attacked for the treatment of employees at their overseas suppliers. Merrill Lynch and Morgan Stanley have been accused of discriminating against women. Microsoft and GE have been written about as maturing companies struggling to find new growth. In each case, it is a reasonable bet that such matters are on the top executives' minds.

Another way to see what executives are thinking is to read their interviews and speeches. Internal memos, if you have access to them, also help. There are numerous such sources to check. Nettie Seabrooks, who started as a librarian at General Motors, was able to use this kind of information to predict what would be the concerns of top executives there and give them information that they would value She became increasingly valuable, and moved into more responsible roles. (For the full account of Nettie's career, see our web site, http://influencewithoutauthority.com/nettieseabrooks.html.)

In addition, you might be able to ask other people in the organization about what senior executives are likely to be focused on these days. That kind of inquiry is legitimate and can always be justified as part of your development "to help you get the bigger picture."

Impact of Organizational Systems

Other areas of influence on those you want to impact are the organization's measures, reward system, procedures, and practices. Organizational members respond to these components of the organization as well as to the way individuals interact with them. For example, the costs that are allocated to different departments can be important shapers of behavior. Can you find a way to alter the formula or challenge particular cost allocations that impact behavior? Similarly, how sales are credited when many departments are involved often affects behavior. Many disputes between departments or locations are caused by the cost or revenue allocation systems; you might reduce resistance or increase cooperation if you can find a way to alter them.

Example of IBM Manager Affecting Measures in Order to Shape Behavior of Managers She Wanted to Influence

Mary Garrett, a marketing manager at IBM, was working on a way to get the co-operation of the CEOs who headed the geographical offices. Their boss, the head of services, could help. Mary began with frequent interaction with him to enhance the relationship, and he decided to add a relevant measure to the way the geographic executives were judged:

> I go to the head of services once every six weeks and tell him how I'm doing. He knows I have to convince his direct reports (the geography heads) and not him. It is internal PR. You have to pilot, get their commitment, invest a little at a time, see it taking off—then you have their hearts and minds.
>
> The head of services is helping me by reviewing progress with them (his direct reports) and supports me, but he won't order them to do what I want. He will help by changing their metrics to recognize this.
>
> Doug, my boss's boss, knows I need some assistance on this one. He said, "Go meet with the CFO; get this included in the metrics. Go to him with your boss." That shows the CFO that the big boss thinks this is important. If progress on this initiative is part of their reporting metrics, they will see it as important. What I want is not in their normal set of metrics. Now, by having it included, they have to be articulate on it and know whether they're ahead or behind plan. I just explained to the CFO (who reports to Doug), "Doug said we want to include this in monthly forecasting reviews." Doug has bought in because he is intellectually intrigued by this area. At a recent meeting with 300 of his top managers, he said, "We haven't cracked the code on this, but Mary Garrett has staked her personal reputation on this; she has it figured out." He was being funny, but signaling that he thinks it is important. He's also saying to me, "You have to sell this to the area CEOs and convince them that it is worth investing in. They make the decision on their own. I won't force it on them." He trusts them as GMs to make trade-offs in their own areas. I'm doing it through pilots and experiments, and then they observe the results.

Depending on your position, you can gain more or less access to the systems and procedures or to those who can signal the importance of what you do. But where you can, think about how systems, measures, and procedures influence behavior, and try to alter them when possible. Because these are less personal than face-to-face influence methods and take a while to take hold, there often will be less interest—and opposition.

Who Influences Them?

Who influences stakeholders is information that may be more difficult to come by, but if you can figure out who your stakeholder listens to, as Mary

Garrett did, you can decide whether you might have access to these influencers. In most organizations, unless you are a total newcomer or hermit, there is probably no more than three degrees of separation to any particular person, and someone you know may at least know who is close to the person or group you are interested in.

Most organizations also have behind-the-scenes experts who seem to know everyone and are sought out for their opinions and their connections to people and what is going on. Find out who they are, and see if you can get access into their network. Provide useful information, ask them for advice (most people like to be paid in the currency of listening to their opinion), and be supportive, and you may gain an ally who has the ear of key people.

It also may be as straightforward as asking your boss for help. As Mary Garrett put it:

> I learned on another project where I was fighting alone. I went to my boss, and he said, "I'm mad at you because you didn't come to me sooner; that's wasting time, since I can fix it in one phone call." I said to myself, "Whoa!" I had thought that once you are an executive, you don't ask for help. He said, "You need to know when to ask for help. No matter how much authority you have, at times you will need help." If I tried this current project on my own, I'd be dead.

In any event, you have to figure out how to get influencers to help you. This requires going through the same process of figuring out what their currencies are so you can offer what they value in return for their help. Don't overlook the possibility that being asked for help is in itself a valuable currency for many managers because it is a sign of respect for their ability and clout and a chance to feel good about being helpful—not to mention that it can create a debt for you that they will someday be able to collect on.

Naturally, the other people have to see as worthy what you are pushing, or none of these currencies are so likely to come into play. And it helps if you have a good reputation, so even if they aren't so sure about the idea, they trust that if you are behind it, it is probably okay. But this is something you can't generate at the last minute.

Educational Systems

Another form of indirect influence is to introduce educational activities to the organization, encouraging the people you want to influence to take part. These don't have to be formal educational programs but "education" defined broadly. For example, would it be useful to arrange visits to organizations already doing something like what you want to introduce? Hearing counterparts talking about their own feelings when the idea was introduced, how they feel now that it is embedded, and even watching it in action can be more persuasive than when you talk about it.

Sometimes, it is possible to bring a relevant program or speaker to the company and invite important stakeholders to attend. For example, in many companies there are occasional talks given to top management "to keep them up to date." If you can get to whoever schedules those talks and suggest a speaker who is a good advocate for the concept or innovation you are behind, you can stimulate interest without even being present. You have to exert influence to get the right person invited, but the person who does the scheduling may be grateful for the suggestion because it is probably a nuisance to manage.

We must, however, acknowledge that this method isn't foolproof. Tom Stallkamp, former president of Chrysler, told us about the time after the merger with Daimler that he wanted to get Daimler executives to consider some of the American methods for radically transforming organizational processes. He brought Michael Hammer, one of the inventors of reengineering and a forceful speaker, to address the executives. According to Stallkamp, Hammer just seemed loony to them; Jurgen Schremmp, the managing director, pulled Tom aside and said, "Who is this guy? We certainly don't want to change so much at once!" Any form of education has to hit the right buttons or it will be wasted.

Management training programs can also be useful. You might be in a position to sponsor one and to influence what is discussed and who is invited to visit it. But even for ongoing training you don't run, there will often be management development and training people responsible who are eager to have support from top management but who aren't powerful enough to directly obtain it. You might suggest a "condensed demo version," offered to the top group just so "they will know what is being taught to middle managers." The demo needn't be billed as education for them, which might make them resistant, but as a way to help them do their senior roles. A variation is to request that a key top manager or two be asked to address the middle managers and then to use the occasion to invite discussion that could be enlightening to the speaker. You don't have to be duplicitous about your invitation; just focus on one aspect of it—the top person's expertise being shared—and let the incidental upward education happen naturally.

If you are a reasonably good presenter, you might be able to get a guest appearance yourself, where you are "providing useful information" about an important topic and not directly advocating for your idea. An intriguing presentation, with well-chosen examples, can launch the right kind of discussion, where the initiative to learn more—and with luck become convinced of value—remains with the participants.

Do you have a company magazine or newsletter? The editor is often eager for articles and features, and you might write an educational piece for that. Nettie Seabrooks, mentioned previously as one of the managers featured on our web site, did just that at General Motors, with no particular agenda. But it certainly didn't hurt her reputation, and some executives may have been informed about things that mattered.

In short, you can seek opportunities to introduce new ideas, stimulate interest and possibly discussion, and discover a convert or new ally along the way.

Mobilizing External Forces

A different source of potential indirect influence is outside the organization. The press, customers, government, trade associations, and so on are potential places to gain indirect pressure for what you want. The question is how to get access to them in a way that is supportive.

One place to start is by writing an article for a local paper about either the general phenomenon that you are interested in or the accomplishments of your organization in that area. Local papers—or radio and TV stations—are often hungry for material, and you can be a provider. Trade association magazines are another place to get published, and you can seek opportunities to make speeches at trade meetings. Not only does this help position you as an expert internally, but also the buzz may get back to the decision makers you ultimately want to influence. The challenge is to get positive publicity for your initiative.

You want to be very careful about being associated with negative publicity because no company management wants that, even though fear of it can be quite motivating in directions you care about. Unless you are prepared to be fired, proceed with caution.

Just as you will want to have your elevator speech ready to talk with internal people on a moment's notice, have it ready as you move around the community, go to meetings or conferences, and talk with friends. It is a very small world, and you don't know whom you might get interested and how that person could help you in unpredicted ways. For a wonderful example, see the box on pages 252–253.

The concern with indirect influence connects to a related set of issues: how to understand, use, and overcome organizational politics, which is the subject of Chapter 15.

Paul Westbrook: Gaining Support for Sustainability at Texas Instruments

A wonderful example of using personal interests outside of work to help promote an important initiative comes from Paul Westbrook, a project manager of worldwide construction at Texas Instruments. Paul is passionate about sustainable practices in companies out of concern for environmental degradation and a long-standing distaste for waste. There is a modest movement growing in the United States around these concerns, but many enthusiasts within companies have trouble getting anyone in power to respond. Texas Instruments has a significant number of environmental and sustainable efforts at its facilities around the globe, but Paul wanted to find the lever to move the company to the next level. Meanwhile, his passion had also led him to use green techniques when building his house, which used passive and active solar energy.

Paul has a BA in mechanical engineering and started at Texas Instruments right out of school 21 years ago. He had always worked in facilities operations of the company, for example, clean room design and management, and enjoyed it. But he had not given up on his dream of raising the bar on more sustainability.

When he heard that there was a possibility of building a new wafer fabrication plant, he thought that it might be a possible starting point. He knew that it was always easier to use sustainable practices in a new building designed from scratch, rather than trying to retrofit existing facilities. He was worried, though, because semiconductor fabs are so expensive to build that usually companies take the last design and do minor incremental changes, rather than attempt breakthrough approaches.

He went to a vice president he had previously worked with, who has always been passionate about sustainability and has often been his sounding board. In fact, she was the originator of the term "ZERO wasted resources," which has become an environmental movement slogan. Together, they started to scheme about how to get the senior vice president (SVP) of manufacturing to buy the idea. In the course of that discussion, Paul asked whether it might be a good idea to bring the SVP to his solar house to see what was possible. She thought it was a great idea and agreed to join the visit.

Paul invited the vice president of worldwide manufacturing, a vice president of an existing fab, and Texas Instrument's chief technology officer on a tour of his solar house. The executives invited on the tour were engineers and were very interested in the engineering aspects of the house. At the end of the tour, Paul showed them his utility bill. The average energy cost for his house had been $60 a month, while regular home energy bills average $150 to $200 a month. He said, "You could see the light bulb turn on." They moved from asking technical questions about how the house functioned and started asking more business-related questions such as whether it could scale to an office building or factory, what kind of support he would need to make this happen, and so on. This then led to conversations about logistics of the project and how to proceed.

Eventually, they decided to go ahead. Paul's boss put him in charge of sustainability, rather than assigning him to just one function such as air conditioning, so Paul can work as an integrator of design ideas and practices. He is constantly seeking full integration.

Paul and his colleagues are committed to having the plant be built in the United States. Because labor rates are so much lower in other parts of the world where many fabs are now built, there is tremendous pressure to keep costs low and constant questions about any added costs for sustainability. To jumpstart the process, Texas Instrument leaders spent three days brainstorming ideas on how to make the facility more environmentally friendly. The team developed a list of "want-to-haves" and "need-to-haves," and rigorously sorted what was needed. To help the process, Paul developed a formula for overall return on investment, and got the team to agree that the sustainable items would be built if it were possible to show the equivalent of a 5 year simple payback. All costs are contained within that formula, making it easier to make decisions.

Along the way, he also developed a way to track the impact of decisions that involve capital spending. He calls it "capital cost trading." When a spending idea is proposed for capital equipment needed for environmental purposes, he looks at all related costs and how they are impacted. For example, if a series of conservation measures looked expensive, Paul was able to show that the investment would make it possible to eliminate an entire chiller, which would have been about as expensive. The conservation measures were not an incremental cost when everything was taken into account. In this way, total costs are kept within bounds. His fellow engineers are now very enthusiastic about designing for sustainability.

Notice that Paul was able to get interest when he showed his personal example in his own house and that, at first, he got only a question about feasibility. The argument, however, was framed in terms of monthly energy savings, a currency that executives definitely valued. He didn't have to make up any numbers, but he did talk to them in terms they cared about, instead of in a currency he cared about far more, sustainability. It doesn't always turn out that you can make such a powerful argument in the other people's currencies, but his experience only reinforces the idea that you need to think of what the audience cares about, not just what you do. And the ability to make an impression outside of work helped a lot.

Note also that he developed accounting tools for demonstrating benefits to make ongoing decisions, which is another form of indirect influence—using systems to influence behavior. At this writing, the fab design is about 50 percent complete, with groundbreaking set for November 18, 2004.

CHAPTER 15

UNDERSTANDING AND OVERCOMING ORGANIZATIONAL POLITICS

Even when you're out to get something done—not to do someone in—you have to play politics.

—Michael Warshaw, "The Good Guy's (and Gal's) Guide to Office Politics," Fast Company, *April 1998*

Organizational politics—a dirty word, a cynical explanation of all that is disagreeable, a descriptive term, or an opportunity? Plenty of people are cynical about politics in organizations, by which they mean underhanded seeking of personal interests. That is one kind of politics, probably more aptly described as sheer nastiness. It doesn't take organizational life to find self-serving behavior.

This kind of behavior is *self-oriented politics,* in which the primary goal is only the benefit of the individual, with no concern for the overall organization or department. The people out for only themselves may use methods that are seen as duplicitous, such as saying opposite things about their opinions to different people, giving false compliments to curry favor, harming colleagues by innuendo, or spreading false rumors.

These kinds of distasteful behavior are certainly unpleasant and do occur. But often, more innocent behavior gets interpreted by others as self-seeking or underhanded because the motives or style of the offender aren't clear. Bad, personal motives are attributed to the person, and no one tests the motives with the person because if you already believe he or she is nasty, it feels too risky to take a chance on unnecessary interaction. Be sure you aren't leaping to negative conclusions.

The second kind of political behavior is awareness of the organization as political, in the sense that different groups have different assignments and interests. You can't be fully effective if you don't understand this more benign but potent form of organizational politics, in which unique and idiosyncratic customs develop and impact behavior.

THE NATURE OF ORGANIZATIONS

The sources of the second form of politics have to do with the nature of organizations. No matter how clever the designers of an organization, it is impossible to plan and predict all the ways that people and groups will have to interact. The *formal* organization is a blueprint, but in everyday life, many improvisations will arise to fill in the gaps that can't be adequately accounted for. These improvisations inevitably create an *informal organization,* in which some individuals and groups do more or less than expected—and needed—to make the organization function. Just think, for example, of how important the assistant to the president can become because some things require immediate attention and others can be stalled. Some people who want appointments are obnoxious while others are pleasant, some executives need information that isn't widely available, certain customers can't be ignored, and so on. Over time, the assistant develops ways of responding that go beyond simple rules or policies set by the president because judgment is needed to cope with new situations. The responses become a pattern, and soon informal arrangements become more routine. The three executives who are favored may get together for coffee with the assistant from time to time, and topics are discussed that aren't formally required. Multiply these kinds of informal arrangements many times, and soon the organization chart would need constant revision by a professional mapmaker to reflect the actual distribution of interaction and decision making. Organizations would be less efficient and effective without the informal organization existing alongside the formal one.

As a result of the informal organization (and partly causing it), individuals accrue more or less influence depending on their individual knowledge, past jobs, personal history, competence, and so on. Not infrequently, people who on the charts should have little power actually have a lot, and vice versa. If you want to get things done, it is important to know who is who and what actual influence they have.

In addition, through the natural bumps in work outcomes and the collision of work styles, organizational members develop a variety of feelings about one another and about whole groups of people. This history is very much present, even though it may just be "understood" and the original sources of tension long forgotten.

Furthermore, parts of organizations, created to accomplish different goals and activities, tend to pursue those goals, sometimes at the expense of the total organization or other parts. This isn't a sign of selfishness or bad corporate citizenship; it is just inherent in the design. Somehow there will have to be decisions, and the effort of each group to influence the decisions in their favor is exactly what politics is about. Thus, *politics* refers to pursuit of interests; it would be strange if each area did not do that. (And, the job of leadership is to find a way to make the overall organizational goals at least as attractive, so components pull together.)

Organizations also all have some kind of history, their preferred procedures or protocols for how to get things done, certain individuals who are the key gatekeepers and trendsetters, and certain symbols that have to be invoked. Many members are aware of these, consciously or instinctively, and operate within the preferred structure.

This way of looking at organizational politics implies that part of your job is to understand the dynamics and inevitable conflicts, accept them as part of organizational life, and learn to work through them to accomplish your work. Savvy organizational members take all of this into account as they proceed. Knowing the landscape is part of effectiveness. But knowing it, and working through and around it, does not demand that anyone descend into personal politics of the worst kind. It might be tempting, but it seldom leads to good long-term results. Therefore, don't put down politics. Don't be "above" the politics. That attitude is not only naïve but also a harsh judgment that reality is "bad" and, in its own way, is just as political a position. Avoidance or scorn means giving away power, while engaging in an underhanded, secretive, or nasty way creates poisonous relationships and eventually will hurt your reputation. Play hard, but fair.

CULTURE DETERMINES THE WAY POLITICS ARE PLAYED

Organizations differ in terms of their cultural beliefs about politics. First, there is great variance in terms of how easily they accept the idea that it is okay for a department or project to actively pursue its own interests. While no one would argue that departmental interests do not count, they might well think that departmental benefits should be only a by-product of doing good work for the organization. In other organizations, the pursuit of departmental self-interest is seen as natural and inevitable, and almost anything is fair game.

The second cultural difference is in terms of how well conflict among departments is accepted. In some, the very idea of conflict and opposing positions is frowned on, and differences are suppressed. Thus, conflict and opposing positions can operate only underground. If you work for or have been around many nonprofit organizations, you will recognize this pattern.

Alternatively, take a look at some companies in New York, where fighting is an art form, or at the auto companies. Certain high-tech companies have traditions of intense arguments and fighting out of a belief that truth resides with those who are loudest and most persuasive.

Get the Lay of the Land

For you, the important lesson is to know what game you are in. You don't have to descend into petty backbiting just because you are in an organization where that goes on, but staying back and saying "tsk, tsk" to yourself will leave you completely out of the action. Conversely, you don't want to assume that everyone will cheerfully wade into arguments just because you prefer it that way. And you need to take into account how legitimate it is to overtly pursue your department's interests and to be upfront about what you are after. *Know what game you are in* is one of the first rules for effectiveness. (This rule is parallel to the relationship advice we give about understanding how individuals prefer to be approached.)

When you have to get something done that is likely to touch other areas, finding out the rules of engagement is part of the work. Just as we advocate understanding what is important to the individuals you want to influence by giving something of value for what you want, understand what is important in the organization. Figure out how the game is played.

Seek Help

If you are relatively new and don't know, ask. You can seek out old timers or people who seem well connected, and ask how things work. In Table 15.1 on page 258, we provide some of the kinds of questions you can ask to understand how things work and how to proceed.

Table 15.1   Questions to Help Determine How to Operate Consistently within the Political Climate of the Organization

What are the hot buttons of various key stakeholders?

Where are the land mines buried; what are the loaded issues?

Who are the powerful but hidden people?

Who are the kingmakers?

Are there people with (established) connections to the top that you have to be careful not to cross?

Who have to be courted to make sure they don't oppose you even if they do not fully agree with your plans?

What are the unspoken rules for getting along?

DIAGNOSE STAKEHOLDERS

All of the preceding is background work to doing a diagnosis of each important player or group in the organization. As a start, if you tune in to the culture and politics, you will do a better job of identifying who is important and will have to be dealt with. Knowing the key stakeholders is critical to success.

Influence happens when you can provide something valuable to the person you want to influence in return for what you want. (Some people might argue that being so clear about how influence works encourages organizational politics, but the politics of interests are built in, as we discussed earlier.) To deal with the natural interests of individuals and groups that might not be compatible with what you want or have to offer, you need to understand each of them very well. Besides the obvious departmental benefits, what are the many other things that they care about? If you can figure that out, you have an increased range of possible areas to satisfy in making exchanges.

The 10 Commandments Exercise

We have often worked with management teams that wanted to reduce the negative politics of their organization or figure out how to make changes that would enable more people to succeed. A useful activity—one that you could do alone or ask veterans to help with—is the 10 commandments exercise. We ask, "If you wanted to help a terrific new hire learn quickly the way things work around here, what are the 10 commandments of the organization that aren't written down, but people know." The list is usually instructive and provokes good discussion.

In general, we advocate a direct approach and conversation about interests, and if you are in an organization where most people acknowledge the legitimacy of personal and departmental interests, you can ask. The question would go something like this: "I need your cooperation, and I know you will need to feel you are benefiting, too, so if you can tell me what matters to you, I will try to find a way to satisfy your goals." If, however, straight talk like that is frowned on or, worse, relationships have become so suspicious that asking feels as if it makes you too vulnerable, you will have to diagnose at a distance. Chapter 4, "How to Know What They Want," and Chapter 3, "Goods and Services: The Currencies of Exchange," give lots of advice on how to do this, but we can summarize and add to it here.

Think about the organizational situation of the various stakeholders. What are the pressures and forces acting on them? In the early part of this chapter, we talked about the way the culture is part of these forces, but there are others. What are their actual work assignments, and who are the other key players the assignments put them in interaction with? How are people measured and rewarded? How pressured are they? What technologies do they use, and what does that do to their ability to get the work done? What are the most typical educational backgrounds of the people in that area? Is there a history of tension with the group you work in? Do they always have problems with certain other areas?

The answers to these questions can help alert you to what is likely to be important to each stakeholder and allow you to frame your request and the payoffs to the stakeholder accordingly. They also can help you decide in advance how you want to talk to each important stakeholder about your plans. What you choose to emphasize will vary with how you see their interests and what they value; any complex influence attempt will have many possible benefits, and you want to be seen in the best light for each one. It isn't a matter of lying, but of knowing what to stress. If you can anticipate, for example, that one group is likely to be threatened by the potential impact of your initiative, then you will want to focus on some other benefits to them when you approach.

KNOW YOURSELF—AND HOW YOU WILL PROTECT YOURSELF

Dealing productively with the political system requires intense attention, complex trade-offs as you decide what to keep pushing and what to back off on, and considerable nerve as you navigate among competing points of view. Thus, it is especially important that you be clear on your objectives and aware of your own attitudes and values. What are your needs—your hot buttons—and where are you most likely to get thrown off balance? Your values and ethics will probably be tested, as you decide when to be completely open, when to say only what is necessary, and when to bluff. Thinking about how to fit what you say about the project to many different people and groups can be a burden and feel overwhelming. You will need great clarity about your objectives and boundaries. The more self-awareness you have, the less you will have to learn on the fly, when you are most pressured.

If you are in a very competitive organization, with a lot at stake for some groups, you may be faced with dirty, behind-the-scenes tactics being thrown at you, like those of the government official who admitted he sent blind copies of memos to embarrass other staffers or pretended to send a copy that he never sent. Stories of office treachery abound. While we don't advocate any of this, you would be wise to be prepared to deal effectively with similar incidents.

The challenge is to defend yourself without slipping into the same underhanded tactics that cover you with the mud being thrown. Chapter 16, "Hardball: Escalating to Tougher Strategies," looks more closely at how to defend yourself, but in general, getting such behavior out in the open is the best way to dry it up. Only if you have clear self-awareness and a measure of confidence can you continue to function when other people are subverting you and your efforts. Further, it is really helpful to think through how you would handle these kinds of situations ahead of time because when they happen, the first instincts are often rage at the injustice, leading to overreaction. You want to be able to stand back and plan your defense.

We illustrate with an extended example and analysis of navigating the organizational politics at a giant company. Fran Grigsby is a friend who is truly talented. She has held important management positions in a number of companies and now runs her own consulting firm. Some years ago, she moved from DEC to "Commuco," and soon found herself faced with a really tricky task in an organization with a tough culture. She was asked to head a project that most observers considered doomed, but it had been started by a respected senior manager who was still around and invested in it, and she had to figure out how to proceed. In this case, she recounts her experience, and what she learned about surviving organizational politics. Because she is a long-time friend, she was willing to reveal more about her thinking than is usually the case, though we have disguised the company and some details. Some of what she says may make you uncomfortable, but she managed to survive and do well, and it is worth learning from her. You might decide, as she did, that you don't want to play in such an arena, but this will help you figure out how to understand and use politics if you want to.

Working through a Truly Difficult Assignment— Killing a $100 Million Project of a Well-Liked Senior Peer and Navigating the Organizational Politics

I was recruited out of DEC to be vice president of program management for the information systems group at Commuco. This group was involved in everything that was not telephones and pagers. I was promised that if I did this functional job for a while, I would get to run a business. One month later, the head of information systems was moved; the new manager reorganized the group and gave me one of the four resulting businesses to run: Project SWITCH.

History of Project SWITCH

It had been going as a project for four years with 200+ engineers and marketing folks designing a complex, high-end, corporate, multipurpose telephone company (telco) switch. The business was being driven by the customers of telcos. Commuco had been oriented to the individual consumer. This was one of very few really big projects, for big companies. Commuco only knew wide-area networks; it didn't know the kinds of companies that were the telco customers.

This was a huge project, which was failing miserably at the time; they had already spent $100 million on it. The accepted truth around the company, which I had already heard as I got to know people, was that its software design was so badly planned and executed that you couldn't test if you were doing it right as you went along. You couldn't chunk it to test any subsystems. That's purely bad design. No software project is so complex it can't be divided up to see how subsystems are going; otherwise you have to get to the end to find out, and that's too late.

The project had been the brainchild of the Advanced Development vice president, my peer, a brilliant guy, who had persuaded the company to let him run the software side of development. In general, advanced development people don't know how to do production code, but he wanted to. It was both ill-designed software by people who didn't know how to do it, and money hemorrhaging at a time when the company couldn't afford it.

The Political Challenges

I was asked to take over this project, which was made a business, with all the elements for the first time under one manager, me. Those engineers, including the advanced development group, were transferred to me, and they also pulled marketing in. Plus there were political issues: There had been four years of hype, how wonderful the product was, how it would be the flagship for the company, visibility to the CEO in waiting. The vice president of advanced development had built his life on it, so all his fans in the company wanted it to succeed. The cash cow product at the time was turning more competitive, so there was pressure to succeed.

(Continued)

It was classic; a new boss who is pretty sure the project is a loser gives it to me, both of us were new. I should have said "No, just send me back to DEC."

It was clear I was new kid on the block in an old boy company, which was so old boy in style it took pride in "knuckle dragging"—old-fashioned male king-of-the-gorillas behavior. Since I was taking over his baby, I knew I'd have to do things the advanced development guy wouldn't appreciate. To counteract all the affection in my group for the vice president of advanced development, I realized I needed to work the internal power base. Whatever I did, I had to have some power support. I needed corporate level political cover.

It was clear to me from the beginning, though never said explicitly, that I would have to kill it. People in other parts of the company would tell me behind closed doors that the software code was so bad that to succeed you would have to throw it away and rewrite it from scratch, which would make it two years late for the market, so you will have to cancel it, even though $100 million was already spent. Everyone but the vice president of advanced development said that. He wanted to just let them keep working and maybe they will come up with something.

My first official task was to evaluate the project and decide what to do with it. That was actually fallacious because it was so clear it was bad. I knew I needed political cover, and I needed alternatives for the future because if it was canceled, we had too many engineers on hand. The question would be what to do with them. This was a healthy time for IT in general, so hiring good people was a challenge. Since after canceling the project we were going to identify new businesses to enter, I hated to lose these great skills we might need again.

I realized I was in trouble. It was a 'Why not just go fall off a cliff' kind of assignment. But I was challenged, "I can do anything," I thought foolishly. I did not worry that the vice president would undercut my decision; he was a logical and trustworthy person. However, I did feel that, in the eyes of the engineers in the organization, I would be seen as the adversary of this popular manager. This could hurt my ability to attract people for new ventures.

First I had to get internal support: I had to wean my own staff away from other loyalties. They all had long histories with this group and Commuco. I had to convince them there was something in it for them to be working with me. I gave them my personal commitment to manage them well and tell them the truth about the future of the group, and if it didn't work, offered them the promise of exciting new markets, interesting new technological challenges (for the engineers), the opportunity to identify opportunities, and do an internal start up. I can't say I completely converted all of them, but my strategy was to do as much as possible to give them a chance to be managed and productive. They had never been either. There was a payoff to them from getting work done, since as professionals they wanted to be productive. I gave them lots of product stuff to do which had nothing to do with this project. I gave them lots of external contact (since Commuco had been internally oriented); for example, I spent a substantial amount on consultants to provide professional education, pull knowledge in, sent them to conferences, and so on. That provided benefits for them. I also tried to hire a good engineering manager who had worked for me before. Someone with good engineering practices and who I could depend on. (Unfortunately, I couldn't get the ones I tried to get.)

Really important: I tried to have fun, like crazy. The stress was off the map; because of it we did all kinds of things (e.g., we gave insane birthday presents, like rubber chickens; top 10 birthday lists; had celebrations for no reason at all; decorated conference rooms; spread Nerf balls, foam bats, and things like that around, give them a reason to laugh, which we did a lot). We had to laugh because of so much stress. That worked really well; we lost only 2 to 8 staff during two really hard years. (And I still work with two of them on a regular basis, because we became close.)

Building Corporate Political Support

The job was to run and evaluate the project at the same time. I thought the only way to evaluate the project was to use Commuco corporate people to do it. If I went outside the company, they would have no credibility. Yet, I needed evaluators with some distance. I went to my boss's boss. I asked him to assemble us a team. He put together a competent cross-functional team from all over. (They were also politically savvy and well-connected.) After several visits to the project, they made the recommendation to cancel, which politically was very useful.

Also, I made the rounds, took several trips to talk to people at headquarters, including the soon-to-be CEO about what we were doing, how we were going about it, what the criteria would be. My message was, "y value add is being a really good manager (not a politician)," so I went around being clean and straight. Yes, this was a political pose, but it was all I had to offer. I couldn't ask anyone to run interference because I didn't even know who to ask. I hadn't been around the company for years to have a network already built to call on.

It went really well. When I canceled the project, there was very little corporate repercussion. I had talked to everyone, so they knew we were thinking about it. But built in to the assignment was that it was already in big trouble, we'd spent a fortune, but had already announced the product and done a market launch! I couldn't take that back, so I was doing the right thing paving the way, because there would be a big load of bricks falling when we ended it. There was the Corporate PR department to get involved, dealing with the press, all the groups in the company that were designing complementary products, and so on. So the real impact

(Continued)

was large, though I did what I could. I didn't get much fallout from the decision. I got a wave of e-mails, mostly from middle managers whose products were connected to our products, or who respected the vice president of advanced development, so they thought it a shame and that we should have found something else. But I got no peer or corporate flack.

I was worried about the vice president of advanced development's reactions but he laid that to rest. It became clear that I did not need to worry about him actively undermining my actions. I met regularly with him, first to familiarize myself with the project and his views about it, then to inform him about my decisions, then to jointly plan who would be laid off and which engineers would end up in his organization and mine. He was obviously sad about the project, and probably embarrassed since the failure had happened on his watch, but he did not talk openly about this. He retained his job because the organization still needed advanced development work done.

What to do with the people if we canceled the project? Our assignment was to get into corporate networking though the company was in other products. We had to find a profitable opportunity to use them. The last thing we wanted to do was lose the hard-to-find talent. At the time, there was new network technology (ATM), so networking was the obvious place. To keep the group productive and find new business, I made working teams to examine possible new businesses. We looked at ATM switches, adapter cards, servers with bits of old engineering from SWITCH, plus two other possibilities. We ran a tightly managed process with deadlines and milestones. That worked really well to get the team feeling they were not just doing failure work. The fact was that there were just no projects to use all 200 people. So when we canceled, I had to lay people off. I wanted to do it once and for all. Classic: quick and clean, but it still had a huge impact. First, I laid off 60 percent of the group.

It never makes sense to keep paying people if you don't have a job for them. I had laid off many people at previous jobs so my skin was pretty thick by this point. However, many of these engineers had poured heart and soul into this project and I empathized with their disappointment at seeing years of their work down the drain (i.e., not getting to the market).

I never have been under so much stress. I wanted it to go perfectly. It was a hero thing. I wanted it all to work, but it couldn't. I wanted to personally make up for four years of overspending, while no one had done anything but look the other way, but it was contrary to fact, and I just couldn't. Everyone knew it was the right decision, but the impact of breaking up the team, the flagship product for this group, connected widely in the company. There still is an "exSWITCH" mailing list (I'm just about the only non-engineer on it), so it was a tight group. No forward momentum could counteract all this, though I was trying. Everyone in the group got it; I didn't get hate mail from them. Not long after (in a kind of *deux ex machina*) the vice president for advanced development went on vacation with his wife and daughter, and he and the daughter were found dead, no one knew why or what happened. It was like a tangible symbol of how everything had fallen in on itself in this project.

His death made it harder to retain people, even those who didn't work directly for him, because he was the technology thought leader for all the businesses in our group. I had done all the right stuff, new projects were going on. I'd given back money that was otherwise being wasted, people were as energized as can be, but there was so much negative about the project work itself, and our inability to find successful new businesses, that it was stressful and sad.

Here I made a major influence mistake (in Commuco terms). There were a few odd businesses looking for homes, clearly not viable as moneymakers, but popular with senior people. I turned down the chance to run one, which was a mistake internally (though I was honest in saying it wouldn't make money). The other businesses didn't have enough political support to carry through the corporate rolling downsizing that was going on by that time. To protect people in the group, I should have taken these popular businesses that would have been supported even though they were not very profitable. Eventually the group was reorganized, and projects were canceled, including mine. Had I chosen politically popular businesses to run, the group would still exist, working on some possible projects. All of us had to go find new jobs. (After three years with the company, I left, because I was offered jobs in the headquarters city, and didn't want to move there.)

What burned me out was dealing with the old boys who thought good management was cursing you out. I saw I was so much the wrong kind of person for that environment. What I mean by Old boys: confrontation, when in doubt, fight, the management practice of having managers present to be excoriated in front of the group. Whenever I or my group came in to present to my manager, their approach was "How many holes in the presentation can you find?"—"I'm bigger and badder than you," throwing weight around—a four-letter word environment, bullying. At a big cross-company management meeting I attended, that was the average behavior. I realized it wasn't just my manager, it was the culture of the whole place. It's odd, because the CEO wasn't like that; he's intellectual, polite—and you usually think of it as coming from the top. I have been told that the culture was from a very successful acquired group, which meant that people were pulled out of there and seeded around, as was my boss. So maybe that was the culture only the three years I was around.

They certainly had no idea what to do with strong women. They didn't wonder if I was strong or tough enough, but my own manager was never comfortable with me. I was still female. But I passed the test, because I was offered jobs at headquarters. From the corporate point of view, I was respected and valued when the business closed down.

(Continued)

There are two components to political savvy: I think a lot about constituencies. Who are the groups and categories I'm dealing with? I do continual sorting in my head, whatever I'm working on. The strategy is churning in my head, whatever is going on. It's like a mental map; I do it naturally. All my life I have enjoyed this kind of categorizing, like working in operations, where you are putting things in circles and boxes. I'm creating plans for each constituency.

For example, I made sure that the evaluation team that was formed were connected, long-time Commucons, who got credibility from who they are, so when they say something, it is given credibility.

Savvy is also personal, 1 : 1, being emotionally intelligent, so you always think of what their interests are, and their reactions to what you are doing. I know I am strong at that.

Also, you have to know which way the wind is blowing, doing things that will put you in a good light. For example, realizing that this is a junk project that will never make money, but vice presidents like it and want it, so do it to preserve the group. It's knowing how to make yourself look good independent of reality. Or for example, noticing external things, like what category of product is getting a lot of press these days. (That's how SWITCH got started; there was a wave of excitement in the press.) It's a gut sense, hard to say. There is a style of presenting things as a manager (you can think of it as creating your own wind), personal PR, that takes a project or opportunity and feels totally comfortable with discussing business plans, futures—where everyone knows the plans are not literally true, but if you have the guts and balls to say I will make it into a $5 billion business, that gains respect, because you are willing to say I can make the wind blow!

LESSONS FROM FRAN GRIGSBY'S POLITICAL EXPERIENCES

- Credibility is invaluable; if you have it from your previous work, preserve it, and if you have to acquire it, look for difficult jobs with visibility (and deliver).

The higher the level you are operating at, the harder it is to tell if you really know what you are doing. Technology, project complexity, and the length of time it takes to achieve results make it hard to determine who is right. Thus past performance—your reputation—is extremely important. It doesn't guarantee a lack of opposition, but it does help gain latitude and some support. It sounds obvious, but do good work as early and often as you can, so that you can acquire some of the armor of credibility.

If you are new to the organization, however, your past performance may not be worth much, and in some insular places, may even count against you. So you need to figure out how to gain early credibility.

One way is to do a great job with something that has been a problem to the organization, especially when others haven't had the courage to deal with it. Of course, that means there will be risk in taking it on, but if you are successful, you will dramatically increase your credibility, as Fran did. You may not be as lucky as one young man we know well who took a first job where there was a huge mess in procedures that had been unsuccessfully wrestled with for months, and using computer techniques he had just learned at school, he solved it in a few days. Instant hero! But you can seek out difficulties to insiders that as an outsider you have a useful perspective on.

You may well then run into the kinds of political barriers that Fran found, so another way you can demonstrate credibility is to understand that the existing culture may have concerns about whatever you are doing, and ask a lot of questions about how things work. Not only does that give you valuable information, but the very act of knowing enough to inquire and then doing so helps make you more credible. After all, to politically-minded others, it is only natural and prudent to check out the scene.

- Keep your antennae up, especially when you are relatively new to the organization.

Fran talks about how she was constantly monitoring the environment, which was at the least, important for survival. It helped her know where to focus, and where to be extra careful. (In football, players in the open field are told to "have your head on a swivel," to avoid being blindsided by a vicious hit; that's not a bad image for operating in a political organization.)

- Be prepared to compromise when it would preserve larger or longer term goals.

Only you can decide when to back off from a dearly held position, but in most cases, that will have to happen some of the time if you want to succeed. It is hard to balance your vision and principles with tactical necessity, and perseverance is important, but don't get into a "my way or the highway" mentality. Actual politicians usually have figured out how to get along with even ideological opponents, and know that they have to give a little to get what they care about. Good politicians are natural exchangers, and preserve relationships despite disputes.

- Work the network, constantly planting ideas or potential plans, and building your connections.

Working the network follows logically from the need for good information about important stakeholders, and for good relationships. Furthermore, ideas that if implemented will force people to change something usually need time for digestion. What sounds frightening or radical at first, can become a lot more comfortable with repetition and slowly acquired bits of information.

- If what you have to do is personally unacceptable, get out as soon as you can find a better alternative.

Even though Fran was successful, ambitious, and quite good at getting things done in a tough, high-pressure, political organization, she didn't want to continue with that kind of life. Some people wouldn't want to work in a quiet, pleasant environment, finding it too sleepy, while others would experience belonging to any large organization as too pressured. Find what suits you.

CHAPTER 16

HARDBALL: ESCALATING TO TOUGHER STRATEGIES WHEN YOU CAN NO LONGER CATCH FLIES WITH HONEY

Throughout this book, we have stressed the value of working toward a win–win outcome. In today's organizations, there is always a future, and the colleague whom you defeat today could be out to get you tomorrow. Better to have that person walk away satisfied.

However, there are times when an (implied) threat or "cost" might be necessary to achieve such a win–win outcome. It is usually a good strategy to approach the other in terms of the benefit in your proposal, but that might not be enough. It is true that behind even positive offers there is an implied downside. It may be no more than the simple reality that without acceptance of the exchange, the other person will miss out on the benefits. But there are times when it might be necessary to up the ante and talk about the negative exchange that could occur if the other person or group doesn't agree. This may involve—by direct statement or implication—a threat to raise costs by direct action or the withholding of something desirable. You may have to get tough to have any chance to move the deeply resistant potential ally. *By hardball, we mean how to put "teeth" into your requests when needed and what to do when others might be playing dirty pool with you.*

This strategy can be tricky, and it can backfire. Even an implied threat can create resistance—especially if the other party gets upset and focuses on retaliation rather than what benefits the organization. We always emphasize leading with the positive because it is better to aim for a win–win

269

outcome. Second, we stress never to personalize the exchange. You are doing this to achieve organization goals, not for personal dominance. But sometimes, making clear that there could also be a negative outcome—and that you are willing to do whatever is necessary—can not only get the other person's attention, but also, in some cases, increase respect for you. Being willing to fight hard for what you believe in often engenders admiration.

What are the circumstances that require a tougher, less mutually rewarding influence strategy? Sometimes, despite the organizational value of what you want and your best efforts, there is just not a match between any positive currency the ally wants and those you can deliver, so you can't create sufficient obligations. This may be a time in which to start negative escalation. For example, suppose you have gone out of your way to help an ally, but he has been deaf to your requests. You have inquired about this perceived inequality, and your colleague is full of excuses and goes on to say that he has a core set of responsibilities he has to fulfill. Rather than writing that person off as a hypocrite and ungrateful sponge, you could say:

> Bill, I understand you are overworked—we all are—and that some of my requests aren't technically within your job scope. But your requests of me have required that I go above and beyond, and I have come through. Now there are two possible ways we can relate in the future. . . . One where we each go out of our way to help the other or one where we just play it by the rules. Which do you want? I want mutual help, but I refuse to be the only one who gives. If you want real give and take, then I expect greater responsiveness to my requests.

That should get his attention and, if he is not deliberately trying to take advantage of you, create a more mutually responsive relationship. You are willing to be collaborative, but you are not willing to be taken for a sucker. Furthermore, the other person's refusal has some direct costs that are an inevitable consequence of his or her refusal to cooperate.

The following sections present some ways to be tough while preserving the possibility of eventual collaboration or alliance.

RAISING YOUR ALLY'S COSTS—GRADUALLY

When you desperately want something from a highly resistant person—because you are convinced that it is needed for the good of the organization—it becomes necessary to expand the currencies and style you use. The basic ground rule is to raise costs or indicate your intent to raise them a little at a time. Gradual escalation is the way to minimize negative responses, allow yourself the most room for preserving the relationship, and increase the number of options you have. You may need to start with warnings before acting. Stressing the negative—"Here's what will happen/not happen if you don't go along"—could be risky, but warning about it is less personal and takes some of the sting out of the extra pressure. In effect, you are saying that it would be too bad if the ally missed out on the benefits from compliance, putting the emphasis on the nature of the transaction and not on the person. It isn't the same as saying, "You're a jerk for refusing, and I'll get you for it"; rather, it is an attempt to show the recalcitrant ally that it is *his or her* behavior that is leading to these significant costs.

This raise-the-costs strategy requires considerable finesse in its execution and should be used with caution. It lowers the risk if you can also hold out the olive branch by stressing how reluctant you are to have to travel down this negative route. This strategy clarifies that your goal is cooperation, not in harming the other.

In the boxed examples on pages 272 through 274, the people working hard to acquire influence move doggedly from step to step. We identify the variety of increasingly intense measures they have devised for upping the ante for difficult allies.

Increasing costs to a colleague doesn't always involve the direct threat of using customers or higher-ups to gain their cooperation. Even without such measures, it is possible to be tough-minded to get what you need.

WHEN YOUR BOSS IS THE DIFFICULT COLLEAGUE

When the person who is really difficult to influence is your boss and he or she is stuck in negative behavior, you have to work hard to find legitimate, nonprovocative ways to escalate the costs (see box on page 272).

WHO HAS THE POWER?— RECOGNIZING YOUR POWER, INCREASING IT, AND USING IT APPROPRIATELY

In the box on pages 273–274, even though Fred is Dave's boss (and has position power over him), we argue that it was really Dave who (potentially) had the power:

Carefully Escalating Costs for
Unresponsive Colleagues: Sonny Day

Albert "Sonny" Day is a commercial insurance salesman who is very aware of the process of gradually increasing the costs of noncompliance with the requests he made on behalf of his customers. Sonny's work involved long-term relationships with his clients. Preserving their business, however, required special services, necessitating the cooperation of many other departments in the company. Sonny constantly had to ask for unusual attention—estimates, reports, calculations, expedited payments—from colleagues in line and staff jobs; but, in a highly compartmentalized company, he didn't always get what was needed to keep large accounts satisfied. He explains how he dealt with such difficult situations:

> Often the departments had too narrow a view; they only thought about the convenience of their own area. So, one of my functions was to provide them with the larger perspective of customer need: In the long run, we were all dependent on the clients.
>
> My initial strategy was to do a lot of asking and requesting, but I always made sure that I followed up. Sometimes it was just a note to that person or a letter or call to his superior. That was crucial.
>
> I started soft and then moved hard. If my requests didn't get anywhere, I upped the ante as far as I had to, until I was really playing hardball. For example, I'd say to someone who wasn't giving any help, "Your lack of response is pissing off my client, and if we don't get a satisfactory answer by tomorrow noon, I will tell the regional manager that you are the reason we lost this account!" I hated doing this; there was always a knot in my stomach, but I did what I had to.
>
> Then, for really tough cases, I used the principle that everyone has an enemy, and I tried to find that person's enemy. I didn't have to raise my voice or make nasty threats; I'd only have to say something like, "I'm having trouble getting anywhere, so I guess it will be necessary to talk to the insurance association." But I would do that kind of thing only as a last resort, when my survival was at stake.

Sonny was in a rigidly segmented company that focused less on customer need than on departmental autonomy, which made it difficult for him to get reasonable consideration of his requests. In other companies more attuned to pleasing customers, any request from a salesperson on behalf of a client would automatically receive a swift response, but Sonny started with a disadvantage. Thus, he was forced into seeking more leverage than he personally preferred, and he eventually changed his employer. But, while he was with this organization, he learned to push harder and harder, as needed.

Notice that, despite his desperation and his willingness to raise costs in stages, Sonny always tried to keep customer need and company benefit at the forefront. He wasn't using tough tactics just for personal gain, although he had a lot to lose in commission income if he couldn't serve his customers. He wasn't asking for anything that was improper or against company interests, however, and he always gave fair warning before doing anything that would make someone look bad.

Backing Off an Interfering Boss: Dave Offenbach*

Dave Offenbach, an engineering manager, found on a new job assignment that his boss was inappropriately hounding one of Dave's subordinates, and he was struggling to find a way to get his boss to back off. Dave explains what he did:

> In March, I was approached by Fred Wilson, director of engineering of the eastern division of our parent company, about a job assignment that he hoped would interest me. Fred and I had never worked together but knew of each other's characteristics and accomplishments. Everyone told me Fred was brash, impersonal, demanding, and short tempered. During our prejob negotiations, Fred (who had been drafted for this division about one year ago) confided to me that corporate had given him approval to do whatever was necessary to make his division productive and efficient. He also explained that when he analyzed the personnel statistics, he found that the group (with a few exceptions) had been formed with lower quartile people. To upgrade the group, he immediately acquired a few key upper quartile employees. Fred was offering me a new position reporting directly to him. His ultimate goal was to return to the northwest division with me as his replacement in the east.
>
> On my first workday, Fred informed me that there were three "dumb ass" engineering managers working for me that he wanted replaced as soon as possible. Because of my recent arrival, I begged off for 30 days so that I might become familiar with the division. Initially, I assumed that Fred was correct in the assessment of the three managers; but as time progressed, one of the three (Ray) appeared to differ from the other two. Ray responded instantly to requests made of him, accepted any task that was put forth, and worked diligently to get good, justifiable solutions. My concerns for the job and the people influenced me to spend more than normal amounts of time observing their work habits and performance. At meetings and in discussions with other organizations, it became apparent that Ray had the respect and confidence of everyone on the program with the exception of Fred.
>
> During lunch with Fred one day, I asked him to explain his reasons for wanting to replace the three. His concerns regarding the other two were understandable, but I pursued his opinions on Ray. Fred considered Ray worthless and felt that all of the problems seemed to originate from Ray's area. His releases were usually late and/or incomplete, he lacked the answers to important questions, and he was continually asking for more people even though the manpower curve for the division was in the reducing mode.
>
> After expressing himself very vividly, Fred intensely questioned my concerns about Ray. Listening to my observations, Fred became very upset. He ordered me to quit wasting time with Ray and to speed up the process of his replacement.

---

*This example is a case written under the supervision of David Bradford "The Misbranded Goat," reprinted from Stanford Business Cases 1983, with the permission of Stanford University Graduate School of Business. Copyright © 1983 by the Board of Trustees of Leland Stanford Junior University. The analysis is ours.

(Continued)

My next move was to check on Ray's background. Assessment of Ray's personnel folder revealed no negative statements. In fact, it was just the reverse. In his last 14 years in our company, he had a variety of engineering and management assignments. In every case, Ray's capabilities in design, management, and cooperation had been praised. This record was later verified when I spoke to his previous supervisors.

Being thoroughly confused at this point, I decided to confront Ray. In the two-hour discussion that followed, Ray stated that prior to my arrival, Fred had told him that he was going to be fired. I asked Ray to explain his perception of Fred's reasoning. His story concurred with Fred's. His releases were late, even though he was working 40 to 50 percent overtime. He repeatedly requested additional personnel, and his area was the major origin of problems. He also had difficulty answering some of Fred's questions related to the early parts of the program. But Ray also pointed out that he had been assigned his area of responsibility only six months prior to Fred's arrival. Since the program was over four years old, the design problems had been created by managers that Ray had replaced. However, each time that he had used this reasoning, Fred had become more and more irate. Ray also expressed the feeling that his workload was considerably greater than in other areas. I closed the discussion with the promise that I would continue to work on the problem and that, in my opinion, the harassment was unjustified. I told Ray that I appreciated the fine job that he was doing and requested that he continue his good performance.

Next, I studied the workload in all areas and found evidence confirming Ray's analysis. I then shuffled available manpower so that the capability was more evenly distributed. I explained to Fred that I had no plans to replace Ray and, in fact, thought that he was doing a creditable job. Fred became furious and made it quite clear that Ray's performance could reflect on me.

In the months that followed, Ray continued to do his tasks well. His group started meeting schedules and eventually eliminated the need for overtime. However, Fred continued his relentless badgering. In meetings and in the group, he continued to try to embarrass Ray, especially when I was present. To my amazement, Fred didn't apply the harassment to me. In fact, he seemed to give me more and more freedom and responsibility as time went on.

- *The power of past performance.* Fred brought Dave in to turn around this division because Dave had been a top performer. Furthermore, Dave was the one with the positive reputation—not Fred. So Dave held the ultimate card of resigning from this project if Fred wouldn't change. He could still have his old job, and it would be Fred's reputation that would be damaged—not a card to play initially, but it is great to have it in your back pocket—just in case.
- *Who needs whom?* Dave would have liked to take over this division once Fred left, but he has other choices. Fred was drafted for this job

and needs Dave's competence to quickly turn around this unit so that Fred can return to the northwest division.

• *The power of information.* Dave has not only done his homework by carefully investigating the situation, analyzing work loads, and so on, but his action in reshuffling personnel produced the results that he wanted. This new data could supersede the old information that Fred had on the engineers.

Let's look at how Dave went about influencing Fred:

• *Credibility through action.* First, he bought himself time to do his homework. Then he took decisive action in terminating the two engineers who weren't competent for that position, thereby increasing his credibility with Fred as a person who could take action.

• *Potential ally.* It would have been easy given what Dave had heard about Fred to stereotype him as an immovable autocrat. Instead, he constantly held on to the possibility of influencing him. Part of what allowed Dave not to fall into that stereotype was seeing that even though Fred got emotional around the topic, he wasn't abusive to Dave.

• *Knowing the other's world.* Dave, in an informal setting over lunch, tried to understand Fred's position. Dave didn't argue with him even when Fred got upset. Dave took Fred's information as something to check out (and paid him in the currency of carefully listening to what he said).

• *Being clear on your goals.* Dave kept focused on what was fair and what was important for the organization to be successful. He remained neither hooked in inappropriately defending his people, nor in a personal battle with Fred.

Having done this careful initial work, the problem of Fred badgering Ray still continued. What could Dave do to get Fred to leave Ray alone? He had already collected data from Fred about the problems with Ray, followed up with his own investigation, explained the history of the problems, reorganized work to improve Ray's performance, and then went back to Fred with evidence that Ray really was a solid performer. Because none of this worked, he had to consider further escalation.

Dave had already shown that he had faith in Ray's ability to deliver because he continued to support him after Fred pointed out that Dave's performance rating could suffer from Ray's efforts. This is a step in the right direction; the willingness to guarantee your own performance to your boss if the boss will let you do it your way is usually enough of a valuable exchange to create the desired latitude. As a next step in raising costs, Dave might make this even more explicit than he did, adding that if Fred continued to harass Ray, Dave could no longer guarantee that his unit would deliver the right level of performance. It was *Fred's* behavior, not Ray's, that could undermine the success of the turnaround.

Part of what Dave had to decide was whether Fred could be confronted more directly. Would Fred respect him for being tough, or would he explode and nail Dave in an undesirable way? He could make alternative attributions: Fred's a bully, he can deal only with a subordinate who says yes to everything, or he is impatient and doesn't believe in coddling people so he will be bugged by Dave's patience with Ray. But based on the clues that Dave was picking up in their interaction, he concluded that Fred was able to take direct pushing back. Fred had not been punitive to Dave ("to my amazement, Fred didn't apply the harassment to me"), which subtly communicated his respect despite Dave's refusal to follow his directions in regard to Ray. That suggested that Fred's style is probably to keep pushing until he meets a tough response. Toughness is one of Fred's currencies. And Fred wanted Dave to succeed so that he could return to the Northwest and leave the eastern division in good hands, which makes confidence in Dave's judgment another important currency. These currencies were apparently more important to Fred than data about Ray's performance.

Finally, Dave chose to escalate: "Look, Fred, you had enough faith in me to bring me on board to help you accomplish the turnaround. I've been getting results, and I want to continue doing that, but you're making it hard for me. We've talked about Ray lots of times. I don't think I can convince you to appreciate him. But, damn it, he works for me and I'm responsible for him. I am absolutely convinced that he can do the job, and he's doing it. If you won't get off his back, it could really screw things up. From now on, if you don't like what he does, talk to me, not him! If you don't agree to lay off him, I can't guarantee that I'll be able to continue our successes. So what do you want: to keep harassing Ray or to let me do the job well, using my best judgment?" Fred sputtered, then agreed.

This kind of pushing back used several forms of negative currencies to create the space that Dave wanted. It stressed performance as the most important outcome and made it clear to Fred that his behavior would prevent the performance he definitely wanted. It acknowledged Fred as the boss but reminded him that, in a hierarchy, Dave has the legitimate "right" to manage and judge his direct reports; continuously violating this right would undermine his ability to manage successfully. If Fred continues to interfere, he will be responsible for results that may be poorer than those he was already getting. And, by referencing his successful track record and the confidence that Fred had shown in him on other matters, Dave implicitly threatened the loss of something valuable. Thus, there were several negative costs that Fred could avoid if he would back off Ray, and he did. Furthermore, he used a tough style of interaction that reflected Fred's own behavior, which reinforced Dave's position in the exchange.

THE ULTIMATE ESCALATION: BETTING YOUR JOB

Dave never got to the point of directly threatening to quit if his boss Fred didn't stop harassing Ray, but that would have been his ultimate weapon. Unfortunately, that's not a total victory. Going back to the northwest division and disparaging Fred would not have altered Fred's behavior and would only have been a form of gratuitous revenge that we don't condone. The person who cuts a fellow employee down behind his back risks ruining his own reputation more than the reputation of the person targeted for revenge.

There are times, however, when all other attempts to influence an important ally, especially your boss, leave no choice but to put your job on the line. Certain issues are too important to allow to die, either because you are convinced that the boss is about to make a giant mistake, you feel grossly unjustly treated, you think the boss's requests are unethical, or you have decided that the job is not worth having if your boss continues certain behaviors.

If all else fails and you consider the issue important enough to take considerable risk, then the last resort is to make an offer that, based on your sound diagnosis of the boss's situation (you hope), your boss cannot refuse. You do this only when the possibility of being fired as a result is no more painful than continuing as is. Chris Hammond, for example, discussed in Chapter 6, used this strategy in dealing with the boss who did not want to give her credit for her sales efforts. She pulled out all the stops, threatening to leave and take with her sales that her boss needed to make his quota and burying them so that he would miss his goals. This is not an everyday exchange strategy and could easily backfire, but it is occasionally necessary. It is an attempt to preserve a partnership that would

---

Successfully Threatening to Quit: Donna Dubinsky at Apple

In another documented situation,* Donna Dubinsky, then of Apple Computer (and subsequently CEO of Handspring and Palm), decided to throw down the gauntlet to her boss's boss, Bill Campbell (and in turn to President John Sculley), when she was sick of having to defend her department's distribution strategy. Donna felt under siege from other areas that had proposed (with the support of company founder Steven Jobs) a change to a just-in-time inventory system that she was certain was inappropriate for Apple's business. Finally, deciding that she would resign if she were not allowed to examine her department's strategy without the interference of a task force, she told Campbell that, if he didn't agree to her terms, she would leave Apple. Because she had been doing an excellent job and was considered extremely promising, Campbell and Sculley agreed to her terms.

---

*The documented instance referred to is in a teaching case series, under the supervision of Todd Jick, by Mary Gentile, "Donna Dubinsky and Apple Computer, Inc., (A) and (B)" (Boston: Harvard Business School Press, 1986). Donna still publicly talks about accumulating go-to-hell money for any job.

---

otherwise explode, and preservation may be preferred by the boss who realizes the alternative.

The Apple ultimatum (see box above) was a high-risk act on Donna's part. She genuinely was not sure that it would work, but she had tried everything else she knew to do. That does not mean that she had no other strategic choices—indeed, she was in that uncomfortable position because she had not reacted positively or actively to questions raised earlier about inventory—but the ultimatum had its intended effect. It showed that she was very serious about finally being ready to do the requisite analysis and willing to put her job on the line for her beliefs.

Donna's strong track record made the outcome a fairly safe bet, and the relative openness of the Apple culture helped, but she did not know at the time what her chances were. The level of her desperation was such that she had openly challenged Sculley about other issues at an off-site training meeting the weekend before, but she did not realize that her outburst at him had impressed him with her integrity. Publicly challenging your company president is not usually a preferred strategy, but it is not always automatic suicide either.

It isn't always necessary to take extreme measures to push back on your boss, and sometimes the inability to achieve influence may reflect either that you have a bad idea or are using inappropriate influence techniques. How much risk to take depends on your own capacity to live with the worst consequences and how long term a view you want to adopt. It is undeniably true that in the long run we are all dead, so ignoring the short term is foolish; but it is equally true that acting only in the short term while pretending that there is no long run is a good way to get bumped off. Judgment is needed.

INTO EVERY LIFE SOME RAIN MUST FALL: ROTTEN APPLES AND HARDBALL

In most of the examples in this book, the potential allies or partners have been difficult but not malevolent. Although it is far less likely to happen than most people assume, every so often you will encounter a genuinely rotten person, boss, or peer, who is so keen to get ahead that he or she is playing it dirty to hurt you, even going so far as to spread untrue rumors about you. (We have heard of people falsely accused of sleeping with the boss, stealing company funds, or even making up false nasty rumors about others.) This calls for a different set of escalation tactics for self-protection, assuming that you are certain that the problem is totally in the other person and not a result of something you have done or are perceived to have done. When that kind of thing happens, it is difficult to think about any mutually satisfactory way of responding; self-protection takes over.

Being nice won't always work as a way of influencing someone who wants to harm you; some measure of toughness is required for a full repertoire of influence strategies. But toughness isn't viciousness. While you could (rarely) encounter a person who will force you into retaliatory viciousness, that is a kind of guerrilla warfare we leave to those who still think that killing for peace is the only way to settle disputes. Instead, we show you how you can be resolute in pursuing your legitimate interests without turning transactions with difficult people into win-lose contests. You almost never want to initiate exchanges in ways that guarantee the creation of a permanent enemy.

We take as an example the sad experience of Rudy Martinez. (See box on p. 280.)

The Calculated Confrontation

Another approach is to take an early exit, collect yourself so that you are sure of what you want to do, and then strongly confront the colleague.

Being Set Up by a Colleague—And What to Do About It: Rudy Martinez

A young lawyer aspiring to become a partner in the corporate law department of a major law firm, Rudy Martinez was innocently chatting at lunch one day with Walt Oliver, a more recent member of the department. Walt began to complain about their boss, Herb Lewis, the department head and one of three senior partners in the group. Herb had been a star in his earlier years, with a reputation for creative thinking. But Walt was unhappy with the laissez faire leadership style Herb had adopted. He complained, "We are like a ship stopped dead in the water. There's no direction. Not only that, but he blocks anybody else from taking initiative."

Rudy realized that Walt was reacting to a recent staff meeting of all 10 members in the corporate department. Walt had been asked to study the feasibility of the department's having a more focused thrust, and, as a result, he had strongly recommended that the department specialize in mergers and acquisitions. When Walt finished, Herb leaned back in his chair and said, "Well, I don't know. . . . I believe in adhoc-racy, letting a thousand flowers bloom. I think each of us should do our own thing." That seemed to kill the interest of the group; all the energy went out of the room.

Rudy agreed with Walt's evaluation of Herb: a nice guy but a black hole for ideas. Herb not only didn't provide any direction, but also, if anybody else took initiative, seemed to kill it.

Normally Rudy wouldn't make waves, but he was startled at how strongly Walt felt about this issue. Walt had reason to be upset, but Rudy had always perceived Walt as too much of a politician to take on the boss openly. Because Rudy was pleased to learn that Walt had feelings similar to his, he agreed that Herb's style was hurting the department.

"Let's all three of us go out to lunch," Walt suggested, "and confront Herb on all this." Rudy hesitated, but Walt seemed determined and said he would make the arrangements.

When Rudy arrived for the lunch meeting, Walt and Herb were already there. After they ordered, Herb opened by saying, "Rudy, Walt has been telling me that you have trouble with my leadership style. What's your problem?"

Rudy was stunned. He looked over at Walt, who just sat there impassively. What should he do? Confront Walt for setting him up? Take on Herb alone or beat a hasty retreat? Rudy decided that retreat was the safest course and mumbled that there must have been some kind of misunderstanding. He said that he wasn't that dissatisfied, quickly thought of a tiny issue that he could mention so that he wouldn't appear to be lying, then made small talk through lunch and left as soon as he could. He subsequently learned that Walt was not above similar tactics with all his colleagues and had frequently tried to sabotage other peers with Herb.

What could Rudy have done at the time or afterward? It is easy to say that Rudy should have somehow known about Walt's reputation, but he didn't. Even with inquiry, he might not have found out. While we hope it never happens to you, it is likely that at some time in anyone's career a dirty player may spring a nasty surprise. Therefore, it is not realistic to suggest that Rudy could have avoided all possibilities. No one can guarantee a total lack of unpleasant surprises, and it is tiring to live in an organization always on its guard, so let's accept that some such events are part of life.

Rudy couldn't let this pass, not only for his own feelings of self-esteem and personal efficacy but also because it would have allowed Walt to initiate and walk away with another win-lose victory. Let's assume that Walt wanted to personally look good at Rudy's expense. What could Rudy do to block that exchange?

Out of the Closet and into the Daylight

One of the best tactics for dealing with anyone who tries to sabotage is to get as much as possible out in the open. Dirty players count on being able to work behind the scenes and undercover, relying on others' reluctance to be explicit when burned. But, since most nastiness makes the initiator look shabby when it is seen in broad daylight, efforts to get everything out in the open are important. That might have turned Walt's win-lose exchange into a lose-win.

Had Rudy been less stunned or less afraid of unpleasantness, he might have looked right at his boss Herb and said, "I am really shocked that Walt has told you that I'm the one with concerns. When he and I talked the other day, he expressed a lot of concerns, too. I don't see how we can go further until we get this cleared up. Walt, are you going to be open about what we discussed? I thought we were going to be helpful to Herb; if this is an attempt to make me look like a troublemaker, I won't play. I want us to have a strong practice group, not make each other look bad."

We have the benefit of time and distance, but, since what we suggest Rudy should have said is more or less what he was thinking all along, it is not completely the result of hindsight.

Instead of being embarrassed in front of his boss, Rudy could have used the opportunity to show his desire to be helpful even while making Walt's game visible. Although it is difficult to formulate a perfect comeback when someone unexpectedly zings you, it isn't necessary to get it just right. The simple principle is: If you genuinely were trying to act for the organization's good, say so, and be open about your reaction to the surprise attack (insofar as it isn't just pure desire to jump up and wring the colleague's neck).

Maybe all Rudy could have mustered would have been an exclamation, "I'm shocked!! I thought we were in this together. What's going on, Walt?" That would

(Continued)

have been enough to get started in a way that didn't leave Rudy totally exposed. If Walt then denied everything, Rudy could explain to Herb that he was misled but that he wants to help the boss be most effective, and, if necessary, he'll do that alone.

None of this would work if Rudy was also trying to do in someone else or nail his boss. If he was genuinely concerned with the future of the division (which, indeed, he was), then saying so need not be excruciating. The Walts of the world are so busy conniving that it never occurs to them someone else might actually want to do the right thing. This is their blind, vulnerable spot. They don't realize how slimy they would look if their victim were to speak up and talk straight. It is even possible that Walt doesn't see himself as nasty, but rather has another explanation for what he did. The effect of his behavior could be very different from his intentions; forthrightly raising the question without attacking allows the apparently malicious person to reveal any benign intentions. Yet, he could also learn the negative consequences of his actions.

Sequel

Sometimes justice occurs. Walt was later turned down for partnership because he was seen as too political. Rudy was made partner but never was one of the movers and shakers in the firm because he wasn't seen as being able to productively "work the system." This is a good example of the dysfunctionality of one type of "being political" and the cost of not having the skills to use the more functional form.

This can be done with cool anger in front of witnesses or a controlled explosion in private. As experienced negotiators will advise, it is probably a mistake to really lose your temper in an organization, but allowing yourself to express anger you genuinely feel can be a useful tactic if deliberately chosen. Controlled anger that is focused with laserlike intensity or a bit of screaming can make it more difficult for the manipulator to be sure of what you will do in the future, which then serves as a buffer against future surprise attacks. You haven't prevented Walt from being successful in front of the boss, but you have blocked him from trying that exchange in the future.

One of the authors found that this worked with a colleague who was, as usual, trying to manipulate and bully him (in this case about office space), by looking right at the colleague and saying in a loud voice, "Don't mess with me, Jack. I teach negotiations!" Jack backed off and was much nicer from then on, because he assumed his ploys wouldn't work.

Spread a Little Sunshine

If direct confrontation is not possible, perhaps all you can do is spread the tale around the organization so that others are warned about the person. As we have noted, however, this has its own dangers. The nasty person probably won't be thrilled with you when word gets back and may be inspired to try for greater damage in return. Because you probably don't have the full revenge and bad temper arsenal he or she has, it's not a great idea to get into a contest of escalating swinishness.

Second, when neutral organization members see you retaliating by talking about the person, they may see only your retaliation and assume that you are the dirty player, talking behind the other's back. Like the basketball player who gets a foul called for swinging back after his opponent unobtrusively elbowed him, there may never be a chance for true justice, and you don't even get the benefit of instant replay. Nevertheless, because reputation is so important in organizational life, as a last resort, you can try to be certain that the person who has nailed you gets the headlines he or she so richly deserves. Just don't abuse the tactic, and remember that some weapons are only for defense.

In general, all tough tactics such as those we have described are far more potent when you only *threaten* to use them. Once launched, the results may be unpredictable and uncontrollable. It is thus better to warn the slime balls of the world of what you will do if they keep on playing dirty pool, in a convincing way, than to retaliate. Just be sure you are prepared to act on your threat if forced to.

Influence, Not Manipulation

The saving grace in organizational life is that anyone who does it only for selfish ends will sooner or later be seen as more interested in advancing personal goals than in helping the organization accomplish its goals and will lose credibility and clout. Although it sometimes takes longer than would be desirable, one bad act is reciprocated with another, and sharks get bitten. A similar process happens to those who use reciprocity illegally (e.g., paying bribes for illegal favors), though again, justice's wheels can grind way too slowly.

Truly difficult people increase the temptation for you to cross the line yourself. It is useful to identify manipulative behavior and make the distinction between that behavior, which is unethical and often sets off equally unpleasant reactions, and skilled influence, which can be used by everyone in an organization without harm.

Table 16.1   Drawing the Line between Influence and Manipulation

Is it manipulation to:	Answer:
Be aware of what you are doing to gain influence?	No
Fit your arguments and language to the other party's interests?	No
Not mention your ultimate goal if not asked?	No
Exaggerate your costs to make the trade seem better.	No
Push yourself to become interested in and concerned for the other person?	No
Do a favor you wouldn't do for everyone?	No
Paint the most favorable picture of the benefits?	No
Fake caring and interest for the other?	Yes
Lie about your intentions?	Yes
Lie about your costs?	Yes
Lie about the benefits?	Yes
Commit to a payment you do not (intend to) make?	Yes
Seek weakness and vulnerability in others to get them indebted in ways that violate their integrity?	Yes

Table 16.1 summarizes our views about the fine line between influence and manipulation.

Influence attempts are not manipulative if you can tell your potential ally your intentions with no loss of influence. Following this rule does not require that you tell everything at once, nor does it prevent you from making your best argument, but it does suggest that outright lies are beyond the pale. Negotiators know: "Always tell the truth, but you don't have to initiate the whole truth."

Be Careful of Assuming Malevolence

Yes, there are occasional rotten apples, but we have seen plenty of situations where each side was certain that his or her own motives were pure while the other's were poisonous, and neither could get past these biases. For example, a group of hospital administrators we consulted with behaved viciously to one another for years, each convinced that "everyone else but me" was willing to trample his own mother to harm the others. Yet, each one, without exception, told us that he hated the way they treated one

Using Currencies Consciously,
but Not Manipulatively

Scott Timmins worked for ODI, a then-thriving consulting firm, as director of consulting operations. As he explains, the position was completely based on influence, and Scott was familiar with the concepts of *Influence without Authority*.

I was director of consulting operations at ODI, responsible for scheduling everyone's travels, among other things. People joked that I was air traffic controller for 50 consultants and 25 to 30 bench consultants (contractors). I had to match the incoming flow for consultant needs, all of which was funneled to me, with all consultants, so they would be where they were needed. My objective was to get client work done with quality and maximize the asset base (time of consultants). The more billable we could make the staff, the better for the bottom line of the business. I had to trade off processes, competencies, and delivery days. Some of the staff did consulting, but mostly they delivered training, so the units of time were in training days (with many programs a week long). Therefore, we often couldn't split the work in a week. If a person was needed for three days, that was it for the week. Most big firms order consultants to go where they are told. We had a permission-based system. We worked on suggestion, and the consultant could say no. Really junior ones felt pressure to take what they were offered, but the more accomplished the person, the more he controlled where he went. So I was trying to maximize usage. I had to connect the work required, the location, and/or client nature with people's interests.

We thought two things made a difference in career acceleration: your ability and the work assignments you got (including who you got to work with). Project leaders also negotiated for whom they wanted. (Everyone was billed at the same price, so all project leaders wanted the best people, which was the scarcest resource.) For each project, I would develop a list of more people than were needed, since some would refuse, rank them with the project leader, then go down the list in order if the top ones said no. The worst answer from a consultant was "maybe." I needed to get it done.

How did I leverage the concepts of exchange when I wasn't face to face? I read the annual professional development plans of every consultant. I knew their developmental goals. I interviewed each to ask what work he or she preferred, what clients they were most and least successful with, and travel requirements (e.g., single mother). You don't want to waste time offering what is not accepted. You want to offer what fits for them. Then they will say yes. That sounds like the easy part, but the reality was different.

If I knew it was a dog client, or tough one, how did I get a yes? Maybe it was the kind of work that the person wanted, or a chance to work for a project leader who was considered strong and could help them develop, or in a part of world they wanted to see. Or, their billability was down, and they needed something. I got 25 to 50 requests per day, and the goal was to put the requests to bed each day. I knew where everybody was supposed to be every day.

(Continued)

I was a junior consultant then, and had no direct reports, no job that others aspired to, but I happened to control one of the key elements in the development of careers—affecting future income and so on. By using this approach and by leveraging my skills, I was able to get cooperation.

I kept records of people's currencies, knew what worked and did not. I kept it in a spreadsheet, all names and what their "buttons" were, and their bad buttons, things that they abhorred, which would lead to an immediate "no." I wanted to decrease the number of noes, because I never had enough time. Increasing the number of yeses per request would get me the time needed. Or, I know that the currency is there, so when I'm stuck and have to ask someone to go to an undesirable assignment, I can say, "I know you don't like traveling to the West Coast, but here is how this assignment is aligned with the work you want, and you can stay an extra day at the hotel on us." We had some perks to offer when we had to. A lot is preparation and tweaking each week, but by the end, it is in your head because you get to know them.

They knew the *Influence* concepts, too, so they were aware that I was consciously seeking to pay in their currencies. They knew my job was to find matches; trust is important. If they knew you were trying to do well by them—though, of course, you were also working for the company good—we did fine. As long as I felt that there was a good reason they were saying no, that was fine. But a consultant can't say no all the time. Some are so good that everyone wants them. At the other end, there are a few for whom it is a struggle to find work, because they are only good at a few things and no one wants to work with them. They had to understand I was caring about them in the process, not just trying to manipulate or sell a bill of goods. After all, they do go to the places and then they know whether I was honest, so that makes it long term, in the context of a relationship, built over time. If the person says no just because they are pissed off over the last assignment, I have to go back and build the trust again. If I convince them when it is not really in their best interest, that will harm me on the next request, which will be in about four days! It also helped that I'd done it; they knew I had lived through what I was asking them to do, so I was credible. I didn't get, "You don't know how hard it is to ride planes, etc."

My wife, Susan, was one of those consultants. She knew IWA [*Influence without Authority*]. I tried it on her in a mechanical way once, and she exploded, "Don't pull that *IWA* BS on me!" It has to be authentic.

Results from Using Currencies Consciously to Influence Consultant Cooperation

We raised billability from about 35 percent to 50 percent during one and a half years. I couldn't have done it much longer, though I learned a lot. It was extremely high pressure and never off. I couldn't get sick or take a vacation. I'd have a sub, but if anything significant happened, I'd be called and have to do it. Say the client cancels; what to do with the suddenly available resources? Or there was an explosion at a session, how do we recover? There was big pressure.

I did get some special requests back from people about where they wanted to go or what special clients they wanted, and I saw it as good to know. Sometimes you can't, but you make trade-offs. The smart ones updated me, kept me informed. Sometimes there were tough trades. If I had to send someone to the ninth level of hell, I would acknowledge, "I know it's lousy, but only you can do it, and I'll pay you back." Some wouldn't do anything just to help the company, and that had consequences, so I'd give the good stuff elsewhere and say why: "That person gave one for the team; you didn't. That's why they go to Bermuda this week."

There were salespeople who would say, "I only want one of these three consultants." Sometimes I had to sell an available consultant to the client advocate. I had to know what they did well and not, so I had to really know consultants. Maybe they were right or not. Is the person good enough? Can you live with it? Water-walkers are easy to place, but there are only a few.

Despite the difficulties, the experience had a positive impact on my career at the company. I had been a road warrior, won an award, was the most billable consultant one year. A mentor offered me a chance to take a turn at the job. I saw it as a way to learn the business, get inside the company. I did it for about 18 months; then my wife and I were offered the opportunity to go to London. We were growing the business there. They needed Susan to train the new people acquired. She had the best reputation for that. She dazzled clients. They wanted her but asked me, too, because they needed systems set up, and I had learned how, so I got the opportunity to go look at operating processes long before I would have otherwise.

We were asked to colead the U.K. business after three months. I joined the European Leadership Council (I was 32), so the whole experience as director of consulting operations accelerated my career. When I left, the company was at $50 million per year and cruising.

another but felt he had to strike first because the others were so ready to attack. When this was revealed, they breathed a collective sigh of relief and began to discover more virtues in one another than any had dreamt of! Think of their experience before leaping to negative conclusions about someone who won't behave as you'd like.

When an escalation strategy does prove necessary, however, another risk is that you will find it highly stressful and back off prematurely. You need to be tough enough to hang in, even if you prefer to make that your last resort.

Humans are apparently wired to cooperate, to create mutual obligation, and to exchange what each other desire. But like all human mechanisms, reciprocity and exchange can be, and often are, abused. The abuse takes several forms (Table 16.2 on page 288).

Table 16.2   Potential Negative Aspects of Reciprocity and Exchange

Corruption
Inappropriate, unethical, or illegal trades
Manipulation
Deceit about intentions, goals, and uses of what is received
Deceit about payment or repayment
Deceit about costs to the giver
Deceit about genuine concern for the trading partner
Creation of obligation that forces reciprocity violating the personal beliefs of the person or group that "owes" repayment
Revenge
Exaggerated sense of obligations and payback
Negative Organizational Climate
Organizations that overdo self-interest at the expense of the organization
Organizations that overuse explicit trades, never developing the kinds of relationships that allow automatic give and take
Organizations that are so afraid of exchange that they can't get anything done
Organizations that operate by fear of retaliation and other negative currencies rather than positive exchanges

We mention each of these unpleasant aspects of reciprocity and exchange, both to make you aware of the dangers and to help you defend yourself.

CONCLUSIONS

Hardball can be dangerous to your organizational (and personal) health, whether you are the one who is throwing it or being hit by it. You want to avoid playing it if you can but not be so afraid of it that you are vulnerable to anyone willing to make your life difficult. Keep looking for exchanges where both sides can win, even if you have to use the possibility of—or actual—negative exchanges to level the playing field.

We urge you, however, to always be looking for the possibility of making the kind of relationships where it isn't necessary to escalate. That means not starting by assuming the worst of others whose behavior does not seem friendly; *threatening* strong reaction before taking it—and making it clear that in the organization's and other person's interests, you would prefer not to have to administer negative consequences; escalating gradually, allowing the possibility of straightening things out earlier in the cycle before the heaviest guns are trotted out; and, if possible, not doing things designed just to injure the other person.

Donna Dubinsky, who early in her career at Apple took on Steve Jobs and John Sculley and eventually helped to found and run Palm and Handspring, talks about always having "go-to-hell" money saved. You can be more courageous if you are not totally dependent on keeping your job. But you are also in a stronger position if you have developed a positive track record of performance and start early at building as large a number of good relationships as you can. Having lots of potential allies is a good idea for acquiring influence and a good idea for being able to play hardball with less fear of striking out. If you need a refresher, read Chapter 6 on building effective relationships again. Avoid these traps in negative exchanges:

Self-Traps to Avoid

- *When somebody is resistant, prematurely backing off.* Learn to use alternative approaches.
- *When somebody plays dirty, retaliating in kind before using threats of negative consequences.* Don't waste nuclear weapons when threats of a slap on the wrist—or a kick in the pants—might work.
- *Being unwilling ever to use negative exchanges.* If you have only honey when a little vinegar is called for, you often get stuck.
- *Using negative exchanges in an attacking way without holding out the possibility of a better future.* Don't fear war, but keep making peace attractive.

APPENDIX A

EXTENDED CASE EXAMPLES AVAILABLE ON THE WEB

To view any of the following case examples in full, paste into your browser: http://www .influencewithoutauthority.com. These are rich, detailed descriptions, and analysis, with action on many organizational levels.

THE CAREER OF NETTIE SEABROOKS: INFLUENCE AGAINST ALL ODDS

As an African American and a woman, Nettie Seabrooks had more than her share of hurdles to leap to acquire influence—especially at General Motors, where her career began. Her remarkable story offers invaluable lessons for gaining influence in the importance of:

- Doing quality work as a way of gaining credibility and positive reputation, which are the entry price for influence. Influence requires more than a technique.
- Cultivating strong relationships.
- Placing the organization's interests first, so you are not seen as self-serving.
- Avoiding self-inflicted traps, such as writing difficult people off, missing learning opportunities, or failing to notice what others want.

To go directly to this case, the address is http://www.influencewithoutauthority.com/nettieseabrooks.html.

WARREN PETERS NAVIGATES A COMPLEX, MULTISTAGED EXCHANGE PROCESS: WORKING WITHIN ORGANIZATIONAL REALITIES

In trying to replace a direct report at his insurance company, Warren Peters ran into conflict with the more senior manager of his favored candidate. Warren had to decide whether to fight for his choice, and once he did, find a way to preserve his relationship while getting the result he wanted. Warren's story illustrates these crucial principles of influence:

- Resisting the impulse to attack when you are attacked
- Listening carefully to your opponents' arguments to distill what is most important to them
- Persistence in the face of objection, using steady patience to meet objections
- Exiting gracefully when necessary

To go directly to this case, the address is http://www.influencewithoutauthority.com/warrenpeters.html.

ANNE AUSTIN CROSSES OVER: SELLING A NEW PRODUCT IDEA, AND GAINING ACCESS TO AN OUT-OF-REACH JOB

Anne Austin had trouble making herself heard when she spotted a new product opportunity from her market analyst's job at a Fortune 500 consumer goods company. But by incredible persistence and deft application of influence skills, she conducted a strong internal campaign to get her product idea accepted and land the job she wanted. Her story shows the importance of:

- Paying attention to exchange in every situation, so efforts are focused
- Keeping your personal goals, as well as task success, in mind
- Taking resistance seriously
- Being assertive, never antagonistic

To go directly to this case, the address is http://www.influencewithoutauthority.com/anneaustin.html.

Lessons from a Determined Influencer: The Rise, Fall— and Eventual Resurrection of Monica Ashley, Revolutionary Product Manager

This complicated example reveals many layers of challenges over several years, and demonstrates how a project management job calls for the ability to determine key players, figure out what is important to them, and utilize a full palette of influence skills to bring a major strategic project to fruition. Monica Ashley had to overcome deep resistance from a powerful technical guru, and she finally won the arguments about going outside for needed technology, but because of her approach, was removed from the product development project and placed in "the penalty box" for a year. If your job brings you into contact with multiple stakeholders who must be won over in order to be successful, you will find the attention required to understand the situation to be well worth your time.

Some of the lessons from Monica's experience include:

- Having the right data is a start, but often not enough for influence.
- Influence requires considerable relationship building and maintenance.
- You have to work your supportive relationships as well as overcome the resisters.
- When people you respect are not doing what you want, do not write them off; inquire and learn.
- The higher you go in management, the more that subtle norms of behavior are in operation, and the more they affect your reputation and career.

To go directly to this case, the address is
http://www.influencewithoutauthority.com/monicaashley.html.

Making a Minor Miracle in Montana: Using Influence to Change People and Groups Outside Your Organization

Timlynn Babitsky and Jim Salomon saw the enormous potential of wind power in Montana, but the locals, unfamiliar with their organization, were skittish. By partnering with several government-sponsored groups, and landing some well-placed publicity, they were able to start a grassroots movement that is tapping into a powerful existing resource and improving people's lives. Important elements of their influence campaign include:

- Finding an issue you care passionately about in order to sustain the effort to overcome complex opposition
- Locating all the relevant stakeholders, and using any connection to them you have
- Using every available communication device to spread variations of your message
- Providing information, access, responsiveness, and homework to relieve time pressure for key stakeholders

To go directly to this case, the address is http://www.influencewithoutauthority.com/montanamiracle.html.

WILL WOOD SELLS E-LEARNING FOR TRAINING: A CASE OF SUCCESSFUL CHANGE IMPLEMENTATION

After being promoted to head of a messy division, Will Wood used careful change planning, considerable influence skill and some calculated maneuvering to implement e-learning, a more effective training tool. But to do it successfully, he had to overcome skepticism and tight budgets. Some of the principles he practiced include:

- Offering a vision of how change would increase efficiency
- Building credibility through better performance
- Tailoring his interaction style to build key relationships
- Preparing for the political implications of the change he initiated

To go directly to this case, the address is http://www.influencewithoutauthority.com/willwood.html.

FRAN GRIGSBY KILLS THE $100 MILLION PROJECT OF A WELL-LIKED SENIOR PEER: CAREFUL NAVIGATION OF ORGANIZATIONAL POLITICS

When challenged with taking over the flawed pet project of a popular long-time manager at Commuco, Fran Grigsby knew she would have to kill it—

without sacrificing a talented staff and her own bright future at the company. Some of the influence principles she demonstrated were:

- Accepting challenges to build credibility
- Keeping your antennae up, so you know which way the political winds are blowing
- Being prepared to compromise in the short term for the sake of the long term
- Getting out as soon as you can find a better alternative, if what you have to do is personally unacceptable

To go directly to this case, the address is
http://www.influencewithoutauthority.com/frangrigsby.html.

APPENDIX B

ADDITIONAL RESOURCES

A. TRAINING PROGRAMS

1. Babson College offers a residential five-day executive development program, *Leadership and Influence,* exploring vision, teamwork, and other leadership competencies needed to influence at all levels of an organization. This highly experiential program is for managers who have direct reports managing others, and combines videos, case discussions, role plays, simulations, and a day of outdoor problem-solving activities linked to influence without authority, and postheroic concepts. Participants request confidential questionnaire feedback on leadership style from peers and direct reports, and utilize the results at the program. With a faculty team led by Allan Cohen, the program runs twice a year and has also been customized for numerous companies. More information available from Babson Executive Education, Babson Park, MA., 02157-0310; phone: (781) 239-4354 or (800) 882-EXEC; or http://www3.babson.edu/bee/programs/leadership.

2. Stanford Graduate School of Business offers a residential five-day *Executive Program in Leadership: The Effective Use of Power,* designed to help experienced managers put effective, collaborative methods of leadership to work for their organizations. Participants discover how to develop and maintain vision and power by tapping into their team's valuable leadership potential and gain hands-on experience through videos, case discussions, role plays, and simulations, linked to influence without authority and postheroic concepts. Participants request confidential questionnaire feedback on leadership style from peers and direct reports, and utilize the results at the program. With a faculty team led by David Bradford, the program runs in the summer and has also been customized for numerous companies. More information available from Stanford Executive Education, 518 Memorial Way,

Stanford, CA 94305-5015; http://www.gsb.stanford.edu/exed/lead; phone: (650) 723-3341 or (866) 542-2205.

3. An online program, *Resolving Interpersonal Issues,* a program for dealing with difficult relationships, based on concepts from Influence Without Authority, is available from Ninth House at http://ninthhouse.com/solution/courses/rii. The Ninth House home page, ninthhouse.com, has more information on their innovative methods of providing learning opportunities.

4. Custom training by Allan Cohen, David Bradford, or several associates, has been designed for half-day, one-day and two-day programs. These can be stand alone or integrated into longer executive development programs. Contacts: cohen@babson.edu or bradford_david@gsb.stanford.edu.

B. Speeches

Keynote speeches and inspirational or informational talks on influence and various applications are available from Allan Cohen or David Bradford. Contacts as above.

C. Survey

A 360-degree instrument on influence, or on influence and leadership, tied to the concepts in *Influence without Authority,* and/or our leadership book, *Power Up,* is available. The questions ask colleagues, subordinates, and boss(es) how the person is doing now, and how the respondent would prefer the person to behave. All questions are tied to actions that can be changed, so that the results are practical and connected to what people want. Sample questions are available at http://influencewithoutauthority.com.

D. Cases on Influence

Extended examples and analyses of people who have exercised, or need to exercise influence, are available at the web site http://influencewithoutauthority.com. (For more details about these examples, see Appendix A.)

Notes

Chapter 2

1. This inscription from a statue called Mantiklos Apollo was cited by Janet Tassel in Mighty Midgets," *Harvard Magazine* (May–June, 1989).
2. Alvin Gouldner, "The Norm of Reciprocity: A Preliminary Statement," *American Sociological Review* vol. 25 (1960).
3. Gresham M. Sykes, *Society of Captives: A Study of a Maximum Security Prison* (Atheneum, New York, 1969).
4. Gary Yukl and J. Bruce Tracy, "Consequences of Influence Tactics Used with Subordinates, Peers, and the Boss," *Journal of Applied Psychology*, vol. 77, no. 4 (1992), pp. 525–535. (See the table on p. 99 of Porter et al. derived from factor analysis, Q sorts, analysis of content validity, etc.)
5. The concept of exchange is central to this book and will be given detailed treatment in subsequent chapters. Some of the classic literature on which we draw are George C. Homans, "Social Behavior as Exchange," *American Journal of Sociology* (1958), p. 63; Peter M. Blau, *Exchange and Power in Social Life* (New York: John Wiley & Sons, 1964); Peter M. Blau, *Bureaucracy in Modern Society* (New York: Random House, 1956); and Peter M. Blau, *The Dynamics of Bureaucracy* 2nd ed. (Chicago: University of Chicago Press, 1963).
6. By their very nature, models are simplified abstractions from reality, highlighting what is important and what to pay attention to. Reality is usually messier, especially when people are involved with their differing perceptions, feelings, and assumptions. In any given instance, you may have to make adjustments and inferences, but a good model helps sort things out. Our influence model takes what had previously been treated by social scientists as descriptive—the presence of reciprocity among people—and makes it prescriptive and proactive. Combined with our research in organizations, the model breaks into steps what often is just taken for granted or feels overwhelming.
7. We use our version of attribution theory throughout the book. The theory was reported in H. H. Kelley, *Attribution in Social Interaction*

298

(Morristown, NJ: General Learning Press, 1971) and F. Heider, *The Psychology of Interpersonal Relations* (New York: John Wiley & Sons, 1958).

Chapter 3

1. Rosabeth Kanter, *The Change Masters* (New York: Simon & Schuster, 1983).
2. See note 1.
3. Peter M. Blau found this in his classic study of tax collectors in *Exchange and Power in Social Life* (New York: John Wiley & Sons, 1964); the expert who gave help in return for thanks soon found that he got so many requests he could barely do his own work, and the "thank-yous" became devalued.

Chapter 4

1. Steven Kerr, "On the Folly of Rewarding A While Hoping for B," *Academy of Management Journal* vol. 18, no. 4 (1975), pp. 769–783.
2. We use our version of attribution theory throughout the book. The theory was reported in H. H. Kelley, *Attribution in Social Interaction* (Morristown, NJ: General Learning Press, 1971) and F. Heider, *The Psychology of Interpersonal Relations* (New York: John Wiley & Sons, 1958).

Chapter 5

1. Rosabeth Kanter, *The Change Masters* (New York: Simon & Schuster, 1983).

Chapter 7

1. Rosabeth Kanter, *The Change Masters* (New York: Simon & Schuster, 1983).
2. See the classic article by Erving Goffman "On Cooling the Mark Out: Some Aspects of Adapting to Failure," *Psychiatry* (1952).

Chapter 8

1. For more on the new leader-subordinate relationship, see David L. Bradford and Allan R. Cohen, *Power Up: Transforming Organizations through Shared Leadership* (New York: John Wiley & Sons, 1998).
2. These statements have been made by clients, or by managers in our training programs.
3. John J. Gabarro & John Kotter, "Managing Your Boss," *Harvard Business Review,* vol. 58, no. 1 (1980), pp. 92–100.
4. See note 1.

Chapter 9

1. The original publication was Robert Rosenthal and Leonore Jacobson, *Pygmalion in the Classroom: Teacher Expectation and Pupils' Intellectual Development* (New York: Rinehart and Winston, 1968).
2. From J. B. M. Kassarjian, "Shaping Spaarbeleg: Real and Unreal" [case] IMD, #GM 537.
3. D. L. Bradford and A. R. Cohen, *Power Up* (New York: John Wiley & Sons, 1998).

Chapter 11

1. This approximate quote was declared at a conference on May 4–5, 2004, in a working group facilitated by one of the authors. Other members were surprised but shared compassionate views of doing what would help the most people.
2. This is an adaptation of R. R. Blake, J. S. Mouton, and R. L. Sloma, "The Union-Management Intergroup Laboratory: Strategy for Resolving Intergroup Conflict," *Journal of Applied Behavioral Science,* vol. 1, no. 1 (1965), pp. 25–57.

Chapter 12

1. Francis J. Flynn, "How Much Should I Give and How Often? The Effects of Generosity and Frequency of Favor Exchange on Social Status and Productivity," *Academy of Management Journal* vol. 46, no. 5 (2003), pp. 539–553.

Chapter 13

1. For more about vision and how to use it, see David L. Bradford and Allan R. Cohen, "Creating Commitment to a Tangible Vision" (Chapter 7), in *Power Up: Transforming Organizations Through Shared Leadership* (New York: John Wiley & Sons, 1998). Chapters 9 through 12 provide more detail on how to lead change. Also, see Peter Vaill with Allan R. Cohen, "Visionary Leadership," in *The Portable MBA in Management,* 2nd ed., Allan R. Cohen, ed. (New York: John Wiley & Sons, 1993).
2. Geoff Bellman, *Getting Things Done When You Are Not in Charge* (San Francisco: Berrett-Koehler, 2001).
3. The accordion method is our adaptation of an excellent concept, "the many-few-many-few technique," developed by Joel DeLuca in *Political Savvy; Systematic Approaches to Leadership Behind the Scenes,* 2nd ed. (Berwyn, PA: Evergreen Business Group, 1999).

INDEX